MERCURY
RADIO ARTS

ALSO BY GLENN BECK

CONFORM

EXPOSING THE TRUTH ABOUT COMMON CORE AND PUBLIC EDUCATION

Written and Edited by

GLENN BECK, KEVIN BALFE, AND KYLE OLSON

Contributors

Sharon Ambrose, Steve Gunn, and Ben Velderman

THRESHOLD EDITIONS / MERCURY RADIO ARTS

New York   London   Toronto   Sydney   New Delhi

THRESHOLD EDITIONS/MERCURY RADIO ARTS
A Division of Simon & Schuster, Inc.
1230 Avenue of the Americas
New York, NY 10020

First Threshold Editions/Mercury Radio Arts
trade paperback edition May 2014

For information about special discounts for bulk
purchases, please contact Simon & Schuster Special Sales at
1-866-506-1949 or business@simonandschuster.com.

The Simon & Schuster Speakers Bureau can bring authors to
your live event. For more information or to book an event,
contact the Simon & Schuster Speakers Bureau at 866-248-3049
or visit our website at www.simonspeakers.com.

Photograph of ripped paper © Dragan Milovanovic/Shutterstock
Photograph of blackboard background © Rangizzz/Shutterstock

Manufactured in the United States of America

1   3   5   7   9   10   8   6   4   2

ISBN 978-1-4767-7388-9
ISBN 978-1-4767-7389-6 (ebook)

To Michael O'Shea, who taught me
to find a mentor—and then become one.
And to Robert Beath, my high school drama teacher,
who instilled a love of learning and exploring the unknown.

CONTENTS

AUTHOR'S NOTE

"America will never be destroyed from the
outside. If we falter and lose our freedoms, it
will be because we destroyed ourselves."
—ABRAHAM LINCOLN

"Men are cast-iron; but children are wax."
—HORACE MANN

America was founded on the revolutionary belief that human
beings receive their rights from God, not the government.
With just a handful of well-chosen words, our Declaration of
Independence effectively stood the entire history of human existence on its head.

Our Founders reaffirmed these "self-evident" truths in the
Bill of Rights, including freedom of religion, speech, press, and
assembly.

Freedom is so deeply ingrained in our national psyche that
we wouldn't think of letting the government tell us where to live,

what kind of car to drive, or what to eat for dinner. But somewhere along the way, too many Americans bought into the idea that the government has the authority to tell us where we must send our children to school, based on nothing more than our zip code. Americans who were always taught to be mistrustful of government and power somehow agreed to entrust bureaucrats with the education of their children.

Many Americans go along with this "zip code" approach to education because, frankly, it works reasonably well for them. Their children attend a government-run school where most students seem to learn reading, writing, and math at an acceptable level. Sure, they might wish their local schools were better in some way, but all in all, the system works okay for them.

Unfortunately, there are a lot of American families having a completely different experience. They are not being well served by their "zip code"–assigned school. Not only are their children not learning much, but their very safety is in jeopardy because their school is so chaotic and dangerous.

It is fundamentally unfair and un-American to force certain children to attend a failing, dysfunctional school simply because their family can't afford to move into the "right" school district. This is not freedom—and it goes against everything our Founders believed about how education should work.

Still, the teachers' unions and their progressive friends in the media and the state legislatures—people we collectively refer to as "controllists"—defend zip code education and argue the only thing ailing government schools is a lack of funding.

Almost every day there are news stories about disputes between a teachers' union and their local school board. These fights invariably revolve around the same issues: teacher pay and benefits, work rules and accountability. It's gotten so absurd that some unions and school boards actually spend time negotiating over how the money from the teachers' lounge vending machine is going to be spent and how much humidity is allowable in each classroom, or "work site," as unions like to call them.

The National Assessment of Educational Progress reports, "We spend more per pupil than any other country, but among industrialized nations, American students rank near the bottom in science and math. Only 13 percent of high school seniors know what high school seniors should know about American history." And remember, these results are based off government-determined standards of what they think our kids should know about science, math, and history. Our personal standards are likely much higher.

It's time to stop the insanity. It's time to focus on the students and their needs, instead of the adult employees and their unions. It's time to make sure every classroom is staffed with an outstanding teacher, and every family has access to an outstanding classroom. It's time to kick down the walls that are keeping children from reaching their full potential.

We can do better—*much better*—than the system the controllists have given us. But it's not going to be easy. Those ivory towers are heavily reinforced and the people who reside in them have a lot of money and power. They control many of our school boards, state legislatures, teacher colleges, and government bureaucracies, and they're not going to relinquish control without a vicious political fight.

The reality is that the controllists know their approach to education isn't working. But instead of admitting that and allowing choice to reign, they're pushing the Common Core national learning standards, which create stifling conformity among our schools. Even some "conservatives" are telling us that the way to fix our education system is by having all of our schools teach students the same concepts at the same time using the same methods.

Does anyone honestly believe the same people who got us into this mess really have a one-size-fits-all magical solution for fixing it?

Of course not. This is just about more power. More money. More conformity.

In my previous book in this series I ended my introductory note with this:

"Information is power. Those without it have nothing. Those with it will always have CONTROL."

Most American slaves were uneducated and illiterate—not because they were incapable of learning, but because their owners forbid it. In some places, like South Carolina, it was actually against the law to teach a slave how to read or write. Why? Because an educated slave was a threat to the status quo.

The same premise applies to today's system of education. The dumbing-down of America is good for one group and one group only: those who currently have all the power and control. By maintaining a failing system they are forcing a collapse that will have only one "savior": the federal government. And that's exactly how they want it.

We now stand at the precipice. On one side is the complete nationalization of education and complete loss of local and parental control. On the other side is a complete educational revolution—one that is rooted in individuality and that follows the principle of "maximum freedom, maximum responsibility."

For the first time in decades we have a real opportunity to convince the country that this kind of revolution is long overdue. People are sick and tired of lower expectations, lower test scores, constant bickering between the schools and unions, and continued increases to their property tax bills to pay for it all.

It's time to combine the incredible technology of the present with the incredible philosophical ideas on education from our past. It's time to restore parents as the rightful leaders of their families and teachers of their children. And it's time to once again put America on top of the world and usher in a new era of education unlike anything this country has ever seen before.

I'm ready to roll up my sleeves and fight for our kids. I hope you're ready to join me.

Glenn Beck
Dallas, Texas
February 2014

PART ONE

THE TRUTH ABOUT EDUCATION

1

YOU CAN'T CRITICIZE
PUBLIC EDUCATION IF YOU HAVEN'T
BEEN IN THE CLASSROOM

"What madness has overtaken our nation? Why the push
to hand innocent children and scarce public dollars to
non-educators? How does 'caring' about education translate into
the experience and knowledge needed to run a school?"

—*DIANE RAVITCH,* Research Professor of Education, New York University

"If you haven't been in the classroom you have no
business in the [school] board room."

—*PATRICIA FOX,* teacher in Orange County, Florida

Randi Weingarten, president of the American Federation of Teachers, an AFL-CIO affiliate with approximately 1.5 million members and more than three thousand local affiliate unions across the nation, has never served in the military, or as a foreign ambassador in the U.S. Department of State.

Given this lack of firsthand experience, she obviously had no right to criticize U.S. military action in Iraq. Everyone knows that if you've never been on the front lines, you have no business debating a war.

Weingarten has also never, to the best of my knowledge, performed a surgery. She's never checked a patient for strep throat or an ear infection, and she's never prescribed pills to treat an injury. Given this lack of real-world medical experience, she obviously had no business supporting Obamacare or discussing the specifics of our country's health-care system.

Of course Weingarten would be quick to remind us that she and her fellow union members are U.S. citizens and taxpayers and that her union represents many thousands of health-care professionals. She'd very likely argue that she has every legal, moral, and professional right to speak her mind on any public policy topic she chooses.

And she'd be absolutely right.

It's unfortunate that Weingarten and her fellow progressives seem to forget this lesson when it comes to education. While most of us have never stood in front of a classroom of students or graded a test, we are citizens and parents and taxpayers and we have the right to speak out about educational issues that affect our families and communities.

Public employees have no business telling the public to mind its own business. That's not how things work in America (or at least it's not how they're supposed to work). It would be like Congress telling citizens to stay out of public policy debates because we've never been congressmen. The voters would quickly correct them in the next election cycle.

The same principle applies in the private sector. You don't hear the owners of professional sports teams telling the fans to keep their thoughts to themselves because they've never owned an NFL team or taken a snap at quarterback. They know better than to say such things because the fans pay the bills.

Yet the education "professionals" expect us—the people who pay the bills—to keep our noses out of their business. Instead of following the golden rule of any other service business—"the customer is always right," they say "the customer should keep his mouth shut." It's a ridiculous concept that should've been corrected long ago—but that hasn't happened.

For all practical purposes, public education has been the exclusive realm of the teachers' unions for the past five or six decades.

Sure, the unions demanded control, but we didn't have to give it to them. Instead of standing up for our kids and fighting for a place at the table, we've allowed the unions to seize power through years of our foolish indifference.

We saw groups with warm and fuzzy names like the "National Education Association" running things, and we assumed that our schools were in the hands of loving educators who put kids first. We had no idea that the union bosses are political animals who have more interest in enhancing their own careers and bank accounts than our children.

The unions took full advantage of our carelessness. They moved quickly to elect union-friendly school board members who rewarded them with fat compensation packages that crippled school budgets and locked local taxpayers into decades of ever-increasing property taxes.

They started pumping millions of dollars into the campaigns of union-friendly political candidates in an effort to guarantee influence over policies and budgets.

They developed a closed system of collective bargaining, where they and their handpicked board members decided how to spend the money and run the schools while taxpayers were all but locked out of the room.

They fought bitterly against suggested reforms like performance pay for outstanding teachers and tougher evaluations for all teachers. They resisted any changes to tenure laws or seniority provisions that guarantee employment for all, regardless of qualifications.

They did everything in their power to maintain their guaranteed clientele of geographically trapped students by fighting anything that even had a whiff of "choice" to it, including the development of charter schools, online schools, home-schooling, and private school voucher programs.

The unions had successfully arranged things exactly the way they wanted them: Government spending on public education continued to rise; salaries and benefits continued to skyrocket; and jobs for compliant dues-payers were basically guaranteed for life.

Everyone else stood by and pretty much let it happen. We were lazy and naïve—and now we're paying the price.

But a few years ago something remarkable happened: taxpayers began to wake up. Perhaps it was the recession or the insane tax bills or the constant bad news about America's educational standing—but, whatever the reason, people started to pay attention again.

And they didn't like what they were seeing.

Federal and state spending on public education has increased nearly 1,500 percent since 1970. Over $2 trillion (adjusted for inflation) has been spent by the federal government alone since 1965, and the total cost of a K–12 public education now stands at more than $151,000 per student. After adjusting for inflation, that's almost 300 percent higher than what we spent on the graduating class of 1970.

Unfortunately, that investment hasn't yielded much of a return. According to a study of government data performed by the Cato Institute and presented to a congressional committee in 2011, "Math and Reading scores at the end of high school are unchanged over the past forty years, while Science scores suffered a slight decline through the year 1999, the last time that test was administered."

Our students also continue to fall behind their peers in other nations. According to 2012 PISA (Programme for International Student Assessment) test scores, American students rank 31st in math, 24th in science, and 21st in reading globally. Our students are outperformed by those in Vietnam, Iceland, Estonia, and Hungary.

It's clear we haven't been getting our money's worth from our education system, and now more and more people are finally demanding change.

That brings me back to the overall argument we're addressing in this chapter, which can pretty much be summed up as the controllists telling the rest of us to mind our own business.

The real reason that line is so dangerous is that it's the one thing that guarantees the status quo will continue. Unions know that when we come to our senses and remember that *we're the owners* and that *they work for us*, the charade will be over.

We shouldn't be surprised by this reaction. In fact, we should expect it. The education "professionals" are simply reacting like teens would react if you left them at home with gobs of your money and no supervision for a year and then you returned and tried to restore law and order. They'd be upset because the party was over. They'd tell you everything was actually fine and beg you to go away again, to give them just a little more time. Teachers' union leaders feel the same way. They'd much prefer we stay out of the house.

Their tactics will be familiar. They will attempt to mock, belittle, and intimidate us, all in the hope that we will once again

defer to their superior intellect and let them handle our schools
however they'd like.

But those days are over.

The time has come for us to form our own union: a group
of concerned parents and taxpayers who believe that enough is
enough. Our power will come through our common goals and
unending focus on a simple yet effective strategy: to use our votes
to elect responsible school board members and state officials who
actually listen to the public. After all, politicians aren't stupid.
They like union money, but they like votes even more. If taxpayers tell them to fix our schools and then we follow up by bouncing
a few who think we're bluffing, we will get the kind of change we
want—and we'll get it fast.

So, to all of the status quo–loving bureaucrats, controllists,
and union leaders, thanks for the tip—I think we *will* start mind-
ing our business.

2

CRITICS OF THE SYSTEM ARE JUST "TEACHER BASHERS"

"When did teacher bashing become the new national pastime?"
—*SAM CHALTAIN,* former national director of the Forum for Education and Democracy

"America hates teachers because America hates learning. How can anyone who tries to instill ideas in the next generation stand a chance in this country that brought us Fox News and reality television?"
—*DAVID SIROONIAN,* New York City history teacher

"Since a teacher's working conditions are a child's learning conditions, attacking teachers is the same as attacking children."
—*RANDY MOUSLEY,* president of United Teachers of Wichita

"Governor Romney and a number of folks try to politicize the issue and do a lot of teacher-bashing."
—*BARACK OBAMA,* U.S. president

Teachers' union officials are the ultimate political animals. The NEA and AFT doled out a combined $19.4 million to the

Democratic Party, its candidates, and allies, in 2012. In addition, they regularly deliver thousands of volunteers and votes to their anointed candidates at every level of government, and they can always be counted on to lob verbal bombs at Republicans.

They can dish it out with the best of them, but they can't take it. When someone criticizes a teachers' union, they often respond by invoking claims of "teacher bashing."

"The trouble is that the current teacher-bashing rhetoric plays right into the hands of conservative politicians who want to slash pay and benefits for teachers," wrote Ashley Lauren Samsa, a public school teacher in Illinois.

The "rhetoric" she was referring to included the idea that bad teachers can't be fired because of union contracts. But that's not rhetoric, it's a fact—and it has absolutely nothing to do with cutting pay for teachers. In fact, most conservatives I know agree with me that good teachers should be paid more.

Still, the idea that attacking antiquated concepts, like granting tenure to third-grade public school teachers, is somehow equivalent to bashing teachers themselves is very effective. Most teachers are highly respected—even beloved—in their communities. A 2013 Gallup poll revealed that 73 percent of people have "trust and confidence" in public school teachers. That number rose to 78 percent when filtered to respondents under the age of forty.

A 2006 Harris poll found similar levels of admiration for public school teachers: 75 percent of respondents said teachers have "very great" or "considerable" prestige. A 2013 Pew Research Center poll revealed that 72 percent of people believe that teachers contribute "a lot" to society's well-being.

Despite union leaders' best efforts to conflate the two, teachers and their unions are far from the same thing. In fact, only a very small percentage of teachers take any interest in their union at all. In most states they become dues-paying union members because that is what's required to get a job in a public school. Those dues are usually deducted involuntarily right from their paychecks.

What would happen if union membership were optional in more states? It's hard to know for sure but it's instructive to look at Wisconsin, the birthplace of progressivism, for some evidence. In 2011 the state adopted Act 10, a law that made union membership voluntary for public employees. The state's largest teachers' union quickly lost about 50 percent of its membership and had to send volunteers door-to-door to collect delinquent dues.

The problem is not the teachers; it's the system they've been put into. Which brings me back to the quote by Ms. Samsa about the "rhetoric" over firing bad teachers, which she equates to "teacher bashing." Samsa says that "the key to saving American education is not getting rid of bad teachers; it is making the profession more attractive to the good teachers, thus making school more attractive to students."

I respectfully disagree. (I hope she doesn't consider that teacher bashing.) The key to saving American education is doing *both* of those things. We absolutely must attract more good teachers, but we also have to clear the pond of those who lack the necessary skills or motivation. In what is arguably the most important "industry" in our country we tolerate failure and reward mediocrity far too often. We allow poor teachers to hang around and plague our schools until they choose to retire.

That's not teacher bashing, because it's not really even the bad teachers who are the problem—they should be expected—it's the political forces that defend a system that is so clearly broken that is the problem. Blaming bad teachers for everything that ails us in public education is like blaming someone in line for food stamps for our national debt. That person isn't responsible, they are only living within the rules that society has created.

If we are sometimes guilty of bashing bad teachers it's because we haven't been allowed to do anything about them. Sometimes good teachers do unfortunately get caught in the crossfire, but that's the fault of the unions, not the public.

Union leaders insist on having all teachers compensated and treated the same way. They force us to lump the good ones in with the bad. That's not fair to the hundreds of thousands of outstanding teachers across the nation, but that's the way it is. For years reformers have been calling for changes—like merit bonuses and performance pay—that will allow the best teachers to be recognized and rewarded. But the unions won't stand for it. They insist we take the good with the bad and treat them all the same.

The teachers' union in East Baton Rouge, Louisiana, recently protested because the school board there took out a full-page ad in a local newspaper, naming and congratulating the teachers who had scored well in the state's recently adopted teacher evaluation process. Carnell Washington, the union president, said that publishing their names was a breach of privacy as well as an insult to teachers not named. "It's not a contest to see how many highly effective teachers are in a school," he said. "Publishing this data is unfair to all of the other teachers who may be doing a fantastic job in the classroom."

By demanding real transparency in the system and a real reward/punishment system, critics are not bashing teachers; we are bashing the unions that hold so many teachers back from reaching their full potential. The unions would serve everyone better if they embraced and promoted their outstanding members, rather than spending so much time defending their worst.

It's difficult to talk about reforming education without talking about teacher quality. A lot of people try to walk on eggshells, not wanting to look as though they are pointing a finger at those who stand in front of our kids doing the hard work every day. But if you don't acknowledge that teacher quality is the key to turning all this around, then your solutions aren't going to get us very far.

Teacher quality is influenced by lots of different factors—many of which I cover in this book: unions and collective bargaining; the quality of our teachers' colleges; compensation strategies; administrators and school boards; and federal mandates promoting "teaching to the test." The entire system rises or falls on teacher quality. Aside from parents, it's the most critical ingredient to positive educational outcomes—yet most want to sidestep the issue for fear of alienating a group of people that we all respect.

My only agenda in this book is to figure out how we can help and support the best and brightest teachers. If they succeed, our kids and schools will as well. I'm comfortable with breaking a few eggs in the process and getting some people mad at me (most of whom will likely not even take the time to actually read this book) if that's what it takes to make real progress.

3

PUBLIC SCHOOLS ARE UNDERFUNDED

"Philadelphia needs $1 billion more a year, or nearly $5,000 additional per pupil, in order to educate all students to academic proficiency."
—PENNSYLVANIA STATE BOARD OF EDUCATION

"Many of our public schools have also been badly underfunded, regularly pummeled by budget cuts, rising class sizes, wrongheaded policies, and damaging mandates that have served to further undermine their mission."
—DIANE RAVITCH, Research Professor of Education, New York University

"When people talk about other nations out-educating the United States, it needs to be remembered that those other nations are out-investing us in education as well."
—RANDI WEINGARTEN, president of the AFT

If the public school establishment is good at anything, it's public relations. Union leaders, administrators, and school board members know how to get their message out, whether it's accurate or not. These controllists constantly scream to a compliant media that public schools are woefully underfunded and that no one should be surprised when test scores drop and students graduate without the ability to read their diplomas.

"We can rebuild our public education system," a guest columnist recently wrote in a Seattle-area newspaper. "It will require the state to invest at least $1 billion more each year in K–12 education."

Sure enough, the American people are eating up that message, hook, line, and sinker.

Thirty-five percent of respondents in a recent poll named "funding" as the biggest problem facing public schools. That was by far the most popular answer to the question. (The second most popular response was "lack of discipline," at just 8 percent.)

The theory that money can solve all problems makes sense to most people. Well-compensated teachers, administrators, and other school employees should theoretically produce better-educated students.

There's only one problem: that theory is dead wrong, and the facts prove it.

Roughly 80 percent of most public school budgets are swallowed up by labor costs. In the private sector, higher salaries and better benefits are generally tied to performance. If an employee is productive, and the company does well, their salary grows. But in the era of union domination of public schools, there's little connection between employee performance and compensation.

In most school districts across the nation, all teachers are given automatic, annual raises every year based on years of service and number of graduate classes completed. To put it bluntly, most teachers get a raise for not dying over the summer—their classroom performance, or lack thereof, has nothing to do with it. While Ms. Samsa would undoubtedly convict me of teacher-bashing for that statement, it's simply an indictment of the system and is one of the main reasons why the money we continually throw at education never seems to trickle down to the kids themselves.

School administrators and union officials keep demanding more funding every year and claim that we can't expect better academic results until we "fully fund schools"—but what does that even mean? It's sort of like people who use the "fair share" slogan when it comes to taxes, yet refuse to ever put a specific number on what that fair share should be.

Philadelphia public schools have been in financial and academic meltdown for years. The district's most recent budget deficit was reportedly $304 million. In January 2012, district leaders issued 1,400 layoff notices to employees. Eighteen months later, school leaders laid off another 3,783 employees. Things were so dire that the district required an emergency infusion of cash from the state just to open its doors for the start of the 2013–2014 school year.

There are a number of reasons for the district's downfall, but chief among them is the budget stress caused by unsustainable pay and benefits for employees. An analysis by EAGnews found that the district spent $132 million on health insurance for union members in 2011–2012. Employees contributed less than one-half of 1 percent toward the cost of that benefit.

In that single year, teachers also received automatic "step" raises, costing $16.8 million. That was in addition to a 3 percent general raise, which cost another $14.4 million, and another $36.2 million paid out in unused sick leave.

Want more insanity? The district coughed up $2.3 million to pay for the *personal* legal bills of union members for things such as divorces or buying a home. The district even spent $5.2 million on the union "wage continuation plan"—a program that continues to pay employees who have used up all of their sick days but are still unable to work.

Philadelphia is only one city, so it's important to look at how America stacks up against other countries.

The Associated Press summarized a recent report from the Organisation for Economic Co-operation and Development (OECD) by saying, "The United States spends more than other developed nations on its students' education each year, with parents and private foundations picking up more of the costs."

How much more? Well, if you add up all of the various constituencies that contribute to our educational system, we spend about 7.3 percent of our entire gross domestic product (GDP). The average OECD country spent 6.3 percent.

If you narrow those statistics down to only primary and lower secondary education, the United States spends 3 percent of its GDP versus the OECD average of 2.5 percent. Finland, which is often held up as one of the gold standards of public education, spends right at the OECD average of 2.5 percent.

To say that the United States does not "invest" enough in education is ridiculous and is only meant to distract people from talking about the real issues that are holding us back. Besides, the data makes it clear that more money does not automatically result in better student performance.

A recent study from the nonpartisan, free-market group State Budget Solutions revealed that "from 2009 to 2011, the states that spent the most money as a percentage of total spending did not produce students with better ACT scores or graduation rates."

Texas ranked first in the nation in K–12 spending as a percentage of its total budget, but ranked below the national average for graduation rates and ACT scores. Between 2009 and 2011, forty-five states spent more on education as a percentage of their total budget than Massachusetts, yet Massachusetts finished first in average ACT scores all three years.

Perhaps more money for education would make a difference if that money was actually spent on students. But it usually isn't.

Most new spending goes into the pockets of employees, and that doesn't translate into higher student achievement.

In New York, for instance, the amount of spending per pupil increased by 28.2 percent between 2005–2006 and 2010–2011. Sounds great until you realize that the amount spent per pupil on *employee compensation* increased by 27.7 percent during that same period.

You can see the same trend in other states: Connecticut (26.6 percent increase in spending, 24.6 percent increase in compensation); Louisiana (27.6 percent, 30.9 percent); Maryland (30 percent, 31.5 percent).

When we "invest" more money in public education, we're really just handing out a bunch of raises or benefits without demanding anything in return.

That fact gets increasingly irritating when we look at the spending habits of some school districts around the nation. Take Los Angeles, for example. In 2011–2012, it spent $334 million on employee health insurance, with *no* contribution from employees. It spent another $82 million on retiree health insurance with no contribution from retirees, and another $47 million on automatic, annual raises for teachers, with no connection to performance.

That district's budget deficit? $640 million.

Worse than its financial performance was its academic performance. The district's graduation rate in 2011 was a miserable 61 percent. Only 32 percent of eleventh graders were proficient in math skills, 35 percent in biology/life sciences, and 37 percent in English/language arts.

The evidence all points to one fact: more money for public schools produces wealthier school employees and bigger budgets, and that's about it.

4

TEACHERS' UNIONS PUT KIDS FIRST

"Students Are OUR Priority"
—*MICHIGAN EDUCATION ASSOCIATION,* protest sign

"SEA [The Sweetwater Education Association] is committed
to put each other and our students first. We know that you
can't put students first when you put teachers last."
—*HELEN FARIAS,* Sweetwater school district (CA) union director

"From day one, our organizations came to the table and
advocated for changes that put Illinois kids first and ensured
our teachers can do what they do best: teach."
—*KEN SWANSON,* former Illinois Education Association president

Albert Shanker, the late president of the American Federation of Teachers, likely spent years of his life regretting an honest statement he made in 1985: "When schoolchildren start paying dues, that's when I'll start representing the interests of schoolchildren."

Former National Education Association legal counsel Bob

Chanin probably feels the same way about comments he included in his retirement speech at the 2009 NEA convention:

> NEA and its affiliates are effective advocates because we have power and we have power because there are more than 3.2 million people who are willing to pay us hundreds of millions of dollars in dues each year because they believe we are the unions that can most effectively represent them, the unions that can protect their rights and advance their interests as education employees.

Those two honest remarks have done a lot to dispel a myth that the teachers' unions have been nursing, developing, and depending on for decades: that their labor goals incorporate the needs of students, and that they are the guardians of student interests.

We see this sentiment displayed on union protest signs all the time—"We're here for the students." The idea is even implanted in the name of the nation's largest teachers' union: the National Education Association. This moniker is designed to conjure up pleasant feelings about an entire organization dedicated to quality education and the well-being of children.

Successfully selling that concept does a lot for unions at contract time, when residents of any given community come out of the woodwork to support their teachers in negotiation showdowns with evil school boards. Unions prey on this goodwill by publicly protesting and picketing when things don't go their way at the bargaining table. Isolated school boards, inundated with nasty messages and phone calls from residents, usually end up caving in to union demands.

When they don't cave, unions are often willing to turn up the heat even further. When the union in Framingham, Massachusetts, wasn't getting what it wanted from the school committee, they went into full Saul Alinsky–style attack mode. As the *Boston Globe* reported:

> [T]he union representing Framingham teachers has urged its members to volunteer personal information they know about committee members, including what health clubs they belong to, and where their spouses work. . . .

> "Many of us have felt some degree of stress in coming to work due to the contract struggles and it is not right that the committee put this on us," [union president Sam] Miskin wrote [in an email seeking dirt]. "For all of the stress we have felt, we owe it to the committee to return the favor. . . . The focus will now be on making the committee feel the same stresses that we have."

Unions also use secrecy to their advantage. Despite the fact that school districts and unions are determining how to spend millions of taxpayer dollars, most still negotiate collective bargaining agreements behind closed doors. Citizens are typically left in the dark about the details of a new contract until it's already been ratified and carries the weight of law.

The public believes the unions represent the kids, so the public backs off. School boards, lacking the public relations budgets necessary to match those of the powerful unions, are forced to accept the role of villain with little ability to fight back. But as Shanker and Chanin acknowledged, it's all a big charade.

The truth is that teachers' unions exist to protect the interests of their members, whether those interests are consistent with the interests of students or not. Everyone can judge for themselves whether that is good or bad, but either way, it is a fact. How else can you explain why so many unions see it fit to write "evergreen" clauses into their collective bargaining agreements. These clauses essentially mandate that terms of expired agreements remain in effect until a new agreement is negotiated, regardless of how long it takes.

The Buffalo, New York, school district is well acquainted with how onerous evergreen clauses can be. Back in the 1970s, the unions managed to win a provision providing free cosmetic surgery to employees. This has cost the district as much as $9 million per year and school officials have long been eager to get rid of it. The problem is that there hasn't been a new labor agreement since 2004, so the nipping and tucking has continued unabated at taxpayer expense. At one point the district offered to cancel one hundred scheduled teacher layoffs in exchange for cancellation of the program, but the union—which supposedly cares so much for the well-being of the students in its district—wouldn't go for it.

Carolyn Doggett, former executive director of the 325,000-member California Teachers Association, acknowledged the truth about her powerful union in a speech she gave to the state council last year:

> [A]s we celebrate the 150th Anniversary of CTA, we must remember that we were founded for one reason—and one reason only—and that was to engage in politics. We were founded to engage in the political process in order to create an organized system of public instruction and to elevate the profession of teaching in California. The fact that our establishment in 1863 coincides with the passage of the Emancipation Proclamation may be a beautiful coincidence, but from the very beginning, we were founded in the throes of political activism and social justice.

Given that mission, it's probably not surprising how most unions reacted when asked to accept wage and benefit concessions as a result of the recent recession. Schools, hurt by falling tax revenues, approached unions across the country and asked for various sacrifices for the good of the students.

One of the most common concessions asked for by districts had to do with the "last in, first out" policy that's written into thousands of collective bargaining agreements across the nation. This policy, which forces districts to lay off teachers strictly according to their seniority, means that those with higher paychecks keep their jobs while younger teachers get the pink slips—regardless of performance or any other factors. For obvious reasons, many local and state unions have gone to the mat in recent years to defend these policies.

A study by *Education Next* found that seventy-five of the largest school districts in the country use seniority as a factor in layoff decisions and more than 70 percent of these districts use seniority as the *sole* factor.

A rational person might expect local unions to make exceptions to that rule when the younger teachers facing layoff are clearly among the best teachers on staff. After all, keeping the best teachers is certainly in the best interests of students. But that's not the way the unions see it. Consider what happened a couple of years ago in Milwaukee.

Under terms of their collective bargaining agreement, teachers in the Milwaukee school district had a choice between two generous health plans—both of which were 100 percent paid for by the district.

School board leaders, faced with a multimillion-dollar deficit, asked the union to alter the collective bargaining agreement so that all teachers could be moved to the less expensive of the two options. The board explained that the switch would save the district about $48 million per year, along with the jobs of all 482 younger teachers who faced immediate layoff.

With the cost of both plans fully funded by the district, employees had no incentive to commit themselves to the lower-cost plan, which presumably offered some lower degree of benefits (although that is not stated in media reports). Employees with more seniority had even less incentive to make the switch, since most of them knew they would not be affected by the "last in, first out" layoff policy.

The union responded to the district with a flat "no," calling instead for federal tax money to save the younger teachers' jobs.

"The problem must be addressed with a national solution," said Pat O'Mahar, interim executive director of the Milwaukee Teachers' Education Association (MTEA), "a federal stimulus package that will restore educator positions and allow MPS (Milwaukee Public School) children to keep their teachers."

Local unions wanted to move the burden up to the federal level, but that's not how it worked out. Megan Sampson, a Milwaukee teacher who was named the 2010–2011 "Outstanding First Year Teacher" by the Wisconsin Council of Teachers of English, was laid off as a result of the MTEA refusing to agree to the insurance change. She later complained, along with many others, that she hadn't been kept informed by the union about contract negotiations, or the possible consequences. "Given the opportunity," she said, "of course I would have switched to a different (insurance) plan to save my job, or the jobs of 10 other teachers."

Another example comes from Pittsburgh, where the school board asked the Pittsburgh Federation of Teachers (PFT) to change their "last in, first out" policy so that outstanding younger teachers could be spared in a round of layoffs. The board pointed to a special "turnaround" elementary school that had improved academically due to the special assignment of some of the best younger teachers in the district. The union rejected the idea, and the board eventually voted to lay off 280 employees, including 190 represented by the PFT and many of the younger teachers who'd been assigned to that successful "turnaround" elementary.

It's not just the seniority layoff policy that leads to these kinds of unfortunate results for students. In Strongsville, Ohio, teachers walked out for eight weeks in 2013 over stalled contract negotiations. This happened in the second half of the school year, just as seniors were preparing for graduation and other students were preparing their final assignments.

The district tried to shield students from the labor dispute by hiring temporary replacement teachers but the union responded by making life miserable for the substitutes. They protested outside the schools where their chants could be heard during class. They personally harassed the subs as they came and went from the schools, with one teacher shouting "Rosa Parks would be ashamed!" to an African-American sub. They even handed out leaflets in their neighborhoods, informing residents that they were living near "scabs."

When the strike finally ended, the nearby Cleveland teachers' union filed a request for the names and addresses of the fill-in teachers. (The district denied the request and the union's subsequent lawsuit is still pending.) Why did they want the names? It's anyone's guess—but if the request is eventually granted it's not hard to imagine that these subs might find themselves unable to secure full-time teaching jobs in the future.

The argument that teachers' unions are focused solely on our children is especially hard to take when stories surface about unions spending enormous quantities of time and money defending teachers who clearly have no place in the classroom.

During the 2006–2007 school year, the Swartz Creek, Michigan, school district suspended teacher/counselor Mary Ruth Clark (with pay) due to what officials described as "erratic and worrisome behavior." Clark was examined by a psychiatrist, who wrote that "the patient seems very paranoid. . . . I don't believe she should return to work at this time. . . ." She was also examined by a psychologist, who wrote that she should be allowed to return to work only if she "becomes involved in individual psychotherapy on a weekly basis."

The district told Clark that she could return to work if she obtained a clean bill of mental health from a professional. According to district officials, she never provided such documentation.

In 2008, Clark asked the Michigan Tenure Commission to force the district to choose between immediate reinstatement or termination. The district chose to fire her, and she challenged that decision.

At a hearing, the Tenure Commission ruled that the district had sufficient grounds for termination, but it also noted that the district lacked updated information on her psychological condition, so it ordered her reinstatement.

The district fought that order for several years, until the Michigan Education Association, Clark's union, filed a lawsuit. In May 2011, almost five years since the initial episodes of erratic behavior were witnessed, a judge ordered her reinstatement.

Nobody—least of all the union officials who filed the lawsuit—had any idea about the current state of Clark's mental health, but they fought tooth and nail for her reinstatement anyway. Are those really the actions of an organization that puts kids first?

Former NEA president Mary Hatwood Futrell may have summed it up best when, in 1982, she explained the overriding mission of their powerful union:

> The major purpose of our organization is not the education of
> children. It is or ought to be the extension and/or preservation
> of our members' rights. We earnestly care about the kids learn-
> ing, but that is secondary to the other goals.

There are plenty of great union members who care deeply about our kids. Put your trust and faith in them—not in the unions themselves.

5

TEACHERS NEED UNIONS AND COLLECTIVE BARGAINING

"Collective bargaining provides a foundation and security for public school employees upon which they build policies that enable them to meet the needs of the students they serve. It is this foundation that helps to attract the best and brightest minds into the teaching profession and to retain those individuals. . . ."
—*PENNSYLVANIA STATE EDUCATION ASSOCIATION*

"Teachers without due process or collective bargaining rights cannot safely speak out for what is best for students."
—*TEACHERS FOR SOCIAL JUSTICE*

A headline on a pro-union website recently proclaimed that "Teachers Need Strong Unions."

If that's the case, many of the teachers themselves don't seem to be aware of it. As we've seen recently, when teachers get a chance to dump their mandatory union memberships, they do so in big numbers.

Perhaps the best example of this comes from Wisconsin,

where state lawmakers adopted a law in 2011 that offered emancipation to thousands of public sector union members. As a result, the Wisconsin Education Association Council, the state's largest teachers' union, lost approximately thirty thousand members, or about one-third of their total membership. Teachers in 13 percent of the state's four-hundred-plus school districts have already voted to decertify their local unions, and that number is expected to grow.

Once they were given the choice, thousands of teachers asked themselves if they were getting their money's worth from their unions, and their answer was a resounding "no."

Michigan tried to follow Wisconsin's lead by passing a series of right-to-work laws in 2012, giving all public sector employees the right to decide if they want to be union members. It sounds promising, but most employees never even got the chance to enjoy their freedom.

The right-to-work law didn't take effect until six months after the legislation passed, meaning that it did not affect local school districts until their current labor contracts expired. As a result, numerous unions throughout the state rushed back to the bargaining table to negotiate new or extended contracts designed to keep their members trapped for years into the future.

In the Taylor, Michigan, school district, the union and school board agreed to a new four-year contract, as well as a ten-year "union security clause" that kept all teachers trapped in the union for the next decade. Getting this deal done quickly was so important that the union accepted the type of concessions—including a 10 percent pay cut for teachers—it never would have in the past.

Three Taylor teachers sued for their freedom but eventually lost in court.

"This is really a union insecurity clause," said an attorney for one of the rebellious teachers, "because rather than proving its worth to its members, the union is forcing all teachers to continue paying dues or agency fees through 2023."

Most of the teachers who leave their unions are likely higher-quality educators. Ineffective, dangerous, and troublesome teachers are far less likely to quit because they clearly benefit from the protections that strong unions can provide for teachers who have no business being near a classroom.

As Douglas County, Colorado, school board president John Carson recently said, "The union is just a little group of people who have figured out a great way to be paid to be political activists. They do provide support for some teachers who should go. They will go to bat for teachers who are low performers or who have disciplinary issues. They don't really do anything else."

Carson left out another group of teachers that unions will go to bat for: those who are sexually abusive or have behavioral problems. In New York City, for instance, the local union has negotiated an arbitration process for teachers accused of wrongdoing. The process has traditionally been very slow, leaving many teachers drawing full salaries and benefits for months or years while doing absolutely nothing.

And when these teachers finally reach the hearing phase, they stand a decent chance of reinstatement, regardless of their crime. That's because the arbitrators are jointly employed by the school district and the union, and are very aware that their continued employment is based on giving the union its share of victories, deserved or not.

High school teacher Norman Siegel was accused of pressing his genitalia against a female student's leg. An arbitrator ruled that the charge was likely true, but Siegel was only punished with a forty-five-day unpaid suspension, according to the *New York Daily News*.

Then there's the case of gym and health teacher Willie Laraque, who was accused of bending a male student over a desk, leaning in to him, and saying, "I'll show you what is gay." The *Daily News* reported that Laraque is back in the classroom after paying a $10,000 fine.

Sometimes the unions even score big financial victories for teachers after they're fired and imprisoned. One of the most egregious examples comes from 1980, when a teacher from Ann Arbor, Michigan, was terminated after five students testified that he sexually molested them. The teacher challenged his dismissal with the legal assistance of the Michigan Education Association. In 1984, while the case was still pending, the teacher murdered his wife with an axe. But the union pressed forward with the defense, and nine years later they secured $200,000 in back pay for him.

More recently—again in Michigan—Rose City–West Branch high school teacher Neal Erickson admitted to molesting a student for three years. While he was sitting in prison after his conviction, the Michigan Education Association filed a grievance on his behalf, claiming he was due a $10,000 payout when he left the district. Even shackles and orange jumpsuits apparently aren't enough to knock the taxpayer-funded union gravy train off the tracks.

Teachers' unions have always been obsessed about standing up for their least qualified members, regardless of how inept they are in the classroom, or what they have done to hurt students. So is it any wonder that good teachers flee the unions when they get the chance? They are clearly not a high priority for Big Labor. Why would good teachers want to stay in an organization that sends most of their dues money to state and national parent unions so that it can be spent on Democratic political candidates and liberal causes they may not even support?

The Douglas County, Colorado, school board discontinued its relationship with the Douglas County Federation of Teachers in 2012, partially due to the union's misuse of local dues revenue. School board president John Carson explained, "We also told the union, if you want us to collect $1.3 million per year in union dues on your behalf, you have to start spending that right here in Douglas County on the teachers who pay the dues. Their dirty little secret is that almost all of that money had been going to the national AFT [American Federation of Teachers].

"In 2009, for example, out of that $1.3 million about $850,000 went to the national AFT for political purposes. Another couple hundred thousand went to the state AFT. From what we could figure, they were only spending about $4,000 locally for teacher training."

Andrew Buikema, a high school band director from Grant, Michigan, was incensed when he learned that his National Education Association dues would increase ten dollars per member to fund the union's political advertising, which was heavily supporting President Obama's reelection bid in 2011. "I became a teacher to help kids, not to become a political pawn," Buikema said.

The truth is not that teachers need strong unions, as the headline mentioned earlier suggests; it's the other way around: unions need teachers and the dues money they provide. After all, how else would they be able to pay the generous salaries of their leaders, like AFT president Randi Weingarten (who makes $407,323) and her NEA counterpart, Dennis Van Roekel (who makes $362,644)?

They also need these dues in order to maintain their political muscle in Washington, D.C., and various state capitals. In 2012 the NEA spent $18.1 million on political contributions (95 percent of it going to Democratic candidates) and another $5.9 million on lobbying. Without these payments it's very possible that politicians might finally stop pretending that ideas like tenure and seniority pay make sense for our kids.

Unions know that their members don't join because they want to; they join because they're forced to. When governments allow teachers to make a choice, unions fight back hard to protect the status quo.

6

TEACHERS NEED TENURE

"I have only taught in Duval County (Fla.) for seven years,
but the most important moment was Day One of my fourth
year. It meant that I had reached 'tenure' status. . . ."
—*CHRISTOPHER HARVEY, Florida teacher*

"Teachers also need protection against ambitious,
my-way-or-the-highway administrators who come in with dictatorial
methods and are willing to remove anyone who questions their
judgment. If tenure is removed, teachers in many school districts
will no longer have the ability to question changes that could
have a negative impact on them and the children they serve.
—*RANDY TURNER,* English teacher, Joplin, Missouri

"Teacher tenure—at both the K–12 and university level—is
enormously important, not just to individual teachers, but also
to society as a whole. Tenure is protection against shortsighted
or vindictive administrators. Tenure is what enables teachers to
collaborate with each other instead of competing, to speak up for the
rights of students, and to fight for justice in the classroom, the school
community, and the larger community that the school serves."
—*RETHINKING SCHOOLS, editorial*

Teaching is a difficult and frequently thankless job.

It takes the right type of person to be willing to go to work every day, put up with a ton of nonsense and politics, and still do their best to teach our kids.

Sometimes the best teachers are those who have been at it for years and have acquired a great deal of skill and insight. Sometimes the best are the beginners, straight out of college, who are bursting with the type of enthusiasm and fresh ideas that make students want to learn and get ahead in life.

But one thing is certain: it's absolutely crucial for every classroom to have a high-quality teacher. That's why strong state tenure laws, which essentially give lifetime job protection to K–12 teachers who follow the rules and stay out of trouble, are such a bad idea.

The union types will almost always describe tenure, which is often granted after a teacher's first three to five years on the job, in its most simplistic terms and shake their heads in wonderment when someone objects. They remind us that tenure was created to protect teachers against unfair termination. And they're right— but times have changed.

Years ago, before teachers' unions were common, teaching jobs were often handed out as rewards to loyal supporters of successful local politicians. Those teachers could be—and often were—fired for just about any reason, fair or unfair.

But the world has evolved a great deal since then, and there are now many safeguards in place against unjust termination. "So much has changed about our larger legal framework," said Tim Daly, president of TNTP (formerly The New Teacher Project). "A law about teacher tenure, by far, is not the only thing that would protect you."

What should protect teachers is what protects anyone who must continually justify their job: success. Good teachers continue working, bad ones go away. And if a good teacher is fired without cause or because of some political grudge or ideological difference with a principal, you can be sure that parents will hold that principal accountable. Administrators who value their jobs will heed the public's demands.

Despite the common sense inherent in a system where people must compete for their jobs every year, union supporters have a way of making tenure laws seem logical, fair, and simple.

"Tenure for K–12 teachers is not guaranteed lifetime employment," wrote an educator who blogs anonymously as "Ceolaf." "Rather, after teaching three years with good evaluations, tenured teachers cannot be fired at the drop of a hat or at the whim of an administrator. Rather, the principal must document the teacher's problems, let him/her know about them, give him/her an opportunity to correct them, and then check to see whether they are corrected. If all of these steps are documented, the teacher can be dismissed."

What this blogger fails to mention is the time and money that's required to try to fire a tenured teacher, with absolutely no guarantee of success.

New Jersey's termination process, which was recently reformed, was one of the worst in the nation. First, formal tenure charges had to be filed against a teacher. Then an in-depth investigation followed, during which physical and documentary evidence was gathered and statements were taken from witnesses. That typically took about three months.

The case was then sent to the state Office of Administrative Law and a trial would be scheduled. Because there is no constitutional guarantee of a "speedy trial" in tenure cases, they often took one to four years to complete. The teacher's pay was suspended for the first four months, and then reinstated for the duration of the proceedings, no matter how long they took.

James Smith, executive director of school security in Paterson,

New Jersey, said that trying to fire a tenured teacher is a "time-consuming, painstaking process. It takes guts, money and know-how." He should know; the Paterson school district once took four years and spent $400,000 to fire a tenured teacher who was found guilty of physically assaulting a handicapped student.

Illinois investigative reporter Scott Reeder covered this topic in a 2005 report in which he interviewed education labor law attorney T. J. Wilson. Wilson told him:

> When I sit down with school administrators who want to fire someone, I tell them to plan on spending at least $100,000 in attorney fees and that they still may lose. Those administrators are sitting there thinking three new teachers could be hired for the cost of firing one bad one.

> There is always the possibility that the school district may have to cut some program that benefits children, just to pay for the cost of firing a teacher. This is the biggest reason school districts do not try to fire bad teachers.

Reeder wrote that it costs Illinois school districts an average of $219,504 in legal fees "to get a termination case past all the union-supported hurdles."

The other option, and one that is frequently chosen by schools, is to save the money and frustration and keep the lousy teachers around. That's why, when you get past the spin, the truth is that tenure equals lifetime employment for the vast majority of teachers. The New York, Chicago, and Los Angeles school districts, all of which have severe academic problems and their share of lousy teachers, have fired fewer than 1 out of 1,000 tenured teachers in recent years.

Reeder's 2005 study of Illinois schools found that only 61 of

876 districts even attempted to fire a tenured teacher over the previous eighteen years, and only 38 of them were successful. Of the 95,000 tenured teachers employed at that time, an average of seven were fired per year, and an average of only two were fired for performance reasons.

The concept of teacher tenure seems especially absurd when compared to the way private sector employees are treated. In most corporations, annual reviews are the norm and employee compensation is tied to the results. How many private enterprises would survive if their employees could get away with coasting after three to five years on the job?

Former Minnesota Vikings quarterback Fran Tarkenton once applied the concept of tenure to professional football:

> Imagine the National Football League in an alternative reality. Each player's salary is based on how long he's been in the league. It's about tenure, not talent. The same pay scale is used for every player, no matter whether he's been an All-Pro quarterback or the last man on the roster. For every year a player's been in the NFL he gets a bump in pay. The only difference between Tom Brady and the worst player in the league is a few years of step increases. And if a player makes it through his third season, he can never be cut from the roster until he chooses to retire, except in the most extreme cases of misconduct.

> Let's face the truth about this alternate reality. The on-field product would steadily decline. Why bother playing harder or better and risk getting hurt?

Some say that the real problem lies with school administrators who hand out tenure like candy, without closely scrutinizing teachers during their probationary years.

"Yes there are many teachers . . . that possess none of the attributes it takes to be a good teacher," retired teacher Matt Coleman wrote to his local newspaper. "Tenure is not the problem; the failure to evaluate teachers properly and often is. Because of this, tenure has been granted to too many people not suited to be teachers for a variety of untenable reasons."

Most young teachers have the enthusiasm, but do they also have the skills necessary to help kids learn? That should become obvious over the first three to five years, and principals should be aware of who's making the grade and who isn't.

A lot of young teachers quickly realize the job isn't for them and leave on their own. Some people bemoan the fact that about 45 percent of new teachers walk away within their first five years—but they are probably doing everyone a favor by acknowledging early on that they're in the wrong line of work.

Other new teachers, despite their obvious lack of skill or enthusiasm for the job, will try to hang on. Principals shouldn't be shy about letting these young teachers go, but that doesn't happen as often as it should. A recent report from the nonpartisan TNTP, titled "The Irreplaceables," found this to be a very serious issue:

> Principals rarely attempt to dismiss or counsel out chronically low-performing teachers, though we found teachers are nearly three times as likely to plan to leave if encouraged to do so. In fact, principals often work to retain low-performing teachers, even though a brand new teacher will pay off in improved performance about 75 percent of the time.

> Tolerating poor performers keeps ineffective teachers in the classroom indefinitely, demoralizes outstanding teachers, and allows the entire teaching profession to be defined by mediocrity rather than excellence.

A 2009 *Los Angeles Times* investigation found that the Los Angeles school district denied tenure to fewer than 2 percent of probationary teachers, and their evaluations often consisted of single, pre-announced classroom visits that lasted a half hour or less.

In 2010, National Public Radio reported that only one out of every 1,000 teachers is fired for performance-related reasons nationwide. Compare that to one out of every 97 lawyers losing their license to practice law or one out of every 57 doctors having their license revoked, according to the Center for Union Facts. As one New Jersey teachers' union representative bluntly admitted, "I've gone in and defended teachers who shouldn't even be pumping gas."

There is another group of teachers to consider as well: those who are excellent in their first five to twenty years on the job, but then burn out with another twenty years still to go. Some of them leave voluntarily, which is good for everyone, but many others hang on for the increasing salary that automatically comes with seniority, as well as the benefits, security, and promise of a nice pension. Worse, these teachers are frequently encouraged to stay by the "longevity bonuses" written into most teachers' union contracts.

In 2013, Sarasota County, Florida, schools shelled out a staggering $9 million in longevity bonuses "to more than half of the district employees," according to the *Herald-Tribune*. Those bonuses were on top of a 3.25 percent across-the-board pay raise.

The Killeen, Texas, district offers a $1,175 bonus for every five years of employment to its teachers. Ending that practice could save the district $900,000 per year, according to the *Killeen Daily Herald*.

Too much security in any profession or situation breeds laziness. When there is no threat of termination and loss of income and lifestyle, there is less motivation for individuals to keep innovating, improving, and challenging themselves. Who doesn't remember at least a few older teachers from our K–12 days who were seemingly riding out their remaining years to retirement with little in the way of effort? That's human nature. Every employee in every profession needs some degree of accountability and an occasional kick in the pants. Without that they become complacent. And complacent teachers usually result in complacent students.

One educator who regularly (and anonymously) publishes a blog called "Confessions of a Burned Out Teacher" recently made a very honest admission:

> I am burned out, I do not like being in the classroom and will be honest and blunt about my true feelings. I am not willing to quit teaching to get just any ole job so my quest to find a professional position in the education field outside the high school classroom is my goal. I have been a high school teacher since 1998 nonstop so something has kept me there this long. I am not a bad teacher, I am not the best teacher. I am quick to admit that I could be a much better teacher if that is what I really wanted to do.

Michael Smith, an Illinois school superintendent who publishes a blog called PrincipalsPage.com, wrote a great response to the anonymous, "burned out" teacher:

> I've come to understand that people who have tenure love it. I mean LOVE it, love, love, love it. Absolutely love it. And what's not to love? You have a job. You get to keep the job. Forever. And as most of you know, that's a very long time. Tenure is a pretty good deal if you can get it.
>
> But I would like to ask for one exception. If you publicly announce that you're "burnt out," this statement should lead to

the automatic recall of your tenure rights. No exceptions. My
theory is once someone says this out loud, there is no turning
back. If a person establishes that they are "burnt out," then they
can't come back, at least in the same career.

So if you are in your first year of teaching or 30th year and the
"burnt out" bug hits you, you're done. No tenure. No job. No
nothing (except your pension and maybe parting gifts, but
that's it). Because teaching is kind of important and once the
passion has left you, so should tenure.

Compare the anonymous teacher's blog, which is from a real,
working educator, to this quote from actor Matt Damon, who
thinks he knows how teachers think:

> It's like saying a teacher is going to get lazy when they have ten-
> ure. A teacher wants to teach. I mean, why else would you take
> a [expletive] salary and really long hours and do that job unless
> you really love to do it?

Well, Matt, in your utopian world where everyone only does what
they love, I guess you're right. But in the real world, where people
care about their income and benefits and how they're going to pay
their mortgage and put their kids through college, having a job—
sometimes *any* job—matters.

If we really care about our kids, we need to do more than talk;
we need to act. We can't afford to let these types of teachers hang
around and ride it out until retirement. Teaching is one profession
where the question "What have you done for us lately?" is appropriate and crucial to keep asking, even for those who have been in
the classroom for thirty or forty years.

7

PAY SHOULD BE BASED ON SENIORITY, NOT PERFORMANCE

"They know that merit pay undermines collaboration and teamwork.
They know that it corrupts the culture of the school. But corporate reformers
think they know best, so they continue to push for a reward system
that will give bonuses for 'effective' teachers (those whose students get
higher test scores) and, thus, magically, make teaching attractive to the
theoretical 'best and brightest,' those graduates of Harvard, Princeton, Yale,
and Stanford who would stay in teaching if only they could
compete every year for an extra $5,000 or so."

—*DIANE RAVITCH, Research Professor of Education, New York University*

"We all must be wary of any system that creates a climate where
students are viewed as part of the pay equation, rather than young
people who deserve a high quality education that prepares
them for their future."

—*BILL RAABE, NEA's director of collective bargaining and member benefits*

"I get nervous when I hear merit pay because it pits teachers against
each other. We're teaching children. We're not producing widgets."

—*DENNIS DUFFY, union president and teacher*

There are many remarkable people who don't teach for the money, but for the love of the job and their compassion for children. Our system could seemingly not care less about them.

For an example of this in the real world, consider "Sarah," a teacher who took part (anonymously) in a study from the TNTP after voluntarily transferring to a low-achieving school in a low-income neighborhood. The impact Sarah had there was, by all measures, pretty incredible:

> Despite the challenges her low-income students faced, Sarah helped them make extraordinary academic strides compared with other teachers in her school and district. Almost all of her two dozen fourth-grade students spoke Spanish at home, and their English skills were shaky. But when they took required math and reading tests in English that spring, all but one passed the math exam, and all but four passed reading.

By the end of the school year, Sarah had decided to leave her job. Why? Because her extraordinary efforts, and the outstanding performance of her students, were barely noticed by school administrators. "The principal just signed my paperwork," Sarah said after resigning, "and didn't even say a word. It made me feel like he couldn't care less, not about me and not about this school. If he would have said 'What's it going to take for me to get you to stay?' that's all he had to do. Most people, if they had a really dynamic teacher, wouldn't they say 'What's it going to take?' "

The answer to her question seems to be "no." Mediocrity has become the accepted norm in far too many American government schools, particularly low-achieving schools in economically depressed areas. The best teachers are not valued any more than their peers.

This acceptance of mediocrity is tragically reflected in the personnel policies of most public schools. Union pay scales, which are based solely on seniority and the number of college credits earned, allow some of the worst teachers to collect the same salaries and raises as the best teachers, year after year. These unions operate on the belief that all teachers are equally valuable and their compensation should be primarily based on their years of service. As a result, "last in, first out" provisions in union contracts allow some bad teachers to keep their jobs while good (and generally younger) teachers with less seniority are laid off.

In the Westerville, Ohio, school district, for example, a union contract provision stipulated that a coin flip would be used to determine seniority if two teachers were hired on the same day. One might be a great teacher, the other awful; it makes no difference. That is how much importance unions place on teacher quality.

Even worse are union-negotiated salary scales, which dictate how much teachers will make throughout their careers. They are based completely on seniority and the number of graduate-level college credits earned. Nothing in the typical pay scale provides extra compensation for teachers who are positively impacting student learning.

A perfect example is Jeff Charbonneau, a high school chemistry teacher from Washington State who was named the 2013 National Teacher of the Year. An enterprising journalist did a little digging and learned that roughly 25,000 teachers in Charbonneau's state make more than he does, simply because they've worked longer.

LaRae Munk, a former teacher and local union president who has since become a union critic, believes that this kind of thing takes a toll on teachers. "Though most teachers do not rank salary as their highest priority," she wrote, "the single pay schedule does hurt morale, makes teachers feel unappreciated, and prevents districts from attracting and retaining the best educators, which in turns hurts the quality of students' education."

"We bear a lot of responsibility for this," admitted AFT president Randi Weingarten. "We were focused—as unions are—on fairness and not as much on quality."

These pay scales that promote mediocrity are also incredibly expensive. The Los Angeles Unified School District, for example, paid out $47 million in automatic, annual "step" increases for teachers in 2010–2011. The Denver district paid out an additional $21.4 million and the Detroit district spent $15.6 million. There was no promise of better results in the classroom, so what did taxpayers get in return?

This entire system probably sounds ridiculous to people not involved in the education industry—but it sometimes even sounds ridiculous to those who *are* involved. Antonio Villaraigosa, the former Democratic mayor of Los Angeles, called teachers' unions "the most powerful defenders of a broken system."

Given that Villaraigosa was mayor of the city with the second-largest school district in the country (and, before that, a teachers' union organizer) he had a unique view of the damage done by teachers' unions there. "The notion that seniority drives every decision—assignments, promotions, layoffs—is unsustainable," he said. "Imagine if I ran for a third term and said, 'Vote for me, I've been here the longest.' "

In many ways teachers' unions are strikingly similar to the unions of industrial workers. The typical mentality among the leadership of "less work for more money" is far too prevalent. Outstanding efforts by individual employees are frowned upon, because they give "management" a reason to expect better results without an increase in compensation.

How many industrial workers have naïvely busted their butts

at first, only to be pulled aside and told by the union steward to "slow down, you're making everyone else look bad"?

Teachers' unions generally despise capitalism and the very concept of financial profit, particularly in education. They hate the idea of private charter school management companies making money, even if they produce great academic results. Yet, at the same time, they fail to recognize the greed inherent in the system they've created, a system that demands no minimum level of profit or service, guarantees employment, and makes them virtually unaccountable to any of the key stakeholders in education.

Union leaders essentially want the public to believe that all teachers are equal and deserve to be paid and treated that way— but that's clearly not the case. Some teachers are much more effective than others in helping kids learn, yet school policies and pay scales do little to recognize or reward their efforts. That's proven by how little importance schools have traditionally attached to teacher evaluations. For years it's been commonplace for principals to base entire evaluations on short, prescheduled classroom observations and to give nearly all teachers outstanding reviews.

In Florida, those sorts of "drive-by" evaluations recently resulted in nearly 100 percent of the state's teachers being rated "satisfactory." Officials there, motivated by $43 million in federal "Race to the Top" dollars, have tried to address the problem by developing and implementing tougher teacher evaluations. But it hasn't worked—97 percent of Florida teachers were still rated "effective" or "highly effective" in 2012–2013.

The *Los Angeles Times* created a stir in recent years by publishing a series about teacher effectiveness. They included teachers' names, along with the test scores of their students and the amount of personal growth students were making as they progressed through the system and worked with various educators.

One story in this series focused on two fifth-grade classes in the same elementary school and the vastly different experiences the students had due to the difference in quality between the two teachers:

> Year after year, one fifth-grade class learns far more than the other down the hall. With [teacher] Miguel Aguilar, students consistently have made striking gains on some state standardized tests, many of them vaulting from the bottom third of students in Los Angeles schools to well above average. John Smith's pupils next door have started out slightly ahead of Aguilar's but by the end of the year have been far behind.

Aguilar and Smith are on the exact same pay scale. Would anybody be surprised if Aguilar packed up and moved to another school, or another profession, where his outstanding work would be recognized and rewarded?

Unions like to emphasize seniority and education when it comes to compensation, but there's no real evidence that those things actually matter when it comes to effectiveness. Does seniority really improve student achievement? It may be counterintuitive, but it's a question worth exploring.

The recent TNTP study "The Irreplaceables" looked at four large urban school districts around the country and found that "40 percent of teachers with more than seven years of experience are less effective at advancing education progress than the average first-year teacher."

Schools across the nation have been paying nearly $15 billion per year in bonuses for teachers with advanced college degrees, but the TNTP report proves that this might not be money well spent:

> [Those teachers] are no more effective on average, than their counterparts without master's degrees. The more nuanced evidence suggests that master's degrees in math and science do

confer an instructional advantage on teachers of those subjects, yet approximately 90 percent of the master's degrees held by teachers come from education programs that tend to be unrelated to or unconcerned with instructional efficacy.

In other words, we're paying teachers for showing up year after year and earning unrelated degrees that do not actually improve their skills, but we're not rewarding those who actually help kids learn.

"The Irreplaceables" offers a very sobering summary of what this all means for our schools:

> Knowing the power of great teachers, one would expect schools to be sharply focused on keeping far more of their best teachers than their lower performers. Instead they keep all teachers at strikingly similar rates, and about half of the Irreplaceables (the most effective 20 percent) leave within their first five years.

Some school administrators would like to improve the quality of their teaching staffs, but the current union compensation system makes that very difficult to do. The result, according to the TNTP study, is that "about 55 percent of Irreplaceables earn lower base salaries than the average ineffective teacher."

Many organizations, such as school reformer Michelle Rhee's progressive group StudentsFirst, echo that sentiment:

> By removing any financial incentive for individual effort or excellence, these prohibitions only encourage mediocrity. Other professions do not actively prohibit their strongest performers from receiving individual financial rewards. A true performance-based pay system will reward teachers on an individual level for individual achievements in advancing student performance and not solely on seniority and additional degrees.

Some school districts are cutting through the union rhetoric and actually implementing a new performance-based pay system. For example, Michigan's Leslie Public Schools district established a committee of teachers, administrators, and school board members to develop a "total merit pay process," according to the free-market Mackinac Center for Public Policy.

"I think there is a belief in our community that if somebody is doing a good job they should get rewarded for doing a good job whether they've been here 10 years, or 40 years or two years," Superintendent Jeff Manthei told Mackinac's *Capitol Confidential*. "The present system doesn't allow for that. And we want to attract good teachers. The teacher reaction has been positive."

In Wisconsin, where union pay scales are no longer in place, schools have started to recruit outstanding teachers from neighboring districts. That has resulted in some teachers making much more than they were making under the old union system.

"We are particularly finding a trend of schools losing high-performing, well-trained teachers with five to twenty years of school district experience, being recruited to other school districts paying them $5,000 to $15,000 more for the same position," said Oshkosh school superintendent Stan Mack.

"We are hearing some stories about teachers using their ability to get higher pay elsewhere to negotiate higher pay with their current employer," said Barry Forbes, associate executive director of the Wisconsin Association of School Boards.

It is human nature to want to be recognized and rewarded for achievement. Anyone who argues against that is simply arguing for the failing status quo. It's time we start treating teachers as the professionals they are—people with different levels of enthusiasm, passion, skills, and, yes, experience—rather than as robots lined up alongside an assembly line.

8

ONLY PEOPLE WHO GO TO A COLLEGE OF EDUCATION SHOULD BE TEACHERS

"Alternative teacher certification programs that push candidates into classrooms without any real intensive training contribute to the already pervasive sentiment that teaching is something anyone can do."
—NATIONAL EDUCATION ASSOCIATION

Teach For America is a national organization that places temporary teachers in K–12 classrooms in financially and academically struggling school districts. The group is very difficult to get accepted into as it only considers top graduates from top universities. One recent Harvard graduate said that fifteen to twenty of her classmates applied for TFA, but only four or five were accepted. She said one of her closest friends from Harvard was among those turned away, and had to settle for law school at the University of Virginia.

On the flip side, it's not very hard at all to get accepted into our nation's teaching colleges. Once you're in, you don't have to do extremely well to graduate and gain certification to teach in a K–12 school. As the *Wall Street Journal* put it, "entrance requirements to most colleges of education are too lax, and the requirements for graduation are too low."

Most of our nation's teachers come from those colleges. (The Department of Education reports that just 15 percent of teachers enter the profession via alternative programs.) And that has left us in quite a bind. "[Teacher] colleges have become an industry of mediocrity, churning out first-year teachers with classroom management skills and content knowledge inadequate to thrive in classrooms with ever increasing ethnic and socioeconomic student diversity," the National Council on Teacher Quality reported.

A recent study by McKinsey reported that "the U.S. attracts most of its teachers from the bottom two-thirds of college classes, with nearly half coming from the bottom third, especially for schools in poor neighborhoods. Department of Education data shows that only 23 percent of new teachers overall—and about 14 percent of those in high-poverty schools, come from the top third of graduates."

The worst part is that the unions have recognized this trend for years and have done nothing to stop it. Over a decade ago, Sandra Feldman, former president of the American Federation of Teachers, said, "You have in the schools right now, among the teachers who are going to be retiring, very smart people. We're not getting in now the same kinds of people. It's disastrous. We've been saying for years now that we're attracting from the bottom one-third."

How did this happen?

A study conducted by Arthur Levine, former president of Columbia University's progressive Teachers College, concluded "that a majority of teacher education graduates are prepared in university-based programs that suffer from low admission and graduation standards. Their faculties, curriculums and research are disconnected from school practice and practitioners. There are wide variations in program quality, with the majority of teachers prepared in lower quality programs."

Given all of this, one would think there would be more wide-spread acceptance of alternative teacher certification programs—like TFA and others—that allow outstanding young college graduates and established professionals to enter the classroom without having to jump through traditional hoops. After all, as Becca Garcia from the National Center for Policy Analysis explains, "Alternative certification programs have attracted people that are more devoted to the teaching profession. Commitment and enthusiasm bring in quality that is also needed."

But the education establishment fights alternative certification with every resource at its disposal. Their leaders claim it's because traditional teacher training is necessary to adequately prepare instructors for the rigors of the K–12 world, but the real reasons are much less truth and far more selfish.

The truth is that the teachers' unions want to protect their members' jobs, regardless of their performance in the classroom. Remember: the unions protect the teachers, not the students. They don't want state governments and school districts to be tempted to dump union contracts and employment protections (like they've done in Wisconsin) in favor of nontraditional teachers who have little interest in union membership or Big Labor activism. That would cause a significant reduction in dues revenue and political power and eventually spell the end of teachers' unions as we know them.

The teacher colleges want to protect their monopoly over the training market. George Leef, director of research for the Pope Center for Higher Education Policy, explained why most states require a degree from a college of education for teacher certification:

The ed schools have a guaranteed market and are shielded from competition. The professors and administrators are happy with the way things are, and often express resentment at anyone who suggests that their courses and philosophy do not lead to competent teachers.

The problem is that the teacher colleges define "competent" in a different way than most parents might. As a parent, I want more teachers who are effective in instructing kids in the fundamentals and helping them prepare for whatever track they decide to take: college or a career. But like most colleges and universities in general, most of the teacher colleges have also fallen under the control of progressives who reject traditional teaching methods and measures of learning, even in fundamental subjects like reading, writing, and math.

As Leef wrote:

> Under "progressive" educational thinking, it supposedly dampens a student's creativity and spontaneity to insist on following fuddy-duddy old rules about composition and English usage. Besides that, most of the prospective teachers are not very good at writing themselves, having come through schools where they were taught by teachers who were told that it's bad to fuss over writing. We are caught in a downward spiral of falling competence.

Newly minted teachers emerge from college with few English skills, little respect for the discipline, and heads filled with ideas about the fundamental unfairness of America and how capitalism and individualism are terrible things. Then we put these teachers in front of classrooms, tell them they have no seniority and will be the first to be fired, no matter how they perform, and expect them to be world-class instructors.

In 2010, the mean math SAT score for college freshmen majoring in education was just 486, compared with a mean of 516 for all freshmen. Think about that: our teaching candidates are *worse* in math than the general population of college students. "Most colleges and universities have no incentive to change: The education schools are cash cows, milked for the benefit of the rest of the institution and rarely held accountable for being subpar," educators Barbara Nemko and Harold Kwalwasser wrote in a *Wall Street Journal* opinion piece. "Education curricula are almost uniformly out of date and far too theoretical, with minimal classroom-teaching requirements. Too often, these future educators learn to 'teach' math, but they don't necessarily learn how to do the math itself."

The main problem is that modern university officials see tomorrow's K–12 teachers as being much more than instructors charged with the intellectual development of future generations. They see teachers as primary agents of social change who should use their important positions to recruit new disciples of socialist thought. If the teachers do their jobs correctly, they will produce a generation of students who will fundamentally alter American society. They are, to put it in terms President Obama would appreciate, the community organizers of our youth.

Who cares if Johnny can read or write as long as he's ready to join the people's uprising against the one-percenters!

Okay, so maybe that's a slight exaggeration, but it seems to me that our education colleges have lost sight of the forest for the trees. They are concerned with manufacturing teachers who are great in almost everything except actual mastery of the subjects they're going to teach. (In case you're wondering, no, this is not teacher bashing—it's a further indictment of the system. There are plenty of great teachers who've escaped the Matrix; it's just getting harder and harder to do.)

In 2009, the University of Minnesota announced a "Teacher Education Redesign Initiative" to alter admissions standards for its school of education. The proposal, designed by the "Race, Culture, Class and Gender Task Group," declared that teacher candidates "will be able to discuss their own histories and current thinking drawing on notions of white privilege, hegemonic masculinity, heteronormativity, and internalized oppression."

The Task Group suggested that future teachers should:

- Fight for social justice even if it's just in their classroom.
- Understand resistance theory.
- Explain how institutional racism works in schools.

According to the Foundation for Individual Rights in Education (FIRE), a group credited with exposing the proposed policy, "Those with the 'wrong' views were to receive remedial re-education, be weeded out, or be denied admission altogether." Fortunately, under pressure from FIRE, the university eventually dumped the initiative—but other teacher colleges have continued to drift toward the "social justice" approach to K–12 education:

- Prospective teachers at Brooklyn College are met with the declaration: "Our teacher candidates and other school personnel are prepared to demonstrate a knowledge of, language for, and the ability to create educational environments based on various theories of social justice."
- At Marquette University, the College of Education has declared that education should be a tool "to transcend the negative effects of the dominant culture" and all prospective teachers should

demonstrate a "desire to work for social justice, particularly in an urban environment."

- At Humboldt State University in California, the syllabus of a social studies methods class, which is required for prospective K–12 teachers, says, "It is not an option for history teachers to teach social justice and social responsibility; it is a mandate. History teachers do their best work when they use their knowledge, their commitment, and their courage to help the students grapple with the important issues of social responsibility and when they encourage them to direct their lives toward creating a just society."

In 2004, David Steiner, former chairman of the Department of Education Policy at the School of Education at Boston University, and Susan Rozen, director of reading and literacy for Bedford, Massachusetts, public schools, conducted a study of textbooks most commonly used in basic "foundation of education" and "methods" courses at sixteen respected teacher colleges. They found that some of the most commonly assigned texts were books by Paulo Freire, a radical Brazilian educator who was considered the founder of the "teaching for social justice" movement.

Freire's most famous book, *Pedagogy of the Oppressed*, is one of the most commonly used texts in "philosophy of education" classes. Sol Stern, from the free-market Manhattan Institute, explains why this is troubling:

The odd thing is that Freire's magnum opus isn't, in the end, about education—certainly not the education of children. *Pedagogy of the Oppressed* mentions nothing of the issues that troubled education reformers throughout the twentieth century: testing, standards, curriculum, the role of parents, how to organize schools, what subjects should be taught in various grades, how best to train teachers, the most effective way of teaching disadvantaged students. This ed-school bestseller is, instead, a utopian political tract calling for the overthrow of capitalist hegemony and the creation of classless societies.

The 2004 Steiner/Rozen study found that another book popular among these sixteen respected teacher colleges was one by Bill Ayers, the former 1960s Weather Underground terrorist who eventually became a professor of education at the University of Illinois.

In 2009, Ayers was elected vice president for curriculum studies at the American Educational Research Association, the largest group of education school professors and researchers in the United States. This position gave him an incredible level of influence over the content taught in America's public schools.

"Ayers seeks to inculcate teachers-in-training with a 'social commitment' to the values of 'Marx' and a desire to become agents of social change in K–12 classrooms," the Manhattan Institute's Stern wrote.

To be honest, I wouldn't necessarily have a problem with the Freire and Ayers books being used in these schools if they were followed up by books from people like Milton Friedman and Thomas Sowell. If the idea was to present students with *both* sides of an argument and ask them to think critically about it, then you might convince me that a Freire book has a place in the curriculum. But that's obviously not what's happening. This is not critical thinking, it's persuasion and indoctrination into a worldview with the hope that these teachers will pass that worldview on to their students.

Meanwhile, reformers keep pushing for the expansion of alternate teaching certification so that at least some prospective educators can find jobs and help kids learn without having to first be processed through Marxist brainwashing factories.

For-profit companies like IteachU.S. and nonprofits like Teach For America continue to grow in popularity as suppliers of nontraditional teachers—and the teachers they produce have been widely praised by school administrators across the nation. But they continue to face stiff opposition from the education establishment, particularly the wealthy teachers' unions. As Eugene Hickok, the former deputy secretary of education under President George W. Bush, explained, "The National Education Association has declared its objective to make licensure 'a process controlled by the profession.' It is clear to us that the profession has been doing little to ensure that new teachers have the knowledge base they need, and much more to ensure that colleges of education could expand their control of the preparation of public school teachers."

The unions spend millions of dollars of campaign contributions every election cycle to purchase puppet politicians who will protect their virtual monopoly over this process. The result is that any serious effort to wrestle teacher training and certification away from the controllists is going to be a long, hard slog.

To understand just *how* long and hard, consider the healthcare industry. The American Medical Association was founded in 1847 and became one of the largest and most powerful professional organizations in the country. Most people associate the AMA with the setting of standards and assurance of quality, but, according to Dale Steinreich, an adjunct scholar of the Mises Institute, they had other objectives in mind. "In the days of its founding AMA was much more open—at its conferences and in its publications—about its real goal: building a government-enforced monopoly for the purpose of dramatically increasing physician incomes."

As Steinreich explains, their strategy to accomplish this was to limit competition through regulation and "significantly restrict entrance to the profession by restricting the number of approved medical schools in operation and thus the number of students admitted to those approved schools yearly."

It worked. The AMA's control over the schools that could license new doctors drove up costs and incomes and eventually led to the current government takeover of the entire health-care industry. We are on the exact same track for education. With the unions and schools working together, the government will eventually be "forced" to step in to rescue American education with a new, federal approach.

In 2011, Minnesota governor Mark Dayton signed a bill into law that will enable teachers certified through alternative training programs like TFA to work in government schools. By 2013, TFA Twin Cities was flooded with twice as many teacher applications as it could process. Education Minnesota, the state's largest teachers' union, responded by organizing a statewide letter and phone call campaign that convinced Governor Dayton to veto a bill that would have provided TFA with $1.5 million to meet the increased demand.

They reminded Dayton, a pro-labor Democrat, that he works for them.

Meanwhile, to ensure that TFA would fail, the Minnesota Board of Teaching voted to stop granting temporary teaching licenses to all TFA instructors, instead ruling that each *individual* TFA instructor would have to apply for an individual variance. This decision came just weeks before the start of the 2013 fall semester, leaving many schools that had already hired TFA teachers with open positions and few other options.

It's no coincidence that five of the board members who made this decision are teachers' union leaders, while two others represent traditional teaching colleges.

9

SCHOOL CURRICULUM IS BASED ON A CONSERVATIVE, "WHITES FIRST" WORLDVIEW

"Education is deeply rooted in culture. In the United States, whites are most typically brought up in some version of the northern European tradition. This makes problems for everyone else, because educators . . . practice an unconscious form of cultural imperialism which they impose indiscriminately on others. . . . I refer not so much to content as to how learning is organized, how it is presented, its setting, the language used, and the people who teach it, the rules by which they play, as well as the institutions themselves."

—*EDWARD T. HALL,* anthropologist and former college professor

America's historic civil rights movement is being hijacked by radical educators.

It's all part of their effort to take control over what our children learn and think with the hope that future generations will be more accommodating to efforts to dismantle our nation's capitalistic economic system and impose state control and socialism.

Radical educators are very clever to use civil rights, and the racial inequities that have plagued our society for centuries, as a tool to further their Marxist agenda. That's because few Americans disagree with the fundamental arguments of the original civil rights movement—that barriers needed to be removed so that people of all races can have an equal chance to achieve the American dream.

Education is a natural arena for positive action in the struggle for civil rights. By making sure that all children, regardless of race, have equal access to quality schools and quality instruction, we are giving them a better shot at having a successful life. In the process, we are making America a better country for everyone.

But integration of minorities into the capitalist mainstream is not the goal of today's "social justice" educators. In fact, their goal is not one of integration, but rather to drive wedges between groups and ultimately co-opt all people into the fight for "social justice," a rebranded version of the Marxist class struggle.

Educators appeal to students' emotions by putting forth a narrative that portrays whites as oppressors in order to foment racial resentment and portray America's history as fundamentally unjust. This worldview pits race against race and class against class and leads these students to believe that capitalism is exploitative, inherently unfair, and antithetical to their economic interests. No one wants to be on the side of the oppressor.

Mary Grabar, an Emory University professor who is a critic of left-wing educators, sums up their plan pretty well:

The goal is not equal rights or creating opportunities for everyone to do their best. The goal is to distribute wealth more equally. It has an overriding Marxist theme.

The natural inclination [of typical Americans] is that social justice is a good thing. Most Americans are fair-minded. They don't like racism, they don't like poverty, they don't like discrimination in any form. They are inclined to allow these kinds of lessons in the classroom because they think they represent American values. I don't think they're aware of the bigger theories behind this.

We've already seen how so many schools of education in American universities marinate prospective K–12 teachers in leftist ideology, but efforts are also growing to indoctrinate teachers who are *already* in classrooms, through programs like CREATE Wisconsin and teacher training offered by companies like Pacific Educational Group (PEG).

CREATE (Culturally Responsive Education for All: Training and Enhancement) Wisconsin is a state-sponsored initiative that ostensibly exists to help white teachers learn how to more effectively instruct minority students. The program costs taxpayers roughly $1 million per year.

PEG is a national organization that contracts with school districts around the nation and has the same fundamental goal as CREATE. As of early 2014, PEG's website listed 185 school districts as clients, along with teachers' unions, state departments of education, state school board associations, and parent-teacher associations. And before you dismiss them as a group that only services blue states, keep in mind that the Texas Association of School Administrators was listed, too. Both PEG and CREATE Wisconsin have taken the theory of "white privilege" (which was created in the 1960s by the radical Students for a Democratic Society) and adapted it to education. Their argument, on the surface, is that our education system is too biased toward white cultural norms, and a "Eurocentric" understanding of the American experience, for minority students to grasp.

To be fair, some of their basic arguments have some merit. One of their points, for instance, is that far too many minority students struggle in school as a result of cultural differences, and are therefore unfairly assigned to special education classes where all hope for real learning usually ends. A recent survey of the Madison, Wisconsin, school district revealed that black students comprise 24 percent of the student population, but 29 percent of the special education enrollment. Native Americans comprise 1 percent of the student population but 20 percent of special education enrollment.

"There is a huge disparity in overrepresentation, misclassification, and hardship for minority students, primarily for African-Americans and Native Americans, not only in referral to special education, but also in identification as special ed," said Matt Stewart, former education director for the Hmong Cultural Center, who was actively involved in CREATE Wisconsin.

I don't think anyone would argue with asking teachers to take a long look at their strategies for making sure information is being understood by minority students. If that requires a little more effort, so what? But the radical leaders of PEG and CREATE Wisconsin go way past that. Their message is that the current education and economic system are hopelessly biased against minorities and the poor and must be radically changed to meet their needs.

They begin with the argument that too many white educators are blinded by their status at the top of American society to make any serious effort to assist and empower minorities. "[M]ost American teachers not only do not know how to deal with these students, but have been taught through years of white privilege that these children are different, slower, and to be feared," Stewart told an audience at a 2009 CREATE Wisconsin conference.

These groups also like to plant seeds of racial resentment. Consider the following statements, PowerPoint items, and website postings associated with CREATE Wisconsin:

- "In this country the institutional system supports the dominance of white people."
- "More frequently than not, white people take advantage of privileges generated by a racist society."
- "Racism is caused by white people, by our attitudes, behaviors, practices, and institutions. How is it that white people can justify retaining the benefits of being white without taking responsibility for perpetuating racism? How can you justify it for yourself?"
- "We are given a false sense of superiority, a belief that we should be in control and in authority, and that all people of color should be maids, servants, and gardeners and be limited to the less valued work in society."

That last quote seems particularly absurd, considering that millions of white Americans have twice elected an African-American president of the United States. But statements like these, and the mentality they represent, do nothing to promote harmony, trust, and cooperation between races. Worst, they treat society as separate groups of people who all think and act the same way. In other words, they fail to recognize the individual.

According to PEG's training materials, minority groups focus on "color group collectivism," which entails "fostering interdependence and group success," "shared property," and "making life choices on what will be best for the family." The idea they are promoting is that it's wrong and pointless to teach the American work ethic to minority children because they cannot grasp the concept.

What an insult that is to overwhelming number of people who show up to work hard every day in the hope of creating a better future for themselves and their kids. And what a horrible idea it is to convince minority children that they don't have to bother worrying about timeliness, planning for the future, or working hard, because those things are only for white people.

American employers expect their employees to be on time and work hard, regardless of their race. Generally speaking, people who adhere to those fundamental expectations tend to do pretty well in their careers. People who show up late or are lazy usually find the unemployment line. Are the people who run PEG trying to sentence minorities to a lifetime of welfare checks and food stamps?

Even worse is the suggestion that minority children cannot possibly succeed—at least individually—in classrooms as they exist today. Educators are encouraged to segregate students by race, and to teach minority students by using techniques described by PEG as "group homework preparation," "cooperative projects," and "choral reading."

Teachers are told to be flexible with minority students who are consistently tardy or miss a lot of school because that's just part of their culture. They are trained to be tolerant when black children employ what a CREATE Wisconsin presentation calls "an exuberant participation style of shouting out answers or questions," and are taught that if you ask minority kids to do things the standard way, they will fail.

"When I came here the teachers really did believe that they were doing the best job for the population that they worked with," Sharon Brittingham, a school principal, said to a CREATE Wisconsin conference in 2010. "But what had to change was the belief that these children could learn at high levels of expectations."

Any minority parent with an ounce of common sense would get their child as far away from "educators" like Brittingham as fast as possible. Millions of minority children have excelled over the years in traditional schools with traditional curriculums, and have gone on to graduate and have productive careers and meaningful lives. The quickest way to incentivize failure is to plant the idea that they cannot succeed. The quickest way to dash their hopes is to convince them that a mainstream curriculum is something they'll never be able to grasp.

It's one thing for teachers to do their best to ensure that lessons are meaningful for students of all ethnic backgrounds. It's quite another to teach minority students that they aren't subject to normal expectations, and should be treated with a different set of standards and rules. The progressives who espouse this kind of garbage may be serving their own ideological goals, but they are not serving the interests of children.

Radical educators ultimately tip their hand, and expose their true goals, when they discuss their views of America, its history, and its place in the world. They don't like the United States or free enterprise very much, and they want to train teachers to take their anti-American, anticapitalist views into K–12 classrooms and plant them in the minds of impressionable students.

Consider some of the rhetoric from the 2013 "White Privilege Conference 14," an event attended by about two thousand people—including many educators—from forty-one states and four nations. In the past, the conference has been sponsored by the University of Denver, the University of New Mexico, New Mexico State University, the University of Minnesota, the University of Northern Iowa, and Everett (Wash.) Community College, as well as numerous smaller universities and colleges.

A speaker named Bob Jensen said, "Rich people have a lot of problems, a lot of moral problems, partly because they have no soul. Capitalists are not human." He went on to describe American capitalism as "a death cult" and said corporations "are fascist" in nature. He said our free-market system is "inhuman, undemocratic, and unsustainable" and that capitalism forces people to "maximize the worst part of yourself—greed."

A workshop at the conference delivered the message that violating the law is good, that people who follow rules reach a dead end in life, and that the U.S. Constitution was written to benefit only white, property-owning, Christian males.

The desire of these people to indoctrinate students is perfectly clear. The White Privilege Conference sponsors a "Youth Action Project," which is described as "a team of experienced facilitators [providing] a safe and challenging space, geared toward young of ALL ethnic backgrounds, who are committed to understanding and dismantling white supremacy, white privilege, and all other forms of oppression."

That's a nicer way of saying they want to develop a youth movement dedicated to the dismantling of traditional American culture and free enterprise. And they'd love to have the schools' help to do it.

10

THE GOVERNMENT EDUCATION
SYSTEM CAN'T BE REFORMED UNTIL
WE FIRST ERADICATE POVERTY

"Low performance, contrary to the current pseudo reform
movement . . . is not caused by unions, low performance is not
caused by teachers, low performance is caused by the toxic
combination of poverty and segregation."

—*DIANE RAVITCH, Research Professor of Education, New York University*

Most parents probably don't realize that our nation's teachers' unions serve more than one purpose.

First and foremost, they exist to maximize income for their members, protect them from accountability, and suck as much money from government schools as they possibly can—just like any other bureaucracy. But they are also a very active arm of the national Democratic Party. It's therefore not surprising that they've come up with an excuse that serves all of their agendas simultaneously: poverty is to blame for the sorry condition of education in our nation, and nothing will change until it's eliminated.

If that became our nation's official education policy, the unions would have it made. They'd no longer have to worry about calls for better schools and better teachers, because it would be clear to everyone that schools and teachers are just fine—poverty is the real enemy.

The federal government would then start spending billions of additional dollars on the traditional types of welfare programs that the unions and Democrats already endorse. Some of that money would undoubtedly go to government schools to fund the full-service, "wraparound" programs that unions propose. They want schools to not only be education centers but social service centers as well.

That, of course, would continue the vicious cycle of hiring even more government school employees and more dues-paying union members.

Salon columnist David Sirota summarized this strategy pretty well:

> If Americans were serious about fixing the troubled parts of its education system, then we would be having a fundamentally different discussion. We wouldn't be talking about budget austerity—we would be talking about raising public revenues to fund special tutoring, child care, basic health programs, and other so-called wraparound services at low-income schools.

> More broadly, we wouldn't be discussing cuts to social safety net programs—we would instead be working to expand those programs and, further, to challenge both parties' anti-tax, anti-regulation, pro-austerity agenda that has increased poverty and economic inequality.

In short, if we were serious about education, then our education discussion wouldn't be focused on demonizing teachers and coming up with radical schemes to undermine traditional public schools. It would instead be focused on mounting a new war on poverty and thus directly addressing the biggest educational problem of all.

We would be really stupid to fall for this argument, and for a lot of different reasons.

First, while no one disputes the seriousness of poverty in America, leveraging this issue for education is a convenient excuse for schools and unions looking to deflect calls for reforms that include more accountability.

Most experts agree that *all* children can learn—even those living in a state of poverty—with effective instructors. "Good teachers can make a large difference particularly in hard to staff subjects such as math and science within high poverty schools," the progressive organization Stand for Children wrote. A recent study sponsored by the research arm of the U.S. Department of Education found that staffing Teach For America teachers, who are generally placed in poor areas, resulted in math gains equivalent to 2.6 more months of schooling. The study's authors concluded:

> These results suggest that allowing highly qualified teachers, who in the absence of TFA would not have taught in these disadvantaged neighborhoods, should have a positive influence not just on students at the top of the achievement distribution but across the entire math test score distribution.

There's no doubt that poverty and other issues at home can make education more challenging, but poverty should not be used as an excuse for teachers to throw up their hands in defeat—it should instead serve as a rallying call for educators across the nation to work even harder, and devise smarter strategies, to help less fortunate kids learn.

The negative message that learning is not possible in economically depressed areas becomes a self-fulfilling prophecy. Children tend to respond to expectations. Kids in academically excellent school districts often do well, generation after generation, because a high standard has been set for them. Likewise, kids in miserable schools do poorly because that's the standard that's been set for them.

Are we really surprised to see so many kids in poor areas fail when their teachers are shouting from the rooftops that they won't be able to learn anything until poverty is eradicated? The kids start believing that themselves and some, whether consciously or not, basically give up.

Lou Kitchenmaster, a retired teacher from Michigan, wrote an editorial in 2012 that puts the progressive position in perfect perspective:

> None of us would expect our major auto makers to build a high-quality product given damaged or defective materials; however, too many unfairly expect our public schools to accomplish such, regardless of the inherent condition of the "product" they receive.

So he considers poor kids to be "damaged or defective materials"? Is it any wonder they aren't excelling? Would you want your child in this man's classroom?

Here's an ingenious idea for all the woe-is-us educators like Kitchenmaster who just can't seem to accept any blame: let's free you from the burden of dealing with those poor, pathetic "damaged or defective" students by giving them a voucher to enroll at a private school that believes in their abilities and won't let them fail. Their parents, who've never had much in the way of school choice, will welcome the chance to escape.

There are many schools of all varieties—public, charter, and private—that get great academic results from low-income students, mostly because they don't accept failure as an option, and they won't let their students accept it, either.

A good example of this is the American Indian Public Charter Schools in Oakland, California. The total minority enrollment is 99 percent, and 83 percent of students are economically disadvantaged. Yet, academically, American Indian High School ranks *first* among the thirty-three high schools in the Oakland Unified School District. Over the past three years, 100 percent of their graduates have been accepted to four-year colleges.

What makes this school—along with many other charter schools—different is that everyone is held accountable. There are high expectations set for students. There is a culture of success and teachers and principals will not let students fail. Parental involvement is not a bonus, it's a requirement.

Noble Street College Prep in Chicago has a large majority of black and Hispanic students, about 90 percent of whom come from low-income homes. According to recent data, its students have an average ACT score of 20.4 (21.1 is considered "college ready"), compared to 16.3 for students in Chicago Public Schools (CPS). Noble Street's graduation rate is 85.6 percent, compared to 59.4 percent in CPS, and its college enrollment rate is 77.4 percent, compared to 57 percent for CPS.

These kinds of results can only be achieved because the Noble Street staff focuses on setting lofty goals and accomplishing them. Compare that to Chicago Teachers Union president Karen Lewis, who would rather complain about social conditions than set high standards. Lewis, who proudly led twenty-five thousand Chicago teachers on strike in 2012, has blamed everything from poverty to a lack of funding, to "rich white people" for her schools' woes.

At Calcedeaver Elementary in Mobile County, Alabama, 80 percent of students (most of whom are Native Americans) qualify for federally subsidized school lunches. In 2011, 94 percent of their sixth graders met state reading standards while 80 percent *exceeded* the standards. "If you saw [the school facility], you'd have in mind that it's a run-down, rural, isolated school, bursting at the seams, and that students would be prohibited from learning," said Daria Hall, director of K–12 policy at the Education Trust, a group that awarded Calcedeaver with a "Dispelling the Myth" award for proving that poverty does not preclude academic excellence. "They've found ways to work around that."

Hall said that Calcedeaver succeeds because of their "careful attention to instruction day in and day out." The local paper noted that the school's teachers "use test scores and other data to quickly identify those at risk of falling behind, and to help them catch up. The staff even tracks pupils through high school, to make sure they graduate."

There is no surrender to poverty at this school, no wobbly-kneed excuses. The staff recognizes its challenge on a daily basis and rises to it. Hall said the school dispels "the pervasive and destructive myth that poor kids and kids of color can't learn at high levels."

The teachers' unions and their apologists should pay closer attention to schools like these rather than simply trying to use poverty as a means toward some kind of social utopia where learning conditions would be perfect for everyone. And they should listen to more people like Lynnell Mickelsen, a progressive and former defender of the unions who has since come to realize that poverty isn't the problem, it's the way society treats those who are poor that is the problem:

> [T]he argument that we must first end poverty (a task that will not end in our life-times) before we can design schools to work better for students is bullsh-t. And progressives should stop making it.

> It's not an either/or choice. We can do both. We must do both.

11

STATES HAVE FAILED,
SO WE NOW NEED NATIONAL STANDARDS;
"LOCAL CONTROL" IS JUST A RUSE
TO PROTECT MEDIOCRITY

"One way to ensure that young people develop the skills they need
to compete globally is to set clear standards about what schools
should teach and students should learn—and make these standards
uniform across the land. Leaving such decisions to individual states,
communities, and schools is no longer serving the U.S. well."

—*CHESTER E. FINN JR., president of the Thomas B. Fordham Institute and
chairman of the Hoover Institution's Koret Task Force on K–12 Education*

"[Common Core critics] are defending mediocrity
under the mask of 'local control.'"

—*WILLIAM C. HARRISON, former chairman of the North Carolina State Board of Education*

The controllists have a point with this argument, but not the
way they think.

They're right when they say that some states have lowered the bar on learning quality and expectations in order to drive up scores on standardized, fill-in-the-oval state tests. That's been pretty well documented by researchers.

For example, a 2008 analysis by *Education Next* editors found that forty-seven states had such a generous definition of what constituted proficiency in math and reading that most students were found to be competent in those important subject areas. However, using the federal government's more sober-minded definition, those same states had far fewer proficient students.

One specific example can be found in Georgia, where in 2007 officials declared that 88 percent of their eighth graders were proficient readers. *Education Next* editors, however, concluded that officials were wildly overstating things. Using the feds' measurement standards, only 26 percent of Georgia eighth graders were capable of grade-level reading.

So the controllists are right when they argue that states have dumbed things down in the past, but what they fail to mention is *why* this happened. The ironic truth is that states dumbed things down *as a direct response* to the controllists' effort to "fix" our public schools through big-government programs, most notably No Child Left Behind (NCLB).

NCLB was the brainchild of George W. Bush and Ted Kennedy, both big-government progressives. The central feature of the 2001 law is a federal requirement that states must prove their schools are making "adequate yearly progress" toward the goal that 100 percent of students become proficient in math and reading skills. If schools don't make progress, they're hit with stiff penalties from Washington, D.C.

In order to avoid punishment from their federal overlords, some states have made their standardized tests easier for students to pass. Jay Greene, professor of education reform at the University of Arkansas, says this is because states are trying to appear good—without actually *being* good—to ensure they win "bureaucratic approval from the feds."

It's the type of trick most of us learned when we were five years old.

The lesson most people would take from the No Child Left Behind experiment is that a top-down, heavy-handed approach to improving America's K–12 system doesn't work. It also isn't consistent with the concept of federalism where the states are supposed to be laboratories of experiment. But controllists are so committed to their agenda that they're willing to ignore history and double down on their approach. The problem, they say, is that state tests are too easily manipulated. Their convenient answer is a nationalized, one-size-fits-all set of learning standards that will keep states from cutting corners and playing games with our kids' education.

Now these same people are pushing the Common Core State Standards Initiative (CCSI), a collection of new learning standards that tells schools in virtually every state which concepts to teach kids, grade by grade. The controllists tell us these standards are better and more "rigorous" than the ones states are currently using and will lead to a world-class education for our kids.

Highly respected education scholar Ze'ev Wurman, who was involved in evaluating the quality of Common Core for California disagrees. He says the new learning standards are not only mediocre, but that they'll actually lead to academic atrophy for America's schools.

> I believe the Common Core marks the cessation of educational standards improvement in the United States. No state has any reason left to aspire for first-rate standards, as all states will be

judged by the same mediocre national benchmark enforced by
the federal government.

That cookie-cutter approach to education has a lot of parents
justifiably mad. One of them described Common Core as a "truly
standardized factory-style education" that will result in schools
teaching "exactly the same thing at exactly the same speed to
achieve the same goals." In fact, one might say Common Core
is "spreading the *academic* wealth around" so that every state's
schools are equally mediocre.

What's happened is that we've created this vicious cycle in
which we set federal benchmarks, watch as the states scramble to
meet them, then whine that the states cheated and that the only
way forward is to set uniform national standards. (Economist
Robert Higgs wrote a book about this phenomenon titled *Crisis
and Leviathan,* in which he argues that government intervention
inevitably creates future problems, which results in the government's intervening even more in an attempt to correct them.)
That's exactly what's happening here—but it's a false choice, set up
by the initial insistence by controllists that the federal government
get involved with local education in the first place. Besides, as
Professor Greene of Arkansas points out, most states—acting on
their own free will—have increased and strengthened high school
graduation requirements over time:

> In almost half of the states students now have to pass a state
> test to receive a standard diploma. And 37 states instituted
> their own testing and accountability systems before [No
> Child Left Behind] was adopted. The result of these state and
> local efforts was not always a rigorous education, but they
> clearly show a trend toward higher standards and quality in
> response to consumer demand. Competition produces a race

to the top as long as it is competition for individual taxpayers and business instead of competition for federal government handouts.

Local control worked well enough to make America's education system the envy of the world at one time. We started losing that advantage when local school districts started losing their autonomy.

12

COMMON CORE IS "STATE LED"

"The Common Core State Standards Initiative is a state-led effort coordinated
by the National Governors Association Center for Best Practices (NGA
Center) and the Council of Chief State School Officers (CCSSO)."
—*CORESTANDARDS.ORG*

"Common Core is not a curriculum, a federal program, or a federal
mandate. It was created at the state level. Curriculum remains within
the control of districts, school boards, school leaders, and teachers."
—*THOMAS J. DONOHUE, president and CEO of the U.S. Chamber of Commerce*

"The Common Core State Standards define what students
need to know; they do not define how teachers should teach,
or how students should learn. That is up to each state."
—*JEB BUSH AND JOEL KLEIN, former governor of Florida and former
chancellor of New York City public schools, respectively*

Back when Common Core was still just a twinkle in the controllists' eyes, they understood that any attempt to nationalize our education system would be met with stiff public resistance.

They knew that education in America has traditionally been a matter for local communities to manage. Our Founders explicitly designed our system so that all powers not delegated to the federal government (education included) fell to the states *or the people*; they believed that parents, not government officials, have the moral right to decide what their children are taught.

Thomas Jefferson captured that sentiment perfectly when he wrote, "If it is believed that these elementary schools will be better managed by the governor and council or any other general authority of the government, than by the parents within each ward, it is a belief against all experience."

And that has pretty much been this nation's approach to education, at least until 1965, when Congress passed the Elementary and Secondary Education Act, which gave money to schools to help educate the children of poor families. It was part of President Lyndon B. Johnson's "War on Poverty."

That law gave the federal government a foot in the school door, and progressives have been wedging their way through that a little more every year since.

In 1980, the federal Department of Education opened its doors after President Jimmy Carter cleaved it from the Department of Health, Education, and Welfare. From that moment forward, every American president believed he was expected to have an education agenda that the federal bureaucracy could implement. That, of course, began the power shift from our homes and communities to Washington, D.C.

Despite this, the purveyors of Common Core knew they couldn't come right out and tell Americans, "Hey, we're going to effectively take control of your kids' schools by letting a small group of federal bureaucrats and self-professed education experts decide what gets taught there." They knew that would go over about as well as an announcement that the federal government was going to seize control of the nation's health-care system. These national takeovers require a light touch.

So the controllists decided that Common Core had to appear to be a spontaneous, voluntary decision by the individual states. After all, if the states are running things, then no tinfoil-hat Tea Party members could start making noise about a federal takeover of education.

And, with that, the fabrication that Common Core is a "state-led" effort was born.

Progressives, along with their friends in the media, are so intent on selling the "state-led" notion to people that they repeat that phrase over and over, hoping that they can will it into existence. Start paying attention and you won't believe how much you hear it—it's almost comical.

The controllists sometimes get angry when critics suggest that "state led" is a bit of a fabrication. U.S. Secretary of Education Arne Duncan was downright indignant during a recent speech to journalists: "I believe the Common Core State Standards may prove to be the single greatest thing to happen to public education in America since *Brown v. Board of Education*—and the federal government had nothing to do with creating them. The federal government didn't write [the standards], didn't approve them, and doesn't mandate them. And we never will," he said. "Anyone who says otherwise is either misinformed or willfully misleading."

In typical politician style, Duncan sets up a straw man argument and then destroys it, without ever getting to the real question. In this case he talks about the federal government having nothing to do with the "writing" and "approval" of the standards. Great, I'll concede right now that no federal agency or commission was directly in charge of putting Common Core together—

but that is a completely different issue than whether or not its implementation is being led by states. To get at what's really going on, let's back up a bit.

The Common Core State Standards Initiative, as it's officially known, is the product of three private organizations, two of which have official-sounding names: the National Governors Association (NGA) and the Council of Chief State School Officers (CCSSO). The third private group is Achieve Inc., which boasts on its Web page that it helped take the idea of nationalized learning standards from "a radical proposal into a national agenda."

Between 2007 and 2008 these groups first started to seriously study the idea of imposing one-size-fits-all learning standards in all the states and school districts, a de facto nationalization of America's public schools.

Their plan got its first big jolt when Barack Obama was elected president. His promise to "fundamentally transform" the country was a perfect fit for their agenda. They finally had two things they'd been missing in order to push the plan forward: the right person in the Oval Office, and something to distract everyone from what they were really up to. The historic nature of Obama's inauguration in January 2009, coupled with the economic recovery and the quick push toward Obamacare, was more than enough to do the trick.

As Americans were debating bailouts, individual mandates, and Michelle Obama's finely toned arms, progressives knew they had a golden opportunity to sneak Common Core through the back door. And that's just what they did. Remember what Rahm Emanuel, Obama's first chief of staff, said: "You never want a serious crisis to go to waste." Common Core was that political philosophy in action.

The controllists' plan was almost perfect. They knew they didn't have to sell Common Core to lawmakers in individual state legislatures, where citizens would find out about it and demand it be stopped. Instead, they could just go to the individual state boards of education—entities that most Americans don't even know exist—for permission. In Wisconsin, for example, all it took was one individual, the state superintendent of public instruction, to adopt the standards.

It was a devious and brilliant plan, but that didn't make it foolproof. It wasn't a given that state school board members would agree to Common Core. Some might sense that it was a ploy to slowly nationalize their state's education system. To counter that possibility, progressives wrote special funding for the Common Core "initiative" into President Obama's nearly $800 billion stimulus plan via the "Race to the Top" program. This gave the administration the ability to bribe cash-starved states into adopting Common Core by making it a prerequisite for states to compete for seven-figure education grants. In addition, they delayed the testing component of the standards for several years, thereby giving state bureaucrats several years of zero accountability. Many of these bureaucrats no doubt knew they'd be retired or in a different position by the time the real pain came around.

Education secretary Arne Duncan probably wouldn't put it quite in those same terms, but he does admit that the federal government was certainly involved. "Our big competitive reform fund, Race to the Top, awarded points—40 points out of 500—to states that were collaborating to create common college- and career-ready standards," he said. "It was voluntary—we didn't mandate it—but we absolutely encouraged this state-led work because it is good for kids and good for the country."

Duncan fails to mention that the federal government also incentivized other parts of the Common Core initiative. States received 10 points for "developing and implementing common, high-quality assessments," 24 points for "fully implementing a statewide longitudinal data system," and 58 points for "improving teacher and principal effectiveness based on performance."

In case that still wasn't enough to entice some states, the Obama administration also offered waivers to the federal government's No Child Left Behind law. A state could earn a "get out of jail free" card, so to speak, if it adopted the new Common Core standards, or other standards that are virtually identical. Former Obama administration official Cass Sunstein might call this tactic a "nudge."

It's worth noting that while all this was happening, Microsoft billionaire Bill Gates was in the background, funding NGA, CCSSO, Achieve Inc., and "conservative" groups like the Fordham Institute, and greasing the skids for Common Core among the education establishment by spending the equivalent of a third-world nation's gross domestic product to promote it. Gates, speaking at the 2009 National Conference of State Legislatures, explained:

> Fortunately, the state-led Common Core State Standards Initiative is developing clear, rigorous common standards that match the best in the world. Last month, 46 Governors and Chief State School Officers made a public commitment to embrace these common standards.

> This is encouraging—but identifying common standards is not enough. We'll know we've succeeded when the curriculum and the tests are aligned to these standards.

More on that important curriculum-testing alignment comment in a moment, but first a quick update on Gates's numbers: as of this writing, four states have never adopted Common Core (Alaska, Texas, Nebraska, and Virginia), one state has dropped out of it (Indiana), and one state (Minnesota) only adopted half of the standards.

Kentucky was the first state to adopt Common Core, doing so before the final version was even published. Other states have not been quite as fast to jump. Former Texas education commissioner Robert Scott has publicly testified about the process and the pressure he was subjected to:

> My experience with the Common Core actually started when I was asked to sign on to them before they were written. . . . I was told I needed to sign a letter agreeing to the Common Core, and I asked if I might read them first, which is, I think, appropriate. I was told they had not been written, but they still wanted my signature on the letter. And I said, "That's absurd; first of all, I don't have the legal authority to do that because our [Texas] law requires our elected state board of education to adopt curriculum standards with the direct input of Texas teachers, parents, and business. So adopting something that was written behind closed doors in another state would not meet my state law." . . . I said, "Let me take a wait-and-see approach." If something remarkable was in there that I found that we did not have in ours that I would work with our board . . . and try to incorporate into our state curriculum . . .
>
> Then I was told, "Oh no, no, a state that adopts Common Core must adopt in its totality the Common Core and can only add 15 percent." It was then that I realized that this initiative, which had been constantly portrayed as state led and voluntary, was really about control. It was about control. Then it got co-opted by the Department of Education later. And it was about control totality from some education reform groups who candidly

admit their real goal here is to create a national marketplace for education products and services.

Even more troubling to me was the lack of transparency. . . . These standards were written behind closed doors. . . . We didn't know who the writers were until the project was complete.

Mississippi state senator Michael Watson, who sat on the Senate Education Committee, said he "had no clue" his state was joining the Common Core until he attended an education conference in Washington, D.C. Watson said that the decision was made by the "nine unelected individuals" on the Mississippi Board of Education.

This was no state-led effort. As education analyst Jim Stergios has noted, the public had no say in the matter. In fact, most Americans had never even heard the words "Common Core" until 2011, when the standards were already beginning to take root in their children's schools.

Even American Federation of Teachers president Randi Weingarten—a Common Core supporter—acknowledges the top-down nature in which the standards were imposed on the states. "The public wasn't involved," she said to reporters in late 2013. "Parents weren't involved. The districts weren't involved."

While you might get a Common Core defender to concede that it's not really a "state-led" effort, you'll never get them to admit that states will eventually lose control over their education system because of it. Instead, they'll tell you that the Common Core learning standards only provide teachers with concepts and timelines. They'll explain that the curriculum, which is composed of the lessons and teaching methods, will remain under full local and state control.

That sounds reasonable, if only it were true. As Joy Pullmann of the Heartland Institute has noted, the purveyors of Common Core sold it as a combination of new "rigorous" standards *and assessments* (or standardized tests) used to track student performance. By the 2014–2015 school year, those fill-in-the-oval state tests many of us remember from school will be replaced by national, Common Core–aligned tests administered on computers.

The follow-up question is obvious: Who's designing these new tests?

That task was handed to two testing companies: the Smarter Balanced Assessment Consortium and the Partnership for Assessment of Readiness for College and Careers (PARCC). Those two companies were chosen—and funded—by the federal government. The feds are also taking an active involvement in "vetting" the test questions for "quality purposes." Is anyone willing to bet that progressives in the U.S. Department of Education will strictly limit their involvement with the Common Core tests to "quality control"? Me neither.

So, why does any of this matter? Simple: the questions on the Common Core tests are going to directly impact what gets taught in our children's schools. Neal McCluskey of the Cato Institute has called this "de facto federal curricula."

Why? Well, think about how this works in the real world. If the English portion of a Common Core–related test consistently asks one question about Shakespeare but four questions about an Environmental Protection Agency document, it won't be long before schools tailor their curriculum to include the EPA document. As McCluskey puts it, "Year after year, questions become curricula."

So let's recap where we're at: progressives wrote the Common Core standards, used money from the 2009 stimulus bill to bribe states into adopting them, and are now "vetting" the tests that will eventually shape the curriculum used by school districts all across the United States. In Washington, that qualifies as an organic, "state-led" effort.

Thankfully, a growing number of Americans are figuring out what this really is: the next step in the nationalization of our education system. Columnist George Will may have summed it up best when he described Common Core as "the thin end of an enormous wedge [that] is designed to advance in primary and secondary education the general progressive agenda of centralization and uniformity."

Control and conform—that's the progressive strategy—and Common Core is a gigantic step forward.

13

COMMON CORE IS "RIGOROUS"

"[S]tate leaders have worked together to develop a set of
rigorous academic standards in math and English language arts.
These standards, known as the Common Core State Standards,
set an ambitious and voluntary goal line."

—*JEB BUSH, former governor of Florida*

"This is a real shift from our comfort zone, for some
of us, to a more rigorous approach."

—*COLLEEN HOLMES, Erie, Pennsylvania, teacher*

"We see these rigorous, clear standards as critical to better student results."

—*THE GATES FOUNDATION*

Controllists know that their "Common Core is state led" claim is easily debunked, so their main argument for the one-size-fits-all, nationalized learning approach is that these standards are "rigorous" and "world class." They promise that Common Core is going to pull America's K–12 system out of its decades-long slide and restore it to world prominence.

While most of these controllists admit that students will cover less academic ground under Common Core, they assure us that kids will go "deeper" into each concept and develop "critical thinking skills" that will prepare them for all the new jobs President Obama is busy creating.

The Oregon Department of Education website describes Common Core as "21st century skills for 21st century jobs," and assures parents that the standards "will prepare our students for career success in the rapidly changing world of work."

I included that quote because it gets to the heart of what this Common Core experiment is really about: creating *workers*, not *thinkers*.

I can already hear the groans from progressives, "Come on, you can't blame Common Core for trying to modernize public education. Creating a bunch of 'thinkers' might have been the right mission back in the days of wooden teeth and powdered wigs, but we live in a global economy now and our kids have to compete in it. Get with the times!" That premise is completely false. As Glenn Reynolds explains in his book *The New School*, the purpose of the K–12 system that America adopted in the mid-1800s was actually imported from Prussia and was specifically intended to produce industrial workers.

In any case, let's examine the Common Core standards on its supporters' own terms, and see how well they'll actually prepare students to compete on a global stage. I'll take the math standards first.

Back in 2009, the National Governors Association (NGA) and the Council of Chief State School Officers (CCSSO), the two private groups most responsible for writing the Common Core standards, convened a group of twenty-nine education experts— mostly professors and teachers—and asked them to review and verify that the new standards would create "college and career ready" students.

Stanford professor emeritus James Milgram was the only mathematician on the Common Core Validation Committee, and he refused to sign off on the proposed standards because he believed they were too weak. In testimony to the Texas legislature, Milgram explained that the standards were "in large measure a political document that . . . is written at a very low level and does not adequately reflect our current understanding of why the math programs in the high-achieving countries give dramatically better results."

One of Milgram's objections was that the standards instruct schools to not teach algebra until ninth grade. Milgram and other math experts note that saving algebra until high school means that students won't be introduced to precalculus until college (assuming they even choose that route).

This does not come as a surprise to those who put Common Core together. Jason Zimba, a professor at Bennington College and the lead writer of the math standards, acknowledged as much to the (Baton Rouge) *Advocate*. "If you want to take calculus your freshman year in college, you will need to take more mathematics than is in the Common Core," he said. Zimba also admitted that students following Common Core would likely be precluded from "attending elite colleges" since the Core is "not aligned with the expectations at the collegiate level."

In September 2013, Milgram coauthored a research report with Sandra Stotsky, professor of education emerita at the University of Arkansas, showing that students who don't arrive on a college campus with a solid foundation in precalculus have much less chance of successfully obtaining a college degree in science, technology, engineering, or mathematics (STEM). STEM skills are, of course, the very definition of twenty-first-century jobs skills.

According to Milgram and Stotsky's report: "It is extremely rare for students who begin their undergraduate years with coursework in precalculus or an even lower level of mathematical knowledge to achieve a bachelor's degree in a STEM area. Also, students whose last high school mathematics course was Algebra II have less than a 40 percent chance of obtaining a four-year college degree."

They added: "Clearly, if this country is seriously interested in 21st century mathematics and science, then there is even more reason to question Common Core's mathematics standards."

Even University of Arizona professor William McCallum, one of the lead writers of the math standards, admitted that they are not rigorous compared to other math-savvy countries. "The overall standards would not be too high, certainly not in comparison [to] other nations, including East Asia, where math education excels," he said in 2010.

The problems with Common Core's relaxed approach to math don't end there.

Michelle Malkin, who has taken an active role in exposing Common Core, explains that the math standards "abandon 'drill and kill' memorization techniques for fuzzy 'critical thinking' methods that put the cart of 'why' in front of the horse of 'how.' In other words, instead of doing the grunt work of hammering times tables and basic functions into kids' heads first, the faddists have turned to wacky, wordy non-math alternatives to encourage 'conceptual' understanding—without any mastery of the fundamentals of math."

This "critical thinking" approach to even simple math problems has made it impossible for many parents to understand their children's homework, relegating them to bystander status.

Heather Crossin, an Indiana mother who helped get Common Core repealed in her state, explained her daughter's experience with this "rigorous" new approach to math to *National Review:*

> Instead of many arithmetic problems, the homework would contain only three or four questions and two of those would be "explain your answer." Like, "One bridge is 412 feet long and the other bridge is 206 feet long. Which bridge is longer? How do you know?"

Crossin was unable to help her daughter because the "how do you know" could only be answered with Common Core–style language and reasoning.

Since most parents don't understand the Common Core techniques, students are becoming more dependent on their schools and teachers for their education, and less on help from their parents. This is like a dream come true for progressives who hope to continue to minimize the role of parents in the lives of their children. (Remember Al Gore telling kids, "There are some things about our world that you know that older people don't know.")

According to education scholar and former DOE official Ze'ev Wurman, the end result of this convoluted, backward approach to math education will be to leave American students roughly two years behind their international peers. "It is not difficult to show that the Common Core standards are not on par with those of the highest-performing nations," he wrote.

So, in terms of math, Common Core is definitely not "rigorous"—either by America's historical standard, nor the progressives' gooey "twenty-first-century skills" standard. And the English standards aren't much better.

Sandra Stotsky, the professor who coauthored the Milgram report, is highly regarded in education circles for her work in helping author Massachusetts's English language arts learning standards, which were widely acknowledged to be the best in the nation. Notice the past tense—*were*. Massachusetts officials have since replaced those top standards with Common Core's.

Stotsky now travels the country sounding the alarm over the threat that Common Core poses to English education. She's especially disturbed by Common Core's focus on "informational" texts instead of literature. Under Common Core, only 30 percent of a high school student's reading will be literary based.

The idea is to have students read things that will make them twenty-first-century-job ready. The literature that helps students to become self-aware thinkers and well-rounded human beings is being shelved in favor of more "practical" and "meaningful" texts, like excerpts from a Federal Reserve newsletter or a review of government documents. Erin Tuttle, a mother who helped lead Indiana's anti–Common Core charge, said the new learning standards resulted in her daughter's being assigned fewer novels and more "*Time* magazine for kids."

Hillsdale professor Terrence Moore, who has extensively studied the new English standards, is horrified at how Common Core guts great literature from our schools. Moore warns that this will lead to a generation of students who are clueless about many of the stories that showcased America's founding values and principles:

> Stories, you see, are what shape our view of the world. . . . Whoever controls what today we call "the narrative" controls the politics, the economics, the family, the ways of thinking, and the ways of believing. The most impressionable people, of course, are always the children.
>
> So welcome to the world of Common Core. The Common Core, at least as far as the English standards are concerned . . . is the

attempt to take away the great stories of the American people and replace them with the stories that fit the progressive, liberal narrative of the world. As such, the architects of the Common Core are nothing less than story-killers. . . . They're deliberately killing the greatest stories of the greatest nation in history.

Common Core instructs teachers to present "informational texts"—such as Lincoln's Gettysburg Address—without any background information or context. So while students will still read some important material, they'll read it "cold," which will strip the texts of their historical power and instead allow students to interpret the documents however they choose.

Common Core proponents call this technique "discovering content."

Do these really sound like "rigorous" changes to you? Or does it sound more like a systematic approach to dumb down our kids and further remove parents from the process so that students will be easier to indoctrinate and control?

University of Arkansas professor Jay Greene says the only "experts" who claim that the Common Core standards are of high quality are those on the Bill & Melinda Gates Foundation payroll. "The few independent evaluations of Common Core that exist suggest that its standards are mediocre and represent little change from what most states already have," he said.

So what do the Common Core "experts" really mean when they tell Americans that these standards will make students "college and career ready"?

By "college," they generally mean community college, not selective four-year universities. That may be fine for a lot of people (I am certainly no fan of the current college system and believe that many more people should consider technical schools, apprenticeships, or other alternative opportunities), but the point is that kids should have the *choice* where to go based on their interests, skills, and abilities. In this model there won't be a choice because the vast majority of kids will be wholly unprepared to enter a selective college.

The progressives' overall plan for K–12 education is to replace the ideal with the practical, and to slow down the learning process so that everyone can keep up. This is a lowest-common-denominator approach to education that will set most kids up to simply plug into the system rather than setting them up to reach for the stars and make a better life for themselves and their families. Common Core is how you create an economy of dronelike workers, not an economy of thinkers, doers, and innovators.

The top students in high school—those who are able to overcome everything that's been set up to hold them back—will still be allowed to attend selective, four-year universities (where they'll be taught by tenured progressive professors), but they'll start out way behind. With Common Core having left them unprepared for college-level math and English courses, these schools will either have to lower their standards or spend more time making up the ground that these students lost.

Of course, there is another option, one that would be very attractive to the government, the college and university cartel, and the controllists alike: a fifth year of college. After all, if K–12 is leaving kids behind because of Common Core, then what better way to make up for it than with a freshman year in college that is akin to what we all experienced as seniors in high school? Call it a "transitional year." Everyone, except students and parents who have to pay for it, wins: the government gets to keep kids in school even longer, the colleges get a big boost in revenue, and the controllists get exactly what they want by further stretching out the education process, all under the guise of more rigorous standards.

14

TEACHERS LOVE COMMON CORE,
AND THEY'RE THE ONES WHO REALLY MATTER!

"The Common Core gives me guidance, but it does not tell me what materials to use. That's up to me. It allows me to do something different this year and next year so that when I go out at 40 years, it'll be the best year I ever taught."
—*SUE YOKUM, Pennsylvania teacher*

"Roughly two-thirds of educators are either wholeheartedly in favor of the standards (26 percent) or support them with 'some reservations' (50 percent)."
—*NEA POLL of 1,200 union members*

"Our members support the Common Core Standards because they are the right thing to do for our children."
—*DENNIS VAN ROEKEL, NEA president*

Many teachers are overwhelmed, confused, and, in some cases, angry, over Common Core. Louisa Moats, a renowned teacher and researcher who was a contributing writer on the Common Core State Standards, recently spoke about how teachers are faring with the implementation:

Classroom teachers are confused, lacking in training and skills to implement the standards, overstressed, and the victims of misinformed directives from administrators who are not well grounded in reading research. I'm beginning to get messages from very frustrated educators who threw out what was working in favor of a new "CCSS aligned" program, and now find that they don't have the tools to teach kids how to read and write. Teachers are told to use "grade level" texts, for example; if half the kids are below grade level by definition, what does the teacher do? She has to decide whether to teach "the standard" or teach the kids.

Some teachers are thinking about doing neither and instead leaving the profession altogether. Elizabeth Natale, who's been teaching middle school English for fifteen years, recently wrote an op-ed in the *Hartford Courant*, expressing her frustration:

> Surrounded by piles of student work to grade, lessons to plan, and laundry to do, I have but one hope for the new year: that the Common Core State Standards, their related Smarter Balanced Assessment Consortium testing, and the new teacher evaluation program will become extinct.

> [G]overnment attempts to improve education are stripping the joy out of teaching and doing nothing to help children. The Common Core standards require teachers to march lockstep in arming students with "21st-century skills." In English, emphasis on technology and nonfiction reading makes it more important for students to prepare an electronic presentation on how to make a paper airplane than to learn about moral dilemmas from Natalie Babbitt's beloved novel "Tuck Everlasting."

Even the NEA's own poll (in which they claim that "roughly two-thirds" of teachers favor Common Core) isn't quite as conclusive as the union would have us believe. First, it encompassed just 1,200 teachers out of the three million members in that union. Second, how fair is it to poll employees on whether they like something that their boss is infatuated with?

But even if you trust the poll, it's not exactly a resounding endorsement of Common Core. First, they say that 26 percent support the standards "wholeheartedly" and another 50 percent support them "with reservations." We're then told that the sum of these two groups is "two-thirds." I think someone at the NEA might be spending a little too much time with Common Core math standards because, last I checked, 26 percent plus 50 percent equals 76 percent.

Math errors aside, the truth is that you could completely re-write the headline of this poll to say, "Roughly two-thirds of educators wholeheartedly reject the new Common Core standards, or have reservations about them," and it would be just as accurate as the way the NEA wrote it.

15

ALL THIS ANTI-COMMON CORE TALK IS JUST ANOTHER CONSPIRACY THEORY FROM PEOPLE WHO OBVIOUSLY HATE THE PRESIDENT

"What I want to hear from [Common Core critics] is more
than just opposition. . . . Criticisms and conspiracy theories
are easy attention grabbers. Solutions are hard work."

—*JEB BUSH*, former governor of Florida

"[Republican primary voters] think [that Common Core is] a
secret plot controlled by red Chinese robots in the basement
of the White House. No wonder they don't like it."

—*MIKE MURPHY*, political strategist, speaking about the results of his polling

"The idea that the Common Core standards are nationally imposed is a conspiracy
theory in search of a conspiracy. The Common Core academic standards were both
developed and adopted by the states, and they have widespread bipartisan support."

—*ARNE DUNCAN*, U.S. secretary of education

One of the good things about Common Core (yes, there is
one!) is that this is not something like "death panels" where

people have to be convinced that something bad might one day happen. *This is already happening.* Parents in states where Common Core has been implemented are seeing the results firsthand. All of the backlash we're starting to hear about isn't a result of the Tea Party enraging people; it's because parents ultimately aren't dumb. Unlike their kids, they actually *can* put two and two together, and they see that things aren't adding up.

National Review writer Maggie Gallagher explained how Heather Crossin and Erin Tuttle, the two mothers who helped get Indiana to reverse its adoption of Common Core, went from parents to activists:

> [They] did not get involved in opposing Common Core because of anything Michelle Malkin or Glenn Beck said to rile them up, but because of what they saw happening in their own children's *Catholic* school. When experts or politicians said that Common Core would not lead to a surrender of local control over curriculum, Heather and Erin knew better.

This brings up another good point about a common misconception of how Common Core works. Many parents believe their kids will be shielded from this nonsense because they attend a private, religious, or charter school. That's not the case. Charter schools *are* public schools, so they may not be immune to the changes.

Most Catholic schools are signed up, too. The majority of dioceses have adopted the nationalized, dumbed-down Common Core learning standards so that their students won't be left behind their government school peers. That's right, I said "left behind." See, the controllists have laid a very clever trap: they're not only changing state assessment tests to be in line with Common Core, they're also remaking the ACT and SAT college entrance exams to incorporate this material. That means *any* high school that wants to have its students accepted into prestigious colleges and universities will be forced to use Common Core as the basis of its curriculum. This is the epitome of "teaching to the test"—and David Coleman, the architect of Common Core turned president of the College Board (the company that produces the SAT), was right in the middle of it all.

Heather Crossin says that the principal of her child's Catholic school admitted that their curriculum would have to change due to the new Common Core testing. She told *National Review*, "Eventually, our principal just threw his hands up in the air and said, 'I know parents don't like this type of math but we have to teach it that way, because the new state assessment tests are going to use these standards.'"

If the testing doesn't convince Catholic schools to adopt Common Core, then the prospect of lost money probably will. In Indiana, vouchers allowed students to attend religious schools only if those schools agreed to use standardized state tests. Those tests, the highly acclaimed "Indiana Statewide Testing for Educational Progress" (ISTEP), were later switched to Common Core exams.

Many Catholic professors and academics aren't taking this lying down. One hundred thirty-two of them recently sent a letter to every bishop in the United States explaining the ramifications of these "rigorous" new learning standards and urging them to fight back:

> Common Core adopts a bottom-line, pragmatic approach to education. The heart of its philosophy is, as far as we can see, that it is a waste of resources to "over-educate" people. The basic goal of K–12 schools is to provide everyone with a modest skill set; after that, people can specialize in college—if they end up there. Truck-drivers do not need to know *Huck Finn*. Physicians have no use for the humanities. Only those destined to major in literature need to worry about *Ulysses*.

If a private school or a home-schooling family wants to reject this radical education experiment, they'll have a very difficult time finding textbooks and instructional materials that haven't already been remade in the image of Common Core.

That is a huge problem and it's a big progressive poison pill for the entire education system. Common Core, in fact, has the power to make the whole school choice movement irrelevant. As Emmett McGroarty from the American Principles Project explains, "What difference does it make if you fund different schools if they all teach the same basic curriculum the same basic way?"

It makes no difference at all. Public, private, or charter—everyone will be learning the same things as decided by the same source. Is it really such a big leap to go from that to being worried about exactly what those "same things" are and who is responsible for determining them?

Pearson Education, which creates Common Core–aligned materials, recently apologized for distributing a grammar worksheet for fifth-graders that included politically oriented statements such as:

- "[The president] makes sure the laws of the country are fair."
- "The wants of an individual are less important than the well-being of the nation."
- "The commands of government officials must be obeyed by all."

This can easily be dismissed as a simple mistake or overreach by one editor—and maybe that's all it is. But a national curriculum compounds how quickly these "mistakes" can spread across the country. With the same material going to schools nationwide, the possibility of ideologically driven worksheets or tests winding up in front of thousands of students is much greater.

That's not a conspiracy theory, it's a fact.

16

WE NEED BETTER DATA COLLECTION TO HELP US BETTER EDUCATE OUR KIDS

"Usually, firewalls are set up for our protection. They prevent hackers
from getting into our computers and they block our children from
visiting inappropriate Web sites. But these state firewalls don't help
us. They hurt all of us. They impede our ability to serve students and
better understand how we can improve American education. . . .
Hopefully, someday, we can track children from preschool to high
school and from high school to college and college to career.
We must track high growth children in classrooms to their great
teachers and great teachers to their schools of education."

—*ARNE DUNCAN,* U.S. secretary of education

Up to now we've talked about Common Core in terms of
learning standards. But that's really only half the story.

From the very beginning, Common Core has been about
standards *and* the accompanying standardized tests. The controllists have always spoken of these as a package deal. Why? Two important reasons: First, the tests enforce the curriculum. Without
the standardized exams, states could "cheat" or manipulate their

data—much like they do with No Child Left Behind. The tests are the key to making this a truly national curriculum. Second, and far more sinister, is that standardized testing will yield standardized data.

Once students are being taught the same way across the country and are all taking the same tests as their age-group peers, a stockpile of apples-to-apples data can be generated. This data can then be used by educators and K–12 technology companies to "personalize" the learning process for students. The theory goes that algorithms will help spot a student's problems earlier so that educators can intervene more quickly and effectively.

A Reuters article explains how the process will supposedly work:

> Does Johnny have trouble converting decimals to fractions? The database will have recorded that—and may have recorded as well that he finds textbooks boring, adores animation, and plays baseball after school. Personalized learning software can use that data to serve up a tailor-made math lesson, perhaps an animated game that uses baseball statistics to teach decimals.
>
> Johnny's teacher can watch his development on a "dashboard" that uses bright graphics to map each of her students' progress on dozens, even hundreds, of discrete skills.

Common Core's boosters argue that not only will the data help individual students, it will also benefit groups of students by unlocking the "science" of the teaching and learning processes. The "big thinkers" behind Common Core—most notably Bill Gates and U.S. education secretary Arne Duncan—believe the data generated through the new learning standards and tests will help researchers determine which instructional methods work best for various types of students. In addition, they believe that the data will allow us to identify the most effective teachers so that we can then figure out where they were trained and what makes them so good in the classroom.

In short, controllists argue that Common Core and the related data will allow them to elevate teaching from an "art" form to a hard science.

As you might imagine, there are quite a few issues with all of this. First, there's the obvious problem that teaching is, in fact, both an art *and* a science. Elizabeth Natale, the Connecticut teacher who is considering leaving the profession after fifteen years because of Common Core, explains this side of the data problem pretty well:

> I am a professional. My mission is to help students progress academically, but there is much more to my job than ensuring students can answer multiple-choice questions on a computer. Unlike my engineer husband who runs tests to rate the functionality of instruments, I cannot assess students by plugging them into a computer. They are not machines. They are humans who are not fazed by a D but are undone when their goldfish dies. . . .
>
> Those moments mean the most to my students and me, but they are not valued by a system that focuses on preparing workers rather than thinkers, collecting data rather than teaching and treating teachers as less than professionals.

Okay, so Ms. Natale doesn't love the idea of being measured by this data—and I don't blame her; I certainly wouldn't like it if the entirety of my performance this year came down to a number. But you could also argue that these are the same complaints we always

hear from those who don't want teacher evaluations or performance pay or any of the other good, market-based reforms that I
support.

That brings me to the second problem with all of this data collection: the future implications. Remember, the people behind this
push aren't exactly the most honest brokers. They didn't want public hearings or debate on Common Core and they certainly don't
want any scrutiny over their true long-term agenda. But anyone
with even the most basic knowledge of history understands that
mass data collection can set the table for the largest social engineering project this country has ever seen.

That's a big allegation so let's take a step back. I think once
you see where this came from, the people behind it, and the possi-
bilities for future misuse, you'll agree that this is far from the conspiracy theory that so many Common Core supporters label it as.

If there's one thing the political left and right both believe
about Barack Obama, it's that he is obsessed with using data to
make decisions. That was on full display during the 2008 Democratic primaries, when Team Obama outmaneuvered the Clinton
political machine by using data to identify potential supporters
and to get them to the polls.

Given this, it was no surprise that Obama chose Arne
Duncan—a self-described "deep believer" in data-driven policies—
to be his education secretary.

With two "data" guys now setting education policies for the
nation, it also makes sense that Congress's $787 billion stimulus
bill in 2009 included a hefty sum for the creation of longitudinal data systems used to track a child's progress from preschool
through college, and even to his or her first "real" job.

The Obama administration very cleverly made the creation of
these systems a major consideration when awarding states extra
K–12 aid (via "Race to the Top") during the lean months and years

following the 2008 economic crash. (Remember: "You never want a serious crisis to go to waste.")

In describing the Race to the Top grant criteria to states, the Department of Education helpfully released a summary of the kind of data systems they most wanted to see:

> The Secretary is also particularly interested in applications in which States propose working together to adapt one State's state-wide longitudinal data system so that it may be used, in whole or in part, by one or more other States, rather than having each State build or continue building such systems independently.

In other words, "The Secretary is interested in a national data system, but we can't say that."

As a result of this push, all fifty states now have a longitudinal data system in place. It was a huge achievement, but the administration was just getting started.

The National Center for Education Statistics (NCES)—part of the U.S. Department of Education—worked with state officials to create a standard coding system so the information stored in those fifty individual state databases would be uniform and transferable, ostensibly so it could follow the student if he or she moved to a different state.

The coding process kicked up a public relations firestorm for the federal government after it was reported that codes were being created for roughly four hundred data points, some of them in very sensitive categories, including a student's religious affiliation, medical conditions, and discipline problems, along with his or her family's income and voting status. They would even track how much students work on the weekends.

NCES commissioner Jack Buckley defended the practice by saying the codes were based only on information that states have already been collecting, and that it was up to individual states to decide which data points to track.

The Obama administration's involvement in this large-scale data-collecting scheme didn't end there. In late 2011, the U.S. Department of Education made a historic change to the Family Educational Rights and Privacy Act to allow schools to release student records to third-party organizations *without parental consent.*

Secretary Duncan defended the change by saying it will allow school districts to share student-specific data with K–12 technology companies so that they can provide personalized learning experiences and so teachers and parents can track their students' academic progress.

With all of this as background, let's fast-forward back to today. The combination of the one-size-fits-all Common Core learning standards and the longitudinal data systems have allowed controllists in both the private sector and the federal government to create a structure that's set to fundamentally transform the nation's educational system.

Obviously, this poses a huge security concern for families. Moms and dads now have to wonder who has access to their child's and family's most sensitive personal information, and what they're doing with it. The potential for abuse and exploitation is off the charts. In fact, it's not just potential; there are already examples of it happening.

Last fall, a teenage hacker was arrested and charged with felony computer trespass after he allegedly "accessed and downloaded the records of thousands of students in 2012 and 2013." The hacker allegedly posted the information, which "included student identification numbers and information on free lunch plans," to online message boards. More than fifteen thousand records were stolen and posted, including "130 Sachem High School

North [in Lake Ronkonkoma, N.Y.] students . . . who received 'instructional services in an alternative setting.' "

In Minnesota, a legislative auditor discovered that the state department of education's computer systems "lacked adequate internal controls and comprehensive security plans" and that department employees "had failed to document where private [student] data was held or the internal controls needed to secure it."

The federal government having access, via these interconnected longitudinal data systems, to so much data about our kids is frightening. And it's not just academic information that's at stake.

Under the guise of personalizing the educational process and unlocking the science of learning, some schools will soon start collecting physical and biometric data from students. A 2013 story from *Smithsonian* magazine explained how one New York company is proposing that we allow facial recognition software into the classroom:

> Here's how it would work. Using facial recognition software called EngageSense, computers would apply algorithms to what the cameras have recorded during a lecture of discussion to interpret how engaged the students have been. Were the kids' eyes focused on the teacher? Or were they looking everywhere but the front of the class? Were they smiling or frowning? Or did they just seem confused? Or bored?

The idea is that the software will track which activities best captured students' attention, and which ones caused them to space out. One teacher interviewed for the story speculated that in five years this program will be used in classrooms all throughout the United States.

These algorithms might be used to learn a number of things

about an individual child: his or her attention span, interpersonal skills, and work habits—and that's just for starters.

The *Chicago Tribune*—which is not exactly a media arm of the "black helicopter" crowd—also reports that students could soon be wearing "sensor bracelets" in the classroom to help track their engagement:

> The biometric bracelets, produced by a Massachusetts startup company, Affectiva Inc., send a small current across the skin and then measure subtle changes in electrical charges as the sympathetic nervous system responds to stimuli. The wireless devices have been used in pilot tests to gauge consumers' emotional response to advertising.
>
> Gates [Foundation] officials hope the devices, known as Q Sensors, can become a common classroom tool, enabling teachers to see, in real time, which kids are tuned in and which are zoned out.

As creepy as all of this may sound, it still doesn't match the gross negligence of a Florida school district that failed to notify parents that it was testing student iris scans. According to local news reports, the "Eye Swipe Nano" would identify each student getting on or off a school bus by scanning their iris and would then notify parents of the time and location of the scan.

Due to a "clerical error," parents were not notified prior to the pilot test. Once they were, the resulting outcry caused Polk County officials to put the test on hold. "We were not trying to do anything behind their backs," Support Services director Rob Davis said; "we were trying to be innovative."

I actually believe him—but that only proves the point that the road to hell is paved with good intentions. Even if those who want to collect all of this data would never dream of doing anything sinister with it, they have absolutely no idea where all of this might eventually lead.

And the implications are alarming. "More and more colleges are using predictive analysis to give students a good idea of how [students will] fare in a class before they even sign up for it," the *Smithsonian* wrote. "*By using data from a student's own academic performance* and from others who have already taken the class, *advisers can predict with increasing accuracy how likely it is that a particular student will succeed or fail*" (emphasis added).

This predictive technology appears to have originated at Tennessee's Austin Peay State University. In 2013, the university sold its program, Degree Compass, to Desire2Learn, a company that plans to get this technology into colleges and universities across the United States. After it's implemented, many college students will soon get advice on which classes they should take and which ones they should avoid. It's just advice (at least for now), but it all fits in with Common Core because the same type of social engineering is making its way to our K–12 schools.

In 2007, the National Center on Education and the Economy (NCEE) released a groundbreaking report, titled "Tough Choices or Tough Times." The report recommended that high school sophomores be given a "board exam" to determine who should be given the "right" to attend a community college for two years of career training and who "can stay in high school" to take Advanced Placement courses in preparation for a chance to attend a selective college or university.

With all kinds of student data at their disposal, it's a near certainty that school counselors, teachers, and principals will eventually try to identify the "community college" kids and the "selective college" kids well before their sophomore years in high school. Once separated into groups, each will be shepherded onto a different track and put into classes that are most "appropriate" for their future careers.

The Pearson company, one of Common Core's key advocates, produced a promotional video that hints at what the future of education could look like once the standards and the technology are all in place. In the video, a mother is seen reviewing her son's academic progress, while on the side of the screen is her son's "career projection" and "college projection." It's touching to see the mother nearly tear up when she sees that her son's on track to become a mechanical engineer.

Some of you are probably thinking that I am reading way too much into some dumb report written by a bunch of eggheads back in 2007. I wish that were the case, but the reason why it's so concerning is that, according to the NCEE's own website, the group has been pushing for "the development of a national system of academic achievement standards for students" since its inception in 1985. (Back then, the NCEE was called the "Carnegie Forum on Education and the Economy.") The website also boasts that many of the individuals involved in developing Common Core have deep connections to the NCEE.

In other words, many of the people responsible for Common Core share the goals of the group that, just a few years earlier, was calling for "board exams" for high school sophomores and for the creation of national learning standards that would prepare all high school graduates to attend, at a minimum, community college.

That raises some pretty serious questions about Common Core. Given the people involved, is it really the set of "rigorous," "world-class standards" that controllists tell us it is, or is it essentially a backdoor way into community-college-level national learning standards?

To help you answer that question for yourself, consider this excerpt from a 2010 *New York Times* article:

> Dozens of public high schools in eight states will introduce a program [in 2011] allowing 10th graders who pass a battery of tests to get a diploma two years early and immediately enroll in community college.

> Students who pass but aspire to attend a selective college may continue with college preparatory courses in their junior and senior years, organizers of the new effort said. Students who fail the 10th-grade tests, known as board exams, can try again at the end of their 11th and 12th grades.

Supporters of this plan say it's patterned after programs in "high-performing nations," such as Denmark, England, Finland, France, and Singapore, and is meant to ensure that "students have mastered a set of basic requirements and reducing the numbers of high school graduates who need remedial courses when they enroll in college," the *Times* adds.

Maybe it's all as innocent as its supporters suggest, but forgive me for not having an excess stockpile of trust right now, especially when you consider how much money is at stake in the whole education-data-mining arena. (Rupert Murdoch, chairman and CEO of News Corporation, estimated that K–12 education is a $500 billion industry in the United States alone.)

Microsoft founder Bill Gates understands this well. In fact, he understands it so well that teacher Melanie Schneider hit the nail on the head when she argued that Common Core isn't actually "state led," it's "Gates led."

To see what she means, just follow the money. The Bill & Melinda Gates Foundation has given millions of dollars to organizations for the express purpose of advancing Common Core. These include each of the private organizations that are primarily responsible for development of the standards, like the National

Governors Association Center, Council of Chief State School Of-ficers, and Achieve Inc.

So Gates owns Common Core and has been a very public ad-vocate for it—there's no doubt about that. But here's where it gets a little creepy: the Gates Foundation is also a major investor in most of the data mining systems and devices I mentioned in this chapter.

Remember those biometric "Q Sensors" that kids would wear in class so teachers could figure out which moments interest them? Gates gave $1.4 million to researchers for the development and implementation of these so-called galvanic skin response measurements.

Existing methods "only get us so far," explained Debbie Rob-inson, a Gates Foundation spokeswoman. She said that in order to achieve real gains in learning, educators "need universal, valid, reliable, and practical instruments," such as the biosensors.

The *Chicago Tribune* reported that this investment in biomet-ric sensors was really just indicative of the foundation's "emphasis on mining daily classroom interactions for data." They say that the foundation has spent $45 million on this kind of research under the umbrella name "Measures of Effective Teaching."

To sum up, Gates funded the development of standards and tests to provide uniform national data, and is now funding the devices and systems that will work with that data. Yet this is some-how a *conspiracy theory*?

Maybe the reason why Gates and others have been so suc-cessful at getting these things implemented is that they are smart enough to spend money not just on the technology, but also on public relations and advocacy.

Here's a great case in point. The *Tribune* article in which the biometric sensors are discussed ends with a section titled "Poten-tial for Mission Creep." Traditionally, this is where critics of the technology would talk about their concerns over privacy, security, etc. Instead, the *Tribune* interviewed a woman named Sandi Jacobs. Read this excerpt and pay particular attention to the part I italicized:

> To Sandi Jacobs, the promise of such technology outweighs the vague fear that it might be used in the future to punish teachers who fail to engage their students' Q Sensors.

> Any device that helps a teacher identify and meet student needs "is a good thing," said Jacobs, vice president of the National Council on Teacher Quality, *an advocacy group that receives funding from the Gates Foundation.* "We have to be really open to what technology can bring."

Quoting someone who receives Gates's money about their concerns over a Gates-funded device is not exactly high-quality journalism—regardless of the disclosure. It does, however, go to show just how powerful the foundation is—and just how far its tentacles reach. That's why this quote, found on their website, should give anyone who appreciates local control over education serious pause:

> The Common Core will require transformative change—the type of change that many believe cannot be accomplished.

They're wrong. I do believe that the billions of dollars that Gates and others are putting toward these efforts will bring about transformative change. I—and millions of other Americans—just don't want it.

17

GIVEN THE RISING OBESITY EPIDEMIC, THE FEDERAL GOVERNMENT MUST SET STRICT STANDARDS FOR IN-SCHOOL MEALS AND PROVIDE FREE BREAKFAST AND LUNCH DAILY

"The U.S. government has been feeding kids for almost 70 years. It's a big operation that no one else can handle at these relatively low costs. And since the government is subsidizing lunch, government gets to decide what's for lunch."
—*AYALA LAUFER-CAHANA,* physician, cofounder of Herbal Water Inc.

"Imagine our kids begging and pleading, throwing tantrums to get you to buy more fruits, vegetables and whole grains. Yes, this is possible. It is possible to create this world!"
—*MICHELLE OBAMA,* first lady of the United States

In 2008, Michelle Obama was campaigning in Puerto Rico and told the assembled activists, "We are going to have to change our conversation; we're going to have to change our traditions, our history; we're going to have to move into a different place as a nation."

That sounded pretty ominous coming from the wife of a candidate who saw government as a solution to most problems. What type of revolutionary plan did she have up her sleeve?

As it turns out, one of the changes she had in mind was a poorly planned revision of the national school lunch menu.

Citing an obesity "epidemic," the first lady, along with bureaucrats from the U.S. Department of Agriculture, convinced Congress to approve sweeping changes in the National School Lunch Program. "Healthy" menus suddenly became a requirement for school districts looking to receive federal lunch dollars under the "Healthy, Hunger-Free Kids Act of 2010."

Many schools reacted quickly and decisively. Some districts, like Chicago, jumped in to support the effort by banning brown-bag lunches from home. A school from Richmond, Virginia, took a similar stance, sending the following note home to parents:

> I have received word from Federal Programs Preschool pertaining to lunches from home. Parents are to be informed that students can only bring lunches from home if there is a medical condition meriting a specific diet, along with a physician's note to that regard.

The new program drew high praise from famous figures on both sides of the political aisle. Former U.S. senator Bill Frist (R-TN), who began his career as a surgeon, loved how this bill would target obesity:

> As vice chair of the Partnership for a Healthier America, I join President Obama and the First Lady in celebrating the signing of the Healthy, Hunger-Free Kids Act. This bipartisan legislation will significantly enhance the quality of food for our children for generations to come and is a dramatic step toward reducing childhood obesity.

Former Arkansas governor Mike Huckabee, another prominent Republican, had similar praise:

> Congratulations to First Lady Michelle Obama, Secretary of Agriculture Tom Vilsack, and to the bipartisan support in Congress to pass the Healthy, Hunger Free Child Act. By passing a bill that addresses the nutritional quality of school lunches, an important step is being taken to give children choices that will make them healthier and more productive.

It's so nice to see Republicans and Democrats come together on an issue. It would be even nicer if it weren't an issue they were both so wrong about.

As it turns out, an edict from Washington cannot make kids eat healthy. As the new lunch menus were implemented, millions of students began sticking their noses up at the skimpy entrée portions and generous fruit and vegetable offerings they were served. Many schools reported losing vast amounts of money from reduced sales of lunches, and kids who bought them began throwing a lot of the food away (surprise, surprise, they usually threw out the healthiest stuff). And many kids—particularly student athletes who required a large number of calories—started complaining about being hungry by the end of the day.

Reports about the impact of the menu changes have not been positive. Here's a small sample from media reports around the country:

- Parents in Harlan County, Kentucky, attended a school board meeting to complain about the new lunch offerings. "They say it tastes like vomit," board member Myra Mosley reported.
- In Pierre, South Dakota, students staged a mass revolt, tossing out thousands of pounds of unwanted food. "I know a lot of my

friends who are just drinking a jug of milk for their lunch, and they are not getting a proper meal," middle school student Samantha Gortmaker told a local television station.

- Officials in the Catlin, Illinois, district decided to opt out of the national lunch program after losing $30,000 from a decline in the number of meals that were served and an increase in the amount of food going into the garbage. "Some of the stuff we had to offer, they wouldn't eat," said Superintendent Gary Lewis. "So you sit there and watch the kids, and you know they're hungry at the end of the day, and that led to some behavior and some lack of attentiveness."

- Officials with the Carmel Clay school district in Indiana said they lost $300,000 in one school year when many students rejected the menu changes and stopped purchasing school meals. "I'm a registered dietician," said Amy Anderson, food service director for the school district. "I used to feel that I was an educator and part of the education system. I currently feel like I'm a food cop. I don't get credit for the 98 percent of the kids who are within normal weight range. I only get slammed for the 2 to 3 percent who aren't."

- Officials in New York's Burnt Hills–Ballston Lake school district decided to drop out of the program after losing about $100,000 in food sales in one school year. "(Our staff) worked hard to implement the new regulations, but there were just too many problems and too many foods that students did not like and would not purchase," Assistant Superintendent Chris Abdoo said in a news release. "Students complained of being hungry with these lunches and the district lost money. I'm confident we can do better on our own next year."

To top it all off, the U.S. Government Accountability Office issued a scathing report in 2013 about the many problems with the program:

Six of the eight schools we visited told us they believe food waste has increased because of the new lunch requirements. In particular, [school officials] said that the fruits and vegetables students are now required to take sometimes end up thrown away, and in our lunch period observations in 7 of 7 schools, we saw many students throw some or all of their fruits and vegetables away.

Athletic directors expressed concerns that student athletes were hungrier after school than they were in previous years and staff reported that more students were distracted during the final period of the school day than in previous years.

The report also found that some schools weren't necessarily increasing the number of healthy food options for students.

To comply with both the meat and grain maximums and the required calorie minimums for lunches, some districts added foods that generally did not improve the nutritional value of the lunches. In three of the districts we visited, [officials] reported adding pudding to certain high school menus to bring the menus into compliance with the calorie minimum. Some also added gelatin, ice cream, or condiments such as butter, jelly, ranch dressing, or cheese sauce to become compliant.

While these additional menu items provided additional calories to lunches, they also likely increased the amount of sugar, sodium, or fat in the meal, potentially undercutting the federal law's goals of improving the nutritional quality of lunches.

Incredibly, none of the criticism seemed to faze the first lady or the government controllists overseeing the program. "One thing

I think we need to keep in mind as kids say they're still hungry," USDA undersecretary Janey Thornton said, "is that many children aren't used to eating fruits and vegetables at home, much less at school. So it's a change in what they are eating. If they're still hungry, it's that they are not eating all the food that's being offered."

In other words, you may *think* you're hungry but you're really not. Sound familiar? It's the same "you may think you know what's best for your kids, but you really don't" argument that we always hear during the school choice debate.

Michelle Obama sounded even less concerned. "Right now, we're truly at a pivotal moment," she said, "a tipping point when the message is just starting to break through, when new habits are just beginning to take hold, and we're seeing the very first glimmer of the kind of transformational change that we're capable of making in this country."

But what if the new menus don't bring about that "transformational change"? Mrs. Obama gave a frightening hint about a possible follow-up strategy at the Partnership for a Healthier America summit in Washington, D.C., in 2013. When she envisioned a world where restaurants and grocery stores would be nudged into rearranging their menus, displays, and advertising, all to promote healthier food choices.

"I mean, just think for a minute what this country could look like," she said. "Imagine walking into any grocery store in America and finding the healthiest food options clearly marked and centrally placed so that you know within seconds what's good for your family when you walk in that store.

"Imagine our kids begging and pleading, throwing tantrums to get you to buy more fruits, vegetables, and whole grains. Yes, this is possible. It is possible to create this world!"

And that's what all of this is really about: creating a world that meets the approval of the Obamas and other controllists. It's the

Bloomberg Nanny State and Cass Sunstein's "nudge" strategy all rolled into one.

But before we can imagine a world in which grocery stores are renovated to reflect Michelle Obama's will, the federal government had to first insert itself into the system. Guidelines and food pyramids weren't enough. To make a real difference they needed to be able to fund the meals so they could then say, "If we're paying for the food, we get to decide what it is." It's sort of like the federal government's relationship to state speed limits. Washington doesn't get to set the speed limit itself, but they've gotten state budgets so hooked on federal money that they have de facto control over all sorts of things. *Sure, you can raise your speed limit to 80, but we'll just hold on to that highway grant money next year.* The states almost always cave; they can't afford not to.

The same strategy is in play here—and the data shows that it's working. What started out as a program to help a select group of poor children get a free or subsidized lunch has morphed into a universal, politician-controlled diet and nutrition plan.

In 1969, the first year for which data is available, the National School Lunch Program served 19.4 million students, with 2.9 million of them (15.1 percent) receiving their meal for free or at a reduced price. Twenty years later, the program was feeding 24.2 million students, with 11.3 million (47.2 percent) getting fed for free or at a subsidized price.

Fast-forward to 2013 and you see just how much things have changed: 30.6 million students were served that year, and a full 21.5 million of them (70.5 percent) got them for free or at a reduced price—an all-time high.

With that kind of scale in place, the government can now transition to the menus themselves—telling kids what they can and cannot eat, all under the guise of the obesity epidemic. It won't work, of course, just as other Nanny State laws don't work.

You can't legislate lettuce and expect high school kids to gleefully play along.

What will work? That's a topic for another book, but I find it interesting that a 2010 study by researchers at Ohio State University identified three main factors in reducing childhood obesity, and all of them involve the same theme we are talking about in this book: more support from parents and family.

> A new national study suggests that preschool-aged children are likely to have a lower risk for obesity if they regularly engage in one or more of three specific household routines: eating dinner as a family, getting adequate sleep, and limiting their weekday television viewing time.

Of course, figuring out what actually works in reducing childhood obesity is not really the point of these programs. (If it were, then the government might finally stop categorizing french fries as "vegetables.") The real point is the same thing it always is: conformity, control, and eventually fundamental transformation.

18

SCHOOL SHOULD TEACH STUDENTS ABOUT SEXUALITY BECAUSE PARENTS DON'T

"How in the world do we say it's OK for schools to teach our
children about math, science, history, and numerous other
subjects, yet then get high and mighty with righteous indignation
when biology is taken a step further to focus on sex? . . . It's
clear that parents aren't as dependable on some matters as they
like to delude themselves into believing."

—*ROLAND MARTIN, columnist and former CNN contributor*

"High school students are very sexually active and getting pregnant
so we don't have that luxury to think that they are too young to be
engaged in conversations about contraception and sexual education."

—*CHRISTINE QUINN, former Speaker, New York City Council*

"I remember Alan Keyes . . . using this in his campaign against
me, saying, 'Barack Obama supports teaching sex education
to kindergartners.' Which—I didn't know what to tell him, but
it's the right thing to do to provide age-appropriate sex education,
science-based sex education in schools."

—*BARACK OBAMA, U.S. president*

Professional educators—people who spend thousands of hours with children every year—should understand one fundamental truth about kids: they yearn for boundaries. Whether they care to admit it or not, they want to be told "no." They crave the security that comes with the knowledge that there are adults in their lives who care enough to set limits.

Adults who set boundaries give kids a legitimate excuse to deal with the pressure presented by peers, society, and their rapidly developing bodies. They find shelter in telling their friends, boyfriends, or girlfriends that they just can't, because their mean old mom or dad won't let them.

Educators are important role models in the lives of impressionable students. Kids often make major decisions based on the information and signals they receive from teachers, principals, coaches, and counselors. Parents should have a right to expect these professionals to be responsible and advise kids that sexual abstinence is the wisest and safest course, particularly in their K–12 years.

But that doesn't seem to be the message coming out of many schools these days. The new message, developed largely by politically and socially radical educators, is that sexual activity is natural and good and is fine to be explored at increasingly younger ages.

This is a radical departure from the sex education lessons we experienced, where we were taught the fundamentals of the birds and the bees. Educators back then knew that some parents were too shy or awkward to broach the subject, so schools made sure kids would have basic knowledge to build on as they grew and developed their own points of view.

Today the trend seems to be to promote sexual activity among children, rather than gradually preparing kids for the facts of adult life.

"Oral sex, masturbation, and orgasms need to be taught in education," said Diane Schneider, an official with the National Education Association, in a speech at the UN's Commission on the Status of Women.

Then there's Planned Parenthood, an organization that's hired to present sexual education classes for schools throughout the nation. As Paul Rondeau of the American Life League explains it, "[Planned Parenthood] is funded with our tax dollars to market sex to our children in our schools under the guise of sex education, anti-bullying, diversity and other tolerance. Once sexualized, those children then become PP [Planned Parenthood] sex customers for contraceptives, STD testing, and abortion."

One Planned Parenthood lesson defines "abstinence" as "choosing not to do any sexual activity that carries a risk for pregnancy or STD/HIV," said Rita Diller, national director for Stop Planned Parenthood. "In other words, abstinence has nothing to do with abstaining from sex acts. So long as the student avoids STDs and pregnancy, and is comfortable with what he or she is doing, it's an anything goes scenario."

Last year in Onalaska, Washington, parents learned that a school principal, who was leading a group of fifth graders in a supposed discussion of HIV/AIDS, ended up describing oral and anal sex in graphic terms to the children. According to news reports, one girl came home from the session and told her parents she learned, "You take a man's penis and you put it in your mouth—that's what the girls do to the boys. The boys spread the girls' legs apart and put their mouths down on the vaginas."

Some parents of students at a Philadelphia high school were upset to learn that their school (as well as twenty-one others in the district) was distributing free condoms to students. School officials noted that the twenty-two targeted schools had the highest rates of sexually transmitted diseases in the district and argued that since kids are having sex anyway, it's better if they take precautions.

I guess they never considered the possibility that kids are having sex because everyone *expects* them to, and that the distribution of condoms only serves to reinforce that message. As one father put it, "It's kind of like promoting it, a way of advertising sex."

Despite only three-tenths of 1 percent of Americans self-identifying as "transgendered," Rutgers University created a lesson plan that provides *all* students with tips on how to "come out" as transgendered to their parents. It's a convenient way for progressives to insert themselves directly into parent-child relationships, even when it's not applicable to the vast majority of students.

A report issued last year, titled "National Sexuality Education Standards" and written by a "range of advocates, academics, and public education officials," was designed to "create a strategic plan for sexuality education policy and implementation."

According to the report, sex education should begin in kindergarten. By the second grade students should be able to "identify different kinds of family structures" and "demonstrate ways to show respect for different types of families."

By the time they reach the age of seven, students should also be able to identify all male and female body parts and "provide examples of how friends, family, media, society, and culture influence ways in which boys and girls think they should act."

By the fifth grade, students should be able to "define sexual orientation as the romantic attraction of an individual to someone of the same gender or a different gender" and "identify parents or other trusted adults of whom students can ask questions about sexual orientation."

By the eighth grade, students should be able to "differentiate between gender identity, gender expression, and sexual orientation, explain the range of gender roles, and define emergency contraception and its use."

In other words, these "standards" would ensure that eighth graders understand when to use the "morning-after pill."

It gets worse.

By the end of middle school, students should be able to "analyze external influences that have an impact on one's attitudes about gender, sexual orientation, and gender identity . . . communicate respectfully with and about people of all gender identities, gender expressions, and sexual orientations, explain the health benefits, risks, and effectiveness rates of various methods of contraception, and describe the steps to using a condom correctly."

By high school graduation, students should be able to "define emergency contraception and describe its mechanism of action and assess the skills and resources needed to become a parent."

If it were up to the people who wrote this report, children would be taught from their earliest days in school to accept various gender roles, different types of families, and various forms of sexuality as morally correct. And they would be extremely well versed (as noted by the repeated mentions) about the availability and appropriateness of "emergency contraception."

The problem with all of this is that many parents *don't* believe it's right to have sex before marriage, or to present it to children as normal or acceptable behavior. Many parents *don't* approve of homosexuality or bisexuality, and many have strong moral objections to abortion, even through the use of morning-after pills.

Shouldn't these parents have the right to instill their values into their own children, without opposition or interference from a public school curriculum? Shouldn't educators have to draw the line at telling kids their parents and churches are bigoted or small-minded? And isn't it ironic that the same progressives who tell others to stay out of their bedrooms are all too happy to knock down the front doors of homes and inculcate the children with what they perceive as the "correct" beliefs regarding families and sex.

There's nothing wrong with educators insisting that all students be treated with respect. There's nothing wrong with teaching kids the basics of biology and human sexuality. There's nothing wrong with teachers having zero tolerance for bullying, or encouraging diversity and tolerance. But school employees have no legitimate authority to force their moral code on students, or to openly reject the traditional moral codes of others.

Jay McDowell, a teacher and local union president in Howell, Michigan, is a perfect example of the thin line between teaching and imposing. In the fall of 2010, McDowell took part in a school observance of "anti-bullying day" by wearing a purple T-shirt to symbolize his support for gay teens. At some point during the day, a female student entered his classroom wearing a belt buckle featuring the old Confederate flag. McDowell told her she couldn't wear such an item because it symbolized racism and offended people.

Daniel Glowacki, a sixteen-year-old student in the same class, defended the girl. He told McDowell that her belt buckle should be acceptable if his purple T-shirt was acceptable. Glowacki went on to explain that he's a Christian and does not approve of homosexuality.

McDowell responded by throwing Glowacki and another boy who took his side out of class. The school superintendent investigated the incident and suspended McDowell for a day, which then incited anger among many colleagues who came to his defense.

Glowacki's mother filed a lawsuit on her son's behalf a few months later, and a judge ruled in her favor, determining that McDowell had violated the student's First Amendment right to free speech and expression.

It's ironic—and perhaps appropriate—that this story ends with McDowell being presented with a human rights award by the Michigan Education Association, a state branch of the NEA. He was honored for teaching his students to be "whole people who learn to stand up for what they believe in and learn how to live."

Tolerance is not really tolerance if it doesn't go both ways.

It must be frustrating for decent parents to watch their children fall under the influence of radical educators, and sometimes make foolish decisions based on the predominant cultures in their schools. But no one should be surprised it happens—far too many educators are moral relativists who reject the notion of absolute right or wrong.

These educators are often defended by a compliant media that rejects traditional values. Columnist Betsy Karasik, writing in the *Washington Post*, went so far as to suggest that we are all just too uptight about the recent rash of teacher-student sexual relationships that are being exposed at an alarming rate across the nation.

> Throughout high school, college and law school I knew students who had sexual relations with teachers. To the best of my knowledge these situations were all consensual in every honest meaning of the word, even if society would like to embrace the fantasy that a high school student can't consent to sex. Although some feelings probably got bruised, no one I knew was horribly damaged.

> The point is that there is a vast and extremely nuanced continuum of sexual interactions involving teachers and students, ranging from flirtation to mutual lust to harassment to predatory behavior. Painting all of these behaviors with the same brush sends a damaging message to students and sets the stage for hypocrisy and distortion of the truth. Many teenagers are,

biologically speaking, sexually mature. Pretending that this kind of thing won't happen if we simply punish it severely enough is delusional.

Karasik apparently believes that a high school teacher hooking up with one of their students is totally fine because it's almost always consensual. That's an interesting point of view, especially considering that fifteen- and sixteen-year-olds aren't legally allowed to consent to much of anything in life yet. It's also ironic that on the one hand we have Michelle Obama and the federal government mandating what kids have to each for lunch each day because they are too young to make the right decisions on their own, while on the other hand we have progressives saying that it's totally fine for these same kids to make a decision to sleep with their thirty-two-year-old English teacher.

Despite what Karasik and others believe about all of this being natural, the fact is that teen sexual activity hasn't always been so widespread. Perhaps it's no coincidence that the problem started growing after we kicked God out of the schools.

A 2008 study conducted by Specialty Research Associates shows that the rates of teen sex, pregnancy, and venereal disease, along with crime, illiteracy, drug use, and suicide, started going through the roof almost immediately following the 1962 Supreme Court decision that ended teacher-led prayer in public schools.

With prayer—and the fundamental acknowledgment that there is a greater power who holds us accountable for our behavior—banished from schools, the vacuum was filled by progressive educators with a very different agenda.

19

___

SCHOOLS SHOULD BE THE CENTER OF THE COMMUNITY, OPEN TWELVE HOURS A DAY, SEVEN DAYS A WEEK

> "[T]he most successful schools of the future will be integrated learning communities, which accommodate the needs of all of the community's stakeholders. They will be schools that will be open later, longer and for more people in the community from senior citizens using the gym and health facilities during off-hours to immigrants taking evening English classes after work."
>
> —*U.S. DEPARTMENT OF EDUCATION,* Schools as Centers of Community: A Citizen's Guide for Planning and Design

> "I think the brand-new American school would be year-round—open from 6 to 6. . . . These schools will serve children from age three months old to age 18."
>
> —*LAMAR ALEXANDER,* former U.S. secretary of education

Progressives like to bemoan the decline of the great American middle class. They say it illustrates the fundamental unfairness of wealth distribution in our capitalistic economy. They argue that, left unchecked, our system will soon produce only two classes of people: the super-wealthy and the extremely poor.

What they fail to mention is that the decline of the middle class has as much to do with life choices as anything else. The biggest problem over the last half century has been the rapid disintegration of the nuclear family and the rapid growth of single-parent families that struggle to provide for the physical and emotional needs of their children.

The American divorce rate is at a record high—around half of all first marriages go down the drain, and the percentage only increases for second and third marriages. A lot of couples with children don't bother to get married anymore and they tend to "break up" at a rate that used to be more common to high school relationships.

Fathers too frequently abandon their children, leaving huge financial and emotional gaps in their lives. That forces many mothers into the full-time workforce, often taking time away from critical parent-child relationships. As statistics provided by the National Fatherhood Initiative show, this negative cycle is extremely hard to break:

- Children in homes with no father are far more likely to grow up in poverty. In 2011, 12 percent of children in families with married parents lived in poverty, compared to 44 percent who lived with mothers only.
- Children living in intact families are more likely to attend college and be physically and emotionally healthy, and are less likely to be physically or sexually abused, use drugs or alcohol, engage in delinquent behavior, and become parents as teens.
- Children from homes where the father is absent are significantly more likely to be incarcerated at some point in their lives. Those who never had a father at home have the highest odds of going to jail or prison.

- Sixty-one percent of three- to five-year-olds living with two parents were read aloud to every day by a family member, compared to 48 percent of children living in single- or no-parent situations.
- Students living in father-absent homes are twice as likely to repeat a grade in school.

The point is that an intact nuclear family is far more likely to have a livable income and produce happier, healthier, and more successful children. Given that somewhat obvious fact, it would make a lot more sense for the government to focus on things that would encourage and empower a comeback of the family unit rather than things that simply deal with the symptoms of our current disease.

But that's not the case. In fact, our government has been all too eager to encourage the continued deterioration of the family structure by assuming more and more responsibilities that should be dealt with at home.

That's particularly true when it comes to government schools.

In February 2014, New York City public schools opened on a day in which heavy snow was falling in the city. When the media asked Schools Chancellor Carmen Farina for her rationale in keeping school open on a day in which streets and sidewalks were clearly dangerous, she answered in a way that likely had controllists everywhere jumping for joy.

"Many of our kids don't get a hot lunch and, in many cases breakfast, unless they go to school," she explained. "So it's still a parent's decision whether they send their kids to school or not. My decision is where the kids are safest and the most taken care of, and the answer to that is in schools."

According to her, kids are safer and more taken care of in school than at home—even in the midst of a blizzard. You'll notice that Farina specifically mentioned the idea of a hot lunch and breakfast—something that ties right back to the federal school lunch program that we've already covered. By serving one or two meals a day to students, schools and controllists can begin to make the case that kids must be in school more so that they can eat properly. A recently proposed rule for the National School Lunch Program and the School Breakfast Program would bolster their case even further by allowing officials in low-income districts to serve free meals to all students, regardless of their family's income.

Some progressives are seeing the opportunity this gives them and are pushing this concept beyond school hours. In New Jersey, Governor Chris Christies has started a pilot program to provide free "after school dinner" for kids in six Camden schools.

All this fits perfectly with the controllists' strategy of teaching children that all good things originate with the state. Once kids learn that their parents are not responsible for providing any meals because the government covers that cost for everyone, it's not hard to take the next step and teach them the concept of "free" public handouts for everything, including education, health care, and housing.

A lot of modern lawmakers and educators have become strong proponents of the full-service "community school" model. These people believe that schools should be open throughout the year, pretty much around the clock, and offer everything under the sun, including free meals, child care, health care, counseling services, family planning services—you name it.

Given the money and power inherent in a concept like this, it's not really a surprise that American Federation of Teachers president Randi Weingarten is a supporter:

> We have to do more than simply instruct children seven hours a day. Community schools should be the hub of the community.

Can you imagine a federal law that promoted community schools—schools that served the neediest children by bringing together under one roof all the services and activities they and their families need? Imagine schools that are open all day and offer after-school and evening recreational activities and home-work assistance. And suppose the schools included child care and dental, medical and counseling clinics.

Yes, suppose they did—it'd be like a little commune where our kids could be brainwashed by Big Brother's helping hand from the moment they can walk.

U.S. education secretary Arne Duncan is another advocate of the school taking over as de facto parents:

If children are hungry, they should be fed. It's hard to learn if your stomach is growling. We need to take that on. If students can't see the blackboard, need eyeglasses, we need to do that. If students need a social worker or counselor to work through the challenges they're facing at home or in the community, we need to do that. My vision is that schools need to be community centers. Schools need to be open 12, 13, 14 hours a day six, seven days a week, 12 months out of the year, with a whole host of activities, particularly in disadvantaged communities.

Not only does this concept encourage the continued dissolution of the family, but it also leaves school personnel in the position of essentially raising the children themselves. That should sound more than a few alarm bells in the minds of anyone who believes in strong parenting, small communities, and the power of the individual.

How can we trust the people who are doing such a poor job with our children academically to do any better with them in other areas? They say that "community schools" are more necessary in low-income areas, but schools in low-income areas frequently suffer from mismanagement, poor allocation of resources, and destabilizing situations like high teacher turnover.

How can public schools, which can barely maintain any order or discipline as it is, be expected to provide for the physical, emotional, and medical needs of millions of children? In the Dallas Intermediate School District, for example, suspensions (both out-of-school and in-school) and placements in alternative schools soared from 35,451 to 44,672 between 2011–2012 and 2012–2013. Texas now spends about $227 million annually dealing with school disciplinary issues and security. How much additional taxpayer money would be required to handle all of the other issues that would come along with being de facto guardians of children?

There's also the issue of what our kids would learn with even more hours at school. Many of these educators would relish the opportunity to spend more time feeding students a steady stream of radical, anti-American political ideas, encouraging teen sexual activity, and deemphasizing the importance of traditional values and religion.

It's conceivable to believe that "community schools" like these would spell the end of many already struggling family units. How many parents would simply turn their children's daily needs over to the school and walk away from their responsibilities? And what happens then—do more and more kids become real guardians of the state? Will the need for student housing on K–12 campuses be the next item on the agenda?

Of course, this is not the first attempt that progressives have made toward turning government schools into parents. Through the federal Head Start program these folks have already taken charge of millions of toddlers—and that has not exactly been a rousing success. "Since 1965, taxpayers have spent more than

$180 billion on Head Start," the Heritage Foundation reported in early 2013. "Yet, over the decades, this Great Society relic has failed to improve academic outcomes for the children it was designed to help."

Heritage reached that conclusion by analyzing two federal studies from the last four years that revealed that access to Head Start had little or no effect on children's academic abilities by kindergarten, first grade, or third grade. In some instances, there were actually *negative* social effects as some Head Start graduates were judged to be more shy and withdrawn and have worse peer relationships than their classmates.

Grover Whitehurst of the left-leaning Brookings Institution, who once directed a national Head Start Quality Research Center, has also seemingly come to realize the program's failings:

> The most defensible conclusion is that these [early education] programs are not working to meaningfully increase the academic achievement or social/emotional skills and dispositions of children from low-income families. I wish this weren't so, but facts are stubborn things. Maybe we should figure out how to deliver effective programs before the federal government funds preschool for all.

There is no way that government schools could ever do a better job of meeting the needs of children than mothers and fathers working cooperatively in a loving and structured home, regardless of income. Our focus should be on promoting the concept of a strong family, not on community schools to stand in for them. Substituting schools for parents is like treating a gunshot victim by putting on a tourniquet. Yes, it may stop the bleeding temporarily, but unless you treat the root cause of the problem, the patient is eventually going to die anyway.

20

HOME-SCHOOLING IS HURTING OUR PUBLIC SCHOOLS AND IS BAD FOR THE COLLECTIVE

"Low-income kids earn higher test scores when they attend
school alongside middle-class kids, while the test scores of
privileged children are impervious to the influence of less-privileged
peers. So when college-educated parents pull their kids out of
public schools, whether for private school or homeschooling,
they make it harder for less-advantaged children to thrive."

—*DANA GOLDSTEIN, journalist and fellow at the New America Foundation*

"[T]he long-term consequences for the child being home schooled
or sent to a private school cannot be overstated. . . . The more
appropriate suggestion for our current educational dilemma
is that public education should be mandatory and universal.
Parental expressive interest could supplement but never supplant
the public institutions where the basic and fundamental lesson
would be taught and experienced by all American children:
we must struggle together to define ourselves both
as a collective and as individuals."

—*MARTHA ALBERTSON FINEMAN, Emory University School of Law*

Education controllists hate home-school families for a lot of different reasons. They are insulted by the idea that just anyone—particularly untrained parents—can provide children with anything even remotely approaching the type of enlightened instruction offered by professional educators.

"Parents aren't teachers," wrote one blogger going by the name of "OEA" (meaning the Ohio Education Association, a teachers' union) on a local community message board. "Let your children be educated by those who have chosen education as their life's work."

The National Education Association feels the same way. "The NEA believes that homeschooling programs based on parental choice cannot provide the student with a comprehensive education experience," they wrote. "Instruction should be by persons who are licensed by the appropriate state education licensure agency, and a curriculum approved by the state department of education."

Controllists, many of whom are hostile to organized religion, are also insulted by the traditional views held by many home-schooling parents. They scoff at the idea of religious studies being an integral part of the home-school experience for many families. "Most disturbing is the virulent strain of religious fundamentalism that is found in the lessons being taught homeschooled children, particularly in the United States," wrote Steve Shives, an atheist contributor to Yahoo!

But the primary reason for the home-schooling hatred is that most controllists also view themselves as social engineers whose long-term goals include the revision of America's economic and social structures. They consider the government education system to be one of the most valuable tools at their disposal to sell their agenda to future generations. They know that if they can continue to bring children into their message and worldview, then those kids are likely to grow into adults who are more willing to dismiss traditional values.

Things like free-lunch menus regulated by the federal government or aggressive sex ed curricula aren't important on their own; they're simply individual steps along a much longer path. That's why the exclusion of home-schooled children from their master plan drives them absolutely crazy. And the fact that home-schooling has skyrocketed in popularity in recent years (the number of home-schooled students jumped 70 percent between 1999 and 2007) makes them hate it even more. After all, if you're a controllist, what could be worse than a serious competitor with values completely antithetical to your own?

These people basically believe that children should be at the disposal of the state. They should learn what the state wants them to learn, not what *you* think they should learn. They should be exposed to values that the state deems crucial, not the values stressed at home.

We all remember when President Obama told small business owners, "You didn't build that." The insinuation was that government has a hand in any success that an individual might find. MSNBC host Melissa Harris-Perry takes that concept (which was originally posited by Hillary Clinton's "It takes a village" remark) a frightening step further, suggesting that our children are really not ours, but are instead the property of the community and state:

> We have never invested as much in public education as we should have because we've always had kind of a private notion of children. Your kid is yours and totally your responsibility. We haven't had a very collective notion of "These are our children." So part of it is that we have to break through our kind of private

idea that kids belong to their parents or kids belong to their families and recognize that kids belong to whole communities. Once it's everybody's responsibility and not just the households', then we start making better investments.

Sounds sort of Orwellian and hard to believe, right? It is—but there's a method to their madness and, unsurprisingly, it all revolves around power and control.

Since kids belong to the "whole community," they have a *responsibility* to attend local government schools, even if they don't receive quality instruction.

"It seems to me that if every single parent sent every single child to public school, public schools would improve," wrote *Slate* editor Allison Benedikt. "This would not happen immediately. It could take generations. Your children and grandchildren might get mediocre educations in the meantime, but it will be worth it, for the eventual common good."

University of Illinois professor Chris Lubienski has the same opinion, but he goes even further, tying this idea directly to homeschooling:

The discourse around homeschooling centers on issues of individual rights and private benefits, rather than the public good. It withdraws not only children but also social capital from public schools, to the detriment of the students remaining behind. . . . Homeschooling undermines the ability of public education to improve and become more responsive as a democratic institution. Thus, homeschooling is not only a reaction to, but a cause of, declining public schools. Therefore, it diminishes the potential of public education to serve the common good in a vibrant democracy.

Even the simple headline attached to one of Lubienski's articles is rather odd and worrisome: "Does home schooling promote the public good?"

I'll answer that question with one of my own: "Why is that any of your business?" Education is first and foremost an individual act, pursued for personal growth and benefit. My child is not a pawn in a massive game of eugenics where people are forced to justify their contributions to society every few years in front of some government board.

Beyond that, the truth is that, yes, education *is* important for society—which is the entire reason for writing a book like this. Controllists like Harris-Perry and Lubienski want to dump all kids into public schools to "serve the common good" without ever even stopping to ask if those schools actually *are* serving the public good.

These enlightened thinkers, with their supposed concern for the welfare of all, are also forgetting an important fact: the desires and goals of the state are secondary to the absolute rights of the individual. We are free to pursue happiness and personal fulfillment in the way we understand those concepts. We can choose to be active members of communities or keep to ourselves. We can choose to work for the common good or focus on personal goals. We are free to worship (or not) as we please, and raise our children in the manner we deem correct. And we reserve the right to educate our children within the realm of our personal values, rather than the popular values of the greater community.

21

HOME-SCHOOLERS ARE ACADEMICALLY INFERIOR TO PUBLIC SCHOOL STUDENTS

"The sad and hidden truth about home schooling is that no one knows whether home schooled students are performing well or poorly. We have no shortage of anecdotes—home schoolers who end up at Stanford or who win spelling bees. Astonishingly, however, we know practically nothing about the academic performance of the average home schooler. The studies that grab headlines use a biased and unrepresentative sample of home schoolers."

—*ROB REICH, professor of political science and education, Stanford University*

"The educational harm is the most immediate, direct risk of unregulated homeschooling. It is also the only one in this litany of possible risks adamantly denied by homeschooling advocates, but contrary to their claims, there is also no credible evidence that they do better. There is no credible evidence of accomplishment here at all."

—*ROBIN WEST, University of Maryland professor*

Some controllists try to paint a picture of home-school children as tragically undereducated. They want the public to believe that these children spend a few hours a day memorizing

Bible verses before playing by themselves in their rooms. But that's a completely inaccurate and unfair stereotype. Many home-school students are academically advanced compared to their public school peers, sometimes by a substantial degree.

Brian Ray, president of the nonprofit National Home Education Research Institute (NHERI), helped commission a wide-ranging study that included more than twelve thousand home-schooled students from across the country. The study looked at the performance of these students on three standardized tests: the California Achievement Test, the Iowa Test of Basic Skills, and the Stanford Achievement Test—for the 2007–2008 academic year. Writing in the *Washington Times*, the Home School Legal Defense Association called this the "most comprehensive home-school academic study to date" and summarized the results:

> Five areas of academic pursuit were measured. In reading, the average home-schooler scored at the 89th percentile; language, 84th percentile; math, 84th percentile; science, 86th percentile; and social studies, 84th percentile. In the core studies (reading, language and math), the average home-schooler scored at the 88th percentile.
>
> The average public school student taking these standardized tests scored at the 50th percentile in each subject area.

Professor Michael Cogan also looked at the college readiness of home-schooled kids versus others. According to the *Huffington Post*, the study, which looked at students attending a doctoral college from 2004 to 2009, found that "[s]tudents coming from a home school graduated college at a higher rate than their peers— 66.7 percent compared to 57.5 percent—and earned higher grade point averages along the way."

Another study, this one by Sandra Martin-Chang of Canada's Concordia University, attempted to use a selection process that would bring in both home-schooled and traditionally schooled students. Thirty-seven home-school families participated, and they were matched with thirty-seven demographically alike public school families.

The study found that most home-school parents took a "structured" approach to their kids' education and that that kind of approach was very important in determining academic success. According to a summary of the study at ParentingScience.com, the structured home-school group's performance was significantly better than the public school group's:

> In 5 of 7 test areas (word identification, phonic decoding, science, social science, humanities), structured homeschoolers were at least one grade level ahead of public schoolers.

> They were almost half a year ahead in math, and slightly, but not significantly, advanced in reading comprehension.

The bottom line is that the quality of a home-school education is very much like the quality of any other education: it comes down to the knowledge, passion, and enthusiasm of the instructors. To say that parents, who have more invested in their children than anyone else, would have less of those attributes than a teacher is absurd. Critics of home-schooling hate the *idea* of home-schooling and the freedom from the government school monopoly that it represents. Their attacks on academic success are just a transparent attempt to divert attention from their own failings.

22

EVEN IF HOME-SCHOOLED KIDS
DO OKAY ACADEMICALLY, THEY SUFFER
SOCIALLY BY NOT BEING AT SCHOOL

"Of course, not all homeschoolers are mis-socialized, just as
all public schoolers are not well socialized. But nevertheless,
homeschoolers—a whole of them—are not well socialized."

—*LANA HOPE, former homeschooling parent*

"A lot of them are demented when they're
homeschooled. . . . They learn to be scared of other children."

—*JOY BEHAR, former co-host of* The View

"Public schools offer much more than basic education. They teach our
children how to behave in society. Homeschooled kids miss out on so
much fun and learning. I think kids ought to have a choice to go to
regular school with their friends or stay home with mom and dad. . . ."

—*"OEA," anonymous blogger*

Controllists love to promote the false stereotype of home-school children being isolated from peers and deprived of opportunities to make friends and interact socially. They'd like all of us to picture a poor kid sitting in their room alone while everyone else is out at recess or playing soccer after school. It really goes right back to the previous argument about home-schooled kids not contributing to the common good. After all, if they have no social skills, then how can they be productive members of society?

Fortunately, this stereotype is just not true. Several studies have attempted to provide scientific proof that home-schooled kids integrate just as well into society as anyone else, and the results have been impressive.

Brian Ray, president of the National Home Education Research Institute, points to a 2000 study by the Discovery Institute as one example. According to PBS, this study involved counselors watching videos of kids playing. Some of the kids were home-schooled and others were enrolled in traditional schools. "The counselors, who did not know which children were from each category, noted that the homeschool students demonstrated fewer behavioral problems than their peers." Ray told PBS that this likely has to do with the kind of people the home-schooled kids are around every day. "Public school children have, as their main role models, peers, while homeschool students have as their role models, adults," he said.

While critics lob all sorts of insults at these studies, the truth is that they don't have any better data to back up their contention. All they have are anecdotes and a white-hot hatred for home-schooling.

As most home-school families already know, there are plenty of options when it comes to social interaction for their kids. For example, "homeschool associations" are popping up all over the nation, offering group activities for the children of home-school parents, including field trips, sports, dances, plays, and other events where students get to know each other and make friends.

Some public schools are also opening up sports, music, and other extracurricular programs to home-school students, based on the premise that their parents are still taxpayers who contribute to the operation of local schools. There are also regular after-school activities, sports leagues, YMCAs, Boy/Girl Scouts, and plenty of other groups and organizations available to home-school families.

Meanwhile, there's another side to this argument, one that controllists don't often like to talk about: the socialization offered by public schools is frequently not the kind that sane parents desire.

"Anyone who watches school bus socialization or cafeteria interaction or children on a playground begins to question the kinds of social skills which are being learned," Scott Turansky of the National Center for Biblical Parenting wrote. "Unfortunately, the negative socialization that takes place in the larger school environment is often destructive and parents must spend time retraining their children after long exposure to it. Meanness, teasing, gossip, rudeness, peer pressure, and other destructive social skills contribute to negative socialization."

Maybe the problem we should all be most worried about isn't how home-schooled kids are doing academically and socially, but how public school kids are doing.

23

BUT WHAT ARE THESE PARENTS TEACHING
THEIR KIDS AT HOME? WE NEED MORE
STATE MONITORING TO MAKE SURE
IT'S NOT ALL CRAZY CHRISTIAN BIBLE STUFF!

"[T]he long-term consequences for the child being home schooled or sent
to a private school cannot be overstated. The total absence of regulation
over what and how children are taught leaves the child vulnerable to gaining
a sub-par or non-existent education from which they may never recover.
Moreover, the risk that parents or private schools unfairly impose hierarchical
or oppressive beliefs on their children is magnified by the absence of state
oversight or the application of any particular educational standards."
—*PROFESSOR MARTHA ALBERTSON FINEMAN,* Emory University School of Law

Similar to the argument about a lack of socialization among home-schoolers, this one should also be flipped on its head. Instead of wondering what sort of crazy religious lessons parents are instilling into their kids, maybe we should be wondering what sort of crazy ideological lessons teachers are imparting on their students.

"The long period of self-censorship among educators regarding class and labor issues may no longer hold," reads an excerpt from the book *Organizing the Curriculum*. "We cannot claim to be teaching for social justice if we ignore the class warfare being waged all around us. . . . Bringing labor into the arena of K–12 education will undoubtedly meet political resistance, but an increasing number of educators are motivated to take up the challenge."

The Educational and Labor Collaborative at Adelphi University has similar views on how teachers can help the labor movement:

> Educators, in collaboration with unionists, can break the cycle
> of reproducing the economic structure through schooling, and
> change the cultural climate that denigrates poor and working
> families.

This sort of thing goes all the way back to John Dewey, a leftist American college professor who was born in 1859 and became president of the radical League for Industrial Democracy, which eventually evolved into the infamous Students for a Democratic Society, the 1960s radical student group in which President Obama's friend Bill Ayers was a key leader.

Dewey was a socialist and one of the first to call for educators to use classrooms to promote the coming revolution to their wide-eyed students.

"I believe that education is the fundamental method of social progress and reform," Dewey wrote in 1897. His organization's magazine, *Revolt*, claimed that "we have to frame the issues of socialism and democracy and fight the battles of socialism and democracy in the stockholders' meetings of industrial corporations, in our medical associations and bar associations and our teachers associations, in labor unions, in student councils, in producers and consumers cooperatives—in every social institution in which we can find a foothold."

The danger posed by Dewey's philosophy of using government schools to sell the fundamental principles of socialism was recognized decades ago. President Dwight D. Eisenhower, for example, once said, "Educators, parents and students . . . must be induced to abandon the educational path that, rather blindly, they have been following as a result of John Dewey's teachings."

Needless to say, we have ignored that advice—and the consequences can be found everywhere. Most people are familiar with the radical left-wing bent of tenured college professors, but this kind of union-supported ideology disguised as teaching has made it to the K–12 arena as well.

A few years ago Nick Benson, a Californian who had two grandchildren enrolled at Barstow High School, realized that his grandson's world history teacher, Jim Duarte, had been feeding his students a steady dose of leftist propaganda disguised as classroom assignments. In one instance, students were told to read an article about Utah legislators proposing an increase in the food sales tax while decreasing the general sales tax. Students were then expected to submit the following answers ("correct" answers are underlined) on their worksheets:

> Lawmakers in Utah are "digging a deeper hole" for the poor by raising the food tax, and this allows the rich to pay less in sales tax on everything else.

On the same worksheet, students were shown an editorial cartoon of two people labeled "unions" walking a gangplank. Students then were required to provide the following answers (underlined):

> Because so many states are now in a <u>recession</u>, caused by <u>corporations</u> (<u>bankers</u> and <u>Wall</u> Street), states controlled by <u>Republicans</u> are going after public sector <u>unions</u> and <u>collective bargaining</u> rights.

Another worksheet required students to fill in the following answers (underlined):

> <u>Republicans</u> have tried to keep <u>young</u> people and <u>minorities</u> from voting, and are trying to weaken the <u>union</u>. . . . <u>Millionaires</u>, who could pay more in taxes and not suffer but are paying less, are hurting <u>states</u> and <u>public</u> schools.

This type of nonsense is prompting more and more families to remove their children from government schools when the opportunity presents itself. That's provided a huge opportunity for charter and voucher schools and is one big reason why school choice is flourishing around the country.

But elitist educators save their most severe contempt for their ultimate enemies: parents who choose to sidestep collective education altogether and home-school their children. When kids don't attend an organized school, there's no possibility for them to be exposed to the "social justice" lessons of the education establishment.

As Michael Farris, chairman of the Home School Legal Defense Association, recently wrote in an eye-opening report, "Christian homeschooling parents are effectively transmitting values to their children that the elitists believe are dangerous to the well-being of these very children and society as a whole."

That explains the real reason for the argument that began this section. Controllists hate the idea that an entire army of kids are being taught, in many cases, pro–free market, pro-America, pro-

Bible principles. The controllists' reaction is usually to attempt to convince people that the state *must* get more involved in regulating and monitoring these home-school families before it's too late.

In his report, Farris quotes Catherine J. Ross, a professor at George Washington University, making pretty much this exact case:

> Respect for difference should not be confused with approval for approaches that would splinter us into countless warring groups. Hence an argument that tolerance for diverse views and values is a foundational principle does not conflict with the notion that the state can and should limit the ability of intolerant homeschoolers to inculcate hostility to difference in their children—at least during the portion of the day they claim to devote to satisfying the compulsory schooling requirement.

In other words, Ross might allow parents to teach their children Christian principles at night, after school, but never as part of a daily home-schooling program. And she believes government should have the right to enforce that ban.

While a recent poll revealed that the opportunity to offer religious instruction was the most popular reason for parents to home-school children, there are other major factors involved in the decision, including "concern about the school environment" (mentioned by 21 percent of respondents) and "dissatisfaction with the academic instruction available" at other schools (mentioned by 17 percent).

Yet the state remains mistrustful and sometimes even hostile to home-school families. The Philadelphia school district, one of the biggest failures in the history of American public education, has a policy requiring home-school parents to submit annual portfolios containing their children's standardized test scores, evaluations, and work samples. Ironically enough, these requirements are coming from a school district where 16 percent of eighth graders are proficient in reading, 18 percent are proficient in math, and only 61 percent of students graduate on schedule. If anything, home-school parents could learn a lot about how *not* to teach their children from Philadelphia educators.

24

MANY PARENTS AREN'T EQUIPPED
TO MAKE THE RIGHT CHOICES
FOR THEIR CHILDREN

"Do we really need to give more autonomy to a mom who can't enforce a
bedtime or the dad who disparages school as a waste of time?
Should we trust the judgment of a parent who constantly tells their
kid how stupid he or she is? Certainly, such families need attention and
support, but more autonomy? Really?"

—*JULIE MACK, Michigan education columnist*

"If I'm a parent in poverty I have no clue because I'm trying to
struggle and live day to day. The idea of parents making decisions
simply based on choice is the abandonment of public schools."

—*MICHAEL WALKER-JONES, executive director of the Louisiana Association of Educators*

The concept of choice is fundamental to almost everything we
do in life.

We decide where we want to live, how many kids we want to
have, what kind of car we want to drive, what type of career to
have, and whether to eat at Burger King or McDonald's for dinner.

The U.S. Constitution trusts us to make all of those choices as free individuals participating in a free-market economy. And that type of freedom builds consumer power. Those competing for our hearts, minds, and wallets are forced to shape their products and services to our tastes and demands. Those that refuse quickly find out just how powerful the free market really is.

But when it comes to K–12 education, consumer choice has been severely limited by the government school monopoly. That means competition between different types of schools has been limited, and the resulting pressure for schools to improve has been noticeably absent.

The American government school establishment, which includes administrators, teachers, school support staff, and union leaders, is responsible for putting us in this situation. Their livelihoods are tied to their traditional public school monopoly, and they do whatever it takes to maintain the status quo—students and parents be damned.

The establishment wants government to continue to force the children of average-income families to attend local public schools. They don't want to compete for students—and the government dollars tied to each one—with public charter schools or private schools. They defend this stance with all kinds of ridiculous arguments, but the one that seems to be made (or at least insinuated) with increasing frequency is the idea that parents are just too dumb to make proper decisions about schools. As a result, the reasoning goes, the logical choice for everyone is the local public school, which also happens to conveniently be staffed by public employees who belong to labor unions.

"In some cases, parents are very good in making decisions about their child," Democratic state representative Neil Brannon said during a debate in the Oklahoma legislature over a school choice expansion bill. "But in some cases, I've seen students with disabilities where the parents have disabilities, also. Now are they really the ones who ought to be making the decisions about where that child goes [to school]? I have great concerns about that, and I think we have to be careful. . . . They may think they know best, but do they?"

At least Brannon maintained the possibility that some parents *might* be smart enough to pick a school for their children. Debbie Squires, an official with the Michigan Elementary and Middle School Principals Association, doesn't seem to give parents even that much credit.

"Educators go through education for a reason," Squires told a Michigan House committee in 2012. "They are the people who know best about how to serve children. That's not necessarily true of an individual resident. I'm not saying they don't want what is best for their children, but they may not know what actually is best from an education standpoint."

Her comments prompted Representative Tom McMillin, a school choice advocate, to quip, "Wow, parents don't know what's best for their child."

Squires responded, "I said they may want what's best for their child, but they may not know. And they may not have the capabilities. . . ."

Ann Laing, retired superintendent of Wisconsin's Racine Unified School District, argued that black parents, in particular, lack the sense to choose the right school for their kids.

"I think Milwaukee is a good example of what will happen on a smaller scale here," said Laing, whose district became part of the state's voucher program. "It's pretty much been white families who have taken advantage of private schools, with a few African-American families. The African-American families are the ones who are most prone to enroll their kids in the fly-by-night schools that cropped up after vouchers existed.

"They don't know how to make good choices for their children. They really don't. They didn't have parents who made good choices for them or helped them learn how to make good choices, so they don't know how to do that."

It's hard to decide what's more frightening, an arrogant government school official who truly believes parents lack the sense to choose an appropriate school for their children, or one who knowingly misrepresents the wisdom of parents in an effort to preserve the status quo.

The school choice debate really has nothing to do with the quality of education offered by any particular type of school. It has *everything* to do with the billions of dollars that government spends on K–12 education every year. Traditional public schools have grown accustomed to getting most of that money, with no competition or strings attached. Now some states are asking them to compete with charter and voucher schools, and they don't appreciate the intrusion, or the risk these schools pose to their existing revenue stream.

With parents and students in some areas choosing alternative schools by the thousands, traditional public schools are under attack. When the kids go, the tax dollars attached to them usually go as well. For union leaders and bureaucrats used to ever-increasing salaries and lavish benefits based on the dues paid by teachers, that's a pretty scary proposition. And for everyone else—the teachers, administrators, aides, cooks, bus drivers, and custodians—who work in public schools, it's scary as well. Corresponding jobs may open up in charter or private schools, but they are typically not union positions and the compensation may not be as generous. Teachers with the best reputations for success may not have to worry, but those who've been coasting and taking advantage of the contractual seniority provisions quickly realize that the gravy train is about to make its last stop.

The establishment fights parental choice programs every chance they get because parental choice means the end of the status quo. And since they really, really like the status quo, they've turned to lawsuits as their preferred method of attack against anything that might offer parents a choice in schools:

- The Alabama Education Association, that state's largest teachers' union, is suing to halt the Alabama Accountability Act, which created a tax credit program of $3,500 per year for parents whose children transfer from a failing public school to a private school.
- The U.S. Department of Justice (which, like all Obama administration departments, is an ally of Big Labor) filed a lawsuit to end the Louisiana Scholarship Program, which gives private school vouchers to students who transfer from failing schools. The Justice Department claimed the vouchers threatened desegregation efforts in some public schools, even though those schools are failing and many black students want out. Under intense public pressure the lawsuit was eventually withdrawn.
- The Hartford Federation of Teachers recently tried to convince the school board to stop Achievement First, a high-performing charter school with a long waiting list of students, from opening a second elementary school in the city. The school board wisely voted to ignore the union and allow the expansion.
- In New York, the United Federation of Teachers and new mayor Bill de Blasio have pledged to stop forcing public schools to share their half-empty buildings with charter schools (which are public schools themselves). New York City Public Advocate Letitia James and City Councilwoman Melissa Mark-Viverito have filed a lawsuit that, if successful, could threaten the existence of several very successful charter schools, or at least their ability to expand, because they lack building space of their own.

As the school choice era continues to grow and flourish, these sorts of frivolous attempts at maintaining the public education monopoly will hopefully dry up. Until then, expect to hear more and more controllists insinuate that parents are just too dumb and irresponsible to have more than one option to consider.

25

SCHOOL CHOICE TAKES MONEY AWAY
FROM GOVERNMENT SCHOOLS

"Vouchers take money away from public schools and give it to private schools."
—*PAUL BRAHCE, Madison, Wisconsin, public school principal*

"NEA opposes school vouchers because they divert essential resources
from public schools to private and religious schools. . . ."
—*NATIONAL EDUCATION ASSOCIATION*

"So what 'choice' really means is a diversion of public funds to religious schools
(more than 90 percent of current voucher students attend religious schools) or
diversion of taxpayer dollars to charter schools. In Louisiana, a voucher program
has inspired many fundamentalist religious schools, often operating in inadequate
storefront spaces, offering virtually no credible curriculum and staffed by unqualified
teachers. Lots of Bible studies, but little math, little science, fictional history, no art,
no music, no gym, and no hope for the poor children suckered into attendance."
—*STEVE NELSON, head of the Calhoun School, New York City*

The education establishment constantly complains about charter schools and private school voucher programs siphoning money from government schools. That complaint is usually based on the wrongheaded assumption that traditional government schools have an inherent right to be perpetually funded in their current form—regardless of their performance. The argument is usually made by those who enjoy the status quo and want to scare parents into believing that school choice is some boogeyman that will leave their local public school in shambles.

If we agree that public education exists primarily to serve students, then we logically must also agree that traditional schools should exist only insofar as they consistently meet that goal. And if we agree that parents should have the right to choose the appropriate schools for their own children, then we logically must agree that open competition will generate the fairest and most equitable distribution of education dollars.

If *any* school—public, charter, or private—does not entice enough voluntary enrollment to meet its own expenses, then it's not getting the job done and probably does not deserve continued taxpayer funding. If the public has no interest in keeping a public school open, how can *anyone* justify keeping it open? Just because the principal and teachers don't want to lose their jobs? Just because the teachers' union doesn't want to lose members and dues revenue? Isn't this supposed to be about the students?

The bottom line is that competition between schools is the best formula for success because it incentivizes superior performance. Human institutions are most effective, and provide the best service, when they are forced to compete for resources. They quickly lose that edge, and their value to customers, when they have a virtual monopoly. Why do a great job of serving your customers, year after year, when your customers have no other options? Too much security breeds complacency, which leads to mediocrity. Think about how happy you are with your local cable TV provider. Are they too expensive? Too slow to correct problems?

Do they set four-hour appointment windows for you and then often don't show up? Do they package together a slew of stuff you don't even want but that's required in order to get the stuff you do want? That's the government school model in a nutshell.

Somewhere along the line someone got the idea that education funded by government must be education provided by government. But is that really the way it has to be? If the private school down the road provides great instruction, and many parents would prefer to send their children there, why shouldn't the government invest its education dollars in that school? If the needs of the student are the first priority, then our money should flow to the best schools, period. Parents will identify which schools those are at enrollment time.

Of course, there are those elitist educators (probably more than we realize) who insist that parents are too ignorant to choose the best school for their kids. They argue that children are better off in their predefined local districts, where the "educated" bureaucrats can make the decisions. But do they really believe that this kind of policy serves the best interest of students, or do they simply understand that trapping kids every year in their silo will guarantee a constant flow of government dollars, which will, in turn, keep the bureaucrats employed?

We've watched the lack of competitive pressure affect the overall quality of education in America for too long now. Government schools have had a near monopoly on the education market for decades, and our students have drifted from the top of international academic achievement charts down toward the middle. Schools and teachers could have worked harder for better results once things started going south, but why would they? The students were trapped, the government dollars were guaranteed, and school employees were content and secure.

It may sound awful to say, but no one really seemed to care

much if student test scores dropped a bit from year to year. Maybe a good analogy is our national debt. We all sort of know intuitively that it's out of control and that some generation down the road is going to pay for our spending spree, but right now, most people don't really seem to care all that much. As long as the economy does all right, their favorite government programs don't get cut, and their taxes don't get raised, they stay quiet. That seems to be the way a lot of people think about education as well.

But now the establishment is being challenged by charter schools, voucher programs, home-schooling, and technology, all of which have been attracting students at an impressive rate—and government dollars along with them. Officials at traditional government schools are furious. They hope that if they scream loud enough and long enough, politicians will restore their monopoly and way of life.

When Montana legislators proposed tuition tax credits in 2013, teachers' union president Eric Feaver told the *Missoulian* that public schools are "the greatest institution this nation has ever created." He added: "We're all a part of the whole. The charter school movement breaks us up into cosmic parts, like we don't belong to each other. . . . The whole purpose of [public education] is not just to teach math, or reading . . . but to educate us on how to live together, across the board."

After Louisiana governor Bobby Jindal proposed a voucher program, state teachers' union head Joyce Haynes criticized the idea. "There isn't anything fair," she said, "about using something like that only against the public schools and then taking our children from us, and sending us where we don't know what they're getting."

For the record, when she says "us" she's of course referring to the union, *not* to parents.

Alternative schools were born out of frustration with the government school monopoly and the mediocre instruction it provided. The public school crowd *created* the new competitive atmosphere through its own arrogance and apathy.

The D.C. Opportunity Scholarship Program is a perfect illustration of the ongoing fight between the education establishment and its challengers. According to a 2006 report from the Cato Institute:

> The District of Columbia public school system has been plagued with problems that make it a national debacle. Its academic performance is abysmal, its financial accountability has been nonexistent, it has undergone several iterations of administrative restructuring, and many of its schools are falling apart. Consequently, it is no surprise that parents who can do so often choose alternatives to the public school system, such as charter or private schools. That has resulted in a steady decline in enrollment during the last decade.

> A large proportion of D.C. parents, however, does not have the economic means to send their children to private schools. The D.C. voucher program was designed to give some of those parents the choice of private schooling. The offer of $7,500 for private school tuition has generated a waiting list of interested parents, and expansion of the program is currently being considered.

Obviously, if D.C. public schools were meeting students' needs, then the voucher program would have died on the vine. That clearly has not been the case. The program had 11,215 applicants between its inception in 2004 and 2012 and awarded 4,900 scholarships. Nearly 90 percent of students have been black and from single-parent, lower-income families. As former U.S. senator Joe Lieberman said in 2011, "This program provides a lifeline to many needy children."

What about the program's effectiveness? Well, it depends whether you ask average citizens or ideologically driven politicians. A 2010 evaluation conducted by the U.S. Department of Education determined that there was "no conclusive evidence" that voucher students outperformed their public school peers academically. But the same study also found that voucher students were graduating from high school at an 82 percent rate—12 percentage points *higher* than public school students. A 2012–2013 study found that 90 percent of voucher graduates went on to a college or university, and that more than 90 percent of parents were satisfied with the program.

D.C. residents are also satisfied. A 2011 poll found that 74 percent of them favored expansion of the voucher program. Seventy-five percent said its academic performance was strong enough to warrant expansion, and 77 percent said "all options should be on the table" for the district's most disadvantaged children.

To summarize, students in the voucher program did at least as well in the classroom as government school students, graduated and went to college at a much higher rate, their parents loved the program, and the community supported it. Shouldn't that have been enough to warrant continued federal funding?

Not according to President Obama, congressional Democrats, and the national teachers' unions. A 2011 position paper from House Minority Leader Nancy Pelosi offered several reasons why she and her allies believed the program should be canceled and its funding diverted to the D.C. government school system. "The expired D.C. voucher program was a failure," Pelosi wrote. "The final congressionally mandated independent study of the program found 'no conclusive evidence that [the program] affected student achievement.' "

So the results of one bureaucratic study automatically made the program a failure? Does the significantly higher graduation rate count for anything? Does overwhelming parental satisfaction and community support count for anything? Shouldn't the citizens of a community—rather than elitist politicians and bureaucrats—determine the type of educational programs that deserve to be funded by their taxes?

Not according to Pelosi:

> As the Obama administration pointed out in its statement of opposition to the bill [to restore funding for the voucher program], "the federal government should focus its attention and available resources on improving the quality of public schools for all students." . . . D.C. is already a city of school choice. In the District of Columbia, 38 percent of students enrolled in public schools are enrolled in public charter schools and 27 percent are enrolled in non-neighborhood public schools through a choice program for parents.

The fact that such a high percentage of students had already fled to charter schools should have told Pelosi everything she needed to know: families wanted out of D.C. government schools. And the waiting lists for the voucher program should have told her that families desired more than just public options.

Fortunately, Speaker of the House John Boehner and his allies prevailed, and the D.C. voucher program was saved (at least for now).

Whether Pelosi and her friends like it or not, and despite all of the legal challenges and obstructions, the era of school choice is here to stay. Charter schools are legal and thriving in nearly every state. At least twenty-two states have jumped on the voucher bandwagon in recent years, offering either direct tuition vouchers or tax credits to help cover private school tuition.

The Milwaukee Parental Choice Program, the nation's oldest

voucher program, has grown from about 11,000 students a decade ago to about 25,000 students this year. Indiana's statewide voucher program, now in its third year, has grown from 3,919 participants to more than 20,000. Eighty percent of K–12 students in New Orleans attend charter schools and about 43 percent of Washington, D.C., students attend them.

According to the Institute of Education Sciences, about 2 million children now attend charter schools nationwide. Between 1999 and 2011, charter school enrollment exploded by 600 percent. In the 2010–2011 school year, there were 5,300 charter schools in America and that number continues to grow.

It's hard to imagine that any of these families are mourning the loss of the controllists' grip on their children's future or worrying about the impact to their failing local public schools. They want educational options, and they want government dollars to help support and provide access to the schools *they* choose for their kids.

When people get a taste of freedom, there's no turning back.

Offering this choice does not mean that public schools have to suffer (unless they are terrible, in which case they probably deserve to be scrutinized). In fact, competition from charter schools usually forces traditional government schools to step up their game in order to attract and retain students—and the state aid that's attached to each one.

26

EDUCATION SHOULDN'T BE FOR-PROFIT

"Our schools should use our hard-earned tax dollars to pay for
children's education, not for boosting shareholders' profits."
—*MARK SCHAUER, former U.S. congressman and current
Democratic candidate for governor of Michigan*

"Republicans want to cut funding for public education because,
you see, they have a different plan. It's called for-profit education.
Charter schools are a huge profit center and they are very
attractive to vulture capitalists like Mitt Romney."
—*ED SCHULTZ, The Ed Show*

"Let's get past the idea that 'running a school like a business'
would somehow solve all our problems. . . ."
—*GLEN LINEBERRY, Arizona high school teacher*

Staffing and managing a school is a complicated, time-
consuming, labor-intensive endeavor. Not surprisingly, it's
also very expensive.

Common sense would dictate that the group we pay to do that

staffing and management should be very skilled at what they do. I don't think most reasonable people care which group gets the job as long as they stay on budget, follow the curriculum, and, most important, produce the desired academic results.

But, of course, some people just aren't reasonable.

One of them is former state representative Patrick Rose of Texas, who said, "We ought not be in the business of supporting for-profit education. Any program that takes money out of our public schools would be against our better judgment."

I don't think Representative Rose truly understands how the education business works—and make no mistake, it *is* a business. Government schools pay lots of different people and companies to provide all sorts of essential services. There are the private publishers who provide the textbooks. There are private food companies that provide student breakfasts and lunches. There are private transportation companies that provide busing. There are private groundskeeping companies that trim the hedges and mow the lawns.

So what's the problem if a school (usually a charter school) hires a for-profit company to manage its operations? Well, to progressives, it all stems from their prejudice against the term "for-profit." The very idea of profit seems selfish and unseemly to most of them (unless they are the ones making it) and they consider the business world to be corrupt and unjust. They believe that public education should exist on a higher moral plane, one where the first concern of all educators should be teaching children, not making a filthy capitalistic "profit."

"I think people have been astounded that anyone can make money off of public education," said Nancy Loome, executive director of the Parents' Campaign, a pro-government-school lobbying group in Mississippi. "Our schools struggle to make it on the resources they are provided. If [for-profit management is] trying to make a profit and pay shareholders, they aren't going to be investing very much in educating children."

Other representatives of the progressive-left agree. "Like the privatized prison business model," the *Daily Kos* blogger "War on Error" wrote, "K–12 school privatization is just another humanity-callous opportunity for the 1% Owners to profit from the 99% Serfs."

Diane Ravitch, a professor of education at New York University, agrees. "Corporations aren't going to put more money into the school, they're only going to make money," she said. "This should make people in America angry. There ought to be a public uprising against this effort to destroy public education."

This would all be pretty funny if it weren't so sad. Here we have the very people who are profiting most off the failing status quo arguing that other people might profit if we try to improve the system.

As is typical with this kind of debate, these people are trying to make a simple issue complicated in the hopes that most others will throw up their hands in defeat. For starters, there is no such thing as a "for-profit" charter school. Charter schools are public schools, which are, by definition, *nonprofit*. They are governed by appointed school boards that sometimes choose to hire for-profit companies to staff and manage their facilities because they believe these companies can do a good job of managing existing resources while helping kids succeed.

If those goals are met, who really cares if the management company makes a profit in the process? Especially if that profit implies the success of their business model (i.e., a better education for your children).

Here's an analogy. Let's say you are the parent of a child who needs in-home physical therapy that will be paid for by the state. Your choices are between a state therapist who has had mediocre success and a private therapist with glowing reviews. The cost to the state is the same; the only difference is that the company that employees the private therapist would make a profit. As a parent, which one would you choose?

The answer is obvious, right? You would want the best possible person working with your child. It doesn't really matter if they make money, so long as you are getting the best quality for the same price. Yet some critics make this kind of logical thinking sound almost criminal.

"Legislation is often designed to mask the for-profit agenda," a Mississippi pro-public-education Parents' Campaign document said. "For instance, charter school legislation may stipulate that charter schools must be non-profit entities but leave loopholes allowing charters to 'contract with' for-profit companies to manage and operate the schools. Such loopholes give corporations access to and control over taxpayer dollars meant for public, not-for-profit education."

Loopholes? That's not a loophole, that's Management 101. This idea that private corporations cannot do anything with public money is absurd. We've already talked about the private vendors that service public schools and are paid with public money, but this kind of thing happens in other areas as well. Obamacare, for example, has large public subsidies that go to private insurance companies. Private sanitation companies are paid with tax money to clean our streets.

Despite their rhetoric, the unions understand this. The Michigan Education Association's 2013 annual financial report lists eight different contractors that were paid for janitorial services. Why? Because the union presumably determined that it was cheaper for them to contract for the service rather than hiring full-time cleaners.

The nonpartisan Ohio Alliance for Public Charter Schools

summarized why this whole attack on "for-profit" companies is pretty absurd:

> [This argument] diverts attention from what all of us should be most concerned about—and that's whether schools are success-fully serving students' educational needs.

> The bottom line is clear. Charter schools' use of private, for-profit management companies is no different than traditional schools' use of private, for-profit companies to provide trans-portation or food services, education materials, or professional development activities. It is completely reasonable, routine, and legal. What matters much more than the tax status of a school's management company or any other professional ser-vices vendor is whether charter schools are meeting the needs of students and their families. On that point there can be little dispute.

Are all for-profit management companies successful in running charter schools? Of course not. Some studies show that they sometimes do worse than the average school run by nonprofit interests, while others suggest they do better. But that's exactly the point: it's about local choice; individual decisions based on individual circumstances. If for-profit companies in one area do a terrible job, then obviously they will be kicked out of schools and will go out of business fast.

One of the benefits of hiring a for-profit company is that they sign contracts to run schools for a defined amount of time. If they are not effective, they can be fired at the end of their contracts and the charter school boards can find other options. This happens routinely. According to a 2010 editorial in the *New York Daily News*, "of the 11 charter schools [in New York State] that have been closed for poor academic or fiscal performance, seven have been managed by a for-profit company. At least five other charter schools discontinued their management contract with a for-profit company."

On the other hand, the *Daily News* reported that "10 charter schools managed by a for-profit administered the state's English and mathematics exams in one or more grades. . . . Of the 20 test measures comparing a school's aggregate results with their respective districts, a charter school managed by a for-profit company outperformed its district's average scores in 19."

If charter schools run by for-profit companies can be closed, or can ditch their management companies for poor performance, what are the controllists upset about? Maybe it all goes back to the "slow down, you're making the rest of us look bad" mentality of unions. After all, these for-profit companies generally come in and trim costs—proving to school boards just how much fat has been built into the budget.

Many progressives attack for-profit education by trying to scare people into believing that class sizes will explode and students will suffer. For example, consider how Chris Lehmann, a Philadelphia school principal, explained his opposition to these companies:

> According to a speech made by Michael Moe of GSV Ventures at the Education Innovation Summit, 90 percent of expenditures in public education is in personnel, and Moe stated that if one wishes to make money in the education sector, one must find a way to reduce personnel costs. And most of those personnel are teachers. If schools are to reduce that expense, they can only do so in one of two ways—more students per teacher so that you need fewer teachers or pay teachers less. Why would anyone think either of those things a good idea?

First, that's not always true. For-profit companies are often able to find significant savings in areas other than the teachers themselves. It's funny how a profit motive makes people look at everything— from the cost of chalk to how to save on water and electricity—in a whole new light. But let's assume for a minute that personnel costs must also be adjusted. If having fewer teachers helps students learn, then that's a *good* thing. Any strategy that results in students making positive academic progress is worthy of support. Remember, this is not about the teachers; it's about the students. Would you rather your child is in a class of twenty students led by a mediocre teacher, or twenty-five students led by a world-class educator? Class size is not everything.

Besides, what the controllists conveniently forget is that government schools already pay out a great deal of money to have someone manage them. If it's not a private company, it will be a traditional management team composed of superintendents, principals, and related staff. These people aren't making any less of a profit than the "for-profit" management companies; the money just flows in a different way.

Consider the deeply troubled Rochester, New York, school system. In 2012 they had 292 employees making more than $100,000 per year in straight salary, yet only 43 percent of students were graduating. Only 18 percent of eighth graders were proficient in English and only 19 percent were proficient in math. Would a "for-profit" company cost any less or do any worse than this bloated group of failed administrators? Doesn't there come a time when the risk of doing nothing is greater than the risk of trying out a proven, experienced for-profit management team?

Then there's the equally inept Providence, Rhode Island, district, where the thirty highest-paid administrators made an average of $150,000 in 2012, despite having "the seven worst high schools in the state" academically, according to news site

GoLocalProv, all with math proficiency rates below 5 percent. Would the Providence school board be negligent to consider a "for-profit" management company, or would they be negligent if they did *not* consider one?

Then there are all the union fat cats who make a very, very nice living from money siphoned from public school budgets. A 2013 report by Jason Hart of the nonpartisan group Media Trackers shed some light on union pay scales that's pretty eye-opening: sixty-seven top staffers for the National Education Association, the nation's largest teachers' union, make more than $200,000 per year.

If a for-profit company is willing to run schools without this kind of bloated, top-heavy bureaucracy that has no day-to-day student contact, they certainly deserve an opportunity.

27

CHARTER SCHOOLS DON'T PERFORM
ANY BETTER THAN TRADITIONAL
GOVERNMENT SCHOOLS

"Like previous studies, the one . . . concluded that kids in most charter schools
are doing worse or no better than students in traditional public schools."

—*CLAUDIO SANCHEZ, former teacher and current education correspondent for NPR*

"But if you want to fight the union, at least use the facts. And the
central fact is this: the nonunion charters are not outperforming
the unionized schools. No, it's just the other way around."

—*BEN JORAVSKY, writer for the* Chicago Reader

"A study [of] charter schools by Stanford University showed
charter schools are twice as likely to underperform rather than
overperform. But who cares when you can make a buck? We
want to—we don't want to pay attention to Stanford."

—*ED SCHULTZ,* The Ed Show

The debate between traditional school and charter school supporters has reached the point of absurdity. A perfect illustra-

tion of this is a study that was conducted by Stanford University's Center for Research on Education Outcomes (CREDO) in 2009, which showed that charter schools underperformed government schools by about .01 standard deviations on state reading tests and .03 standard deviations on math tests.

Government school supporters crowed over the results, offering them as proof that charters are failures. (Try to hide your disgust over the idea that anyone would actually be happy about poor educational outcomes solely for political gain.)

CREDO updated their study in 2013 and the results changed a bit, now showing charter schools outperforming traditional schools by .01 standard deviations in reading and scoring about the same in math. This time around, charter school supporters were jubilant, claiming that the report justified their existence.

What really happened—and why the results improved over those four years—was that the worst-performing charter schools closed. *And that's exactly what is supposed to happen.* Not every charter school in every area is going to work. Some, just like some public schools, will be dismal failures. Others will be resounding successes. The difference is that, on the charter side, the bad ones can shut down and the good ones can keep getting better. That doesn't happen on the public side.

The hypocrisy over this is pretty incredible. Union officials in New York City have no problem when a failing charter school is closed, but they screamed bloody murder and filed lawsuits when then-mayor Michael Bloomberg proposed closing dozens of failing government schools.

As the worst charter schools continue to close or reorganize, the overall scores relative to government schools should continue to rise. This process does, unfortunately, take a good deal of time. Charter school officials at poorly performing schools sometimes end up acting a lot like teachers' union leaders. When their school is targeted for closure, they call in political favors or lawyer up and force districts to spend tons of time and money in an effort to shut them down. So, while these performance studies are great as checkpoints, it's still very early in the charter school life cycle and it's the trend that matters most.

There's a larger point here as well. While academic results are paramount, the existence of charter schools is also based around the important concept of parental choice. Different kids thrive at different types of schools for many different reasons. Sometimes it's just a matter of parents finding the right fit or even the right teacher or principal who really cares. Having more than one publicly funded school option is healthy for families that lack the means to pay expensive private school tuition in search of the ideal situation.

Think about it this way: CNN, MSNBC, Fox News, and The-Blaze TV all have very similar business descriptions. Each is a cable network that exists to deliver the latest in news and information to its viewers. Of course, we all know that these networks, despite their similar business models, are all very different in the way they deliver information. If a cable company were to one day tell its subscribers that they could *only* have MSNBC, many would rightfully balk. After all, some people are MSNBC-type people, and some are TheBlaze TV–type people. Same business; vastly different values.

I'm sure by now you see where this is going. While charter schools are technically "just schools," they are lifelines to some families. Why—assuming that academic results are similar— would we not want parents to be able to decide not just *what* their kids are taught, but *how* they're taught and *who* does the teaching?

Besides, competition for students between various types of

schools keeps everyone performing better. That's a positive outcome for families, who should be the ultimate beneficiaries of all
government education policy.

Parents can read the various reports about traditional versus
charter performance in their own districts if they want. They
can visit government schools and charter schools and determine
which environment they prefer. They can meet staff at both types
of schools and decide whom they like and trust the most.

In the end it's *their choice*, as well it should be.

The controllists would much prefer to force all students who
can't afford private schooling to return to their neighborhood
school districts. That would work out just great for the traditional
schools. They'd continue to get their automatic clientele of students every fall without having to work for it, and it would mean
plenty of state dollars for the teachers and their unions. But that's
about it; everyone else would suffer.

The other thing to remember about these performance
reports—and this goes for both traditional schools and charter
schools—is that the headlines usually talk about national averages.
That can be useful in some circumstances, but when we talk about
parental choice we talk about it on a local level. And that's where
some charter schools have absolutely excelled. In New Orleans,
where 85 percent of students now attend charter schools, ACT
scores have been improving at a faster rate than state and national
averages.

In Massachusetts, the CREDO report found that charter
school students receive 1.5 months of additional learning in reading and 2.5 months of extra learning in math during the course of
an academic year, compared with their counterparts in government-run schools. The report specifically mentions K–12 students
in Boston as doing particularly well. "Charter students in Boston
gain an additional 12 months in reading and 13 months in math

per school year compared to their TPS [traditional public school] counterparts."

In Washington, D.C., a district known for its terrible public schools, charters have been thriving as they serve the needs of the community. Charter schools have been graduating students at a rate of about 77 percent over the last few years, compared with a traditional public school graduation rate of approximately 61 percent.

Of course, even those rates are based on a large scale. If you start looking at specific charter schools that are available to parents as alternatives to the failing traditional schools in their area, you start to see why fostering the charter program is so important:

- The Friendship Public Charter School Collegiate Academy graduated 91 percent of its students in four years. One hundred percent of those graduates were accepted into college.
- Since opening more than thirteen years ago, 100 percent of all graduates of the Thurgood Marshall Academy have been accepted into college.
- KIPP DC Academy, a middle school that is the highest-ranked charter school in the city, sees 93 percent of its alumni graduate from high school. That's despite the fact that, according to the school, most of its students enter the academy "two or three grade levels behind their peers."

Charter schools also seem to be having a positive effect on minority populations, though you'd never hear that from the unions or controllists. According to the *Huffington Post*, the 2013 CREDO study "found more pronounced gains for some minorities. Hispanic English-language learners in charter schools were 50 days of reading instruction ahead of the average of their public school peers, and 43 days ahead in math. Charter school black students in poverty were 29 instructional days ahead of public peers in reading, and 36 days ahead in math."

There have also been failures. About 8 percent of charters in the United States have been closed due to poor performance, and "as many as one in five charter schools should be closed because of poor academic performance," according to a November 2012 report from the National Association of Charter School Authorizers.

Last year CREDO director Margaret Raymond said her organization's most recent study found "that the charter school sector is getting better on average and that charter schools are benefiting lower-income, disadvantaged, and special education students." Raymond also said that charter schools have achieved higher academic quality of late due to the ongoing debate about their effectiveness; higher expectations; and parental involvement.

Government school officials like to remind everyone that it's wrong to judge all of their schools by the relatively few really awful ones, or the longer list of mediocre ones. They are absolutely right. Every school district, and every school within each district, deserves to be judged on its own performance and how it responds to the needs of that community.

Why can't that same principle be applied to charter schools? The establishment argues that all charter schools must be great or else they have failed in their mission. That's idiotic. Why do government schools deserve permanent leases on life while charter schools are forced to demonstrate their value every year?

The fact is that all of these schools are "public," whether they are government or charter. The public should decide which of them survives, by voting with their enrollment. Once again, it comes down to freedom and choice.

But government school controllists continue to work overtime to limit choice as much as possible, regardless of their competitors' performance.

Despite such schools' overwhelming success in Massachusetts, many Democratic lawmakers there are fighting efforts to lift the cap on the number of charter schools. In New York City, the newly elected, Big Labor–backed mayor wants to stop forcing government schools to share unused classroom space with charter schools.

Then there's Washington State, which recently became one of the last states to legalize charter schools after a ballot referendum was narrowly passed in 2012. The Washington Education Association, the state's largest teachers' union, had poured millions of dollars into the effort to defeat the proposal, just like it had on three previous occasions when similar measures failed. After the election the union didn't give up, filing a lawsuit that tried to get the courts to overturn the election results and block charter schools on constitutional grounds.

Pretty much everyone, including some progressive, pro-union newspapers, recognized the greed that drove this desperate tactic. "The Washington Education Association does not like charter schools because it cannot control them," the *Seattle Times* opined. "The union believes the $11 million spent by [charter school] advocates manipulated voters into supporting the nontraditional public schools in the election last fall. Those are flimsy reasons on which to base a constitutional challenge."

The Washington Policy Center agreed: "The lawsuit scheme provides additional evidence the union is a reactionary force determined to block change. Union executives want to protect their monopoly, power, and influence within the system, regardless of the cost to disadvantaged children trapped in failing public schools in Washington State."

"Monopoly," "power," "influence," and don't forget, *control.*

PART TWO

THE WAY FORWARD

Finland has gotten a lot of attention in education circles in recent years—and for very good reason: they are ranked at or near the top of most important worldwide education rankings. Even more impressive is that just a few decades ago, Finland didn't even register on the worldwide stage.

The secrets to Finland's successful reforms aren't really secrets at all. They've been written about extensively, and Finnish educators often make trips to the U.S. (and vice versa) to share strategies.

Some in the U.S., especially on the right, are sick of talking about Finland. They say that America has Finnish "envy" and that a small and relatively homogenous country like Finland simply cannot be compared with a large and diverse country like the United States.

In many ways they're right. It would be foolish for us to think we could simply steal another country's system and that it would work right out of the box. But those who think we can't learn from Finland are likely more interested in politics and ideology than true improvement. I say that because it's clear that many things Finland does go directly against traditional conservative principles in education, including many of the things I advocate for in this book. Finns don't care much for school choice, teacher evaluations, or merit pay. That's enough to turn many conservatives away. But look deeper, past the surface ideological differences between the ways our countries view competition, and you'll find the real reasons Finns have been so successful.

First and foremost, teaching as a career choice is highly valued in Finland. Top students select teaching as a career and the degree programs are extremely selective, admitting only the very best of those who apply. This is something we can definitely learn from.

There are no standardized tests needed to prove that a school deserves more government funding, and, far from being "centers of the community," the schools themselves are open fewer hours than American schools. Mandatory education in Finland doesn't start until kids are seven years old.

Once teachers get placed into a school, they stay for a very long time. Given the highly selective nature of these jobs, it's not often that "bad" teachers make it that far, but when they do, principals are tasked with identifying them quickly and removing them from the classroom. How can they get away with that? According to Henna Virkkunen, the Finnish Minister of Education, it's because the teachers' union has a constructive working relationship with school administrators.

"It's a totally different situation in Finland," Virkkunen said. "For me, as Minister of Education, our teachers' union has been one of the main partners, because we have the same goal: we all want to ensure that the quality of education is good and we are working very much together with the union. . . . I think we don't have big differences in our thinking. They are very good partners for us."

Progressives point out that Finland values educational equality far more than America does. You can go to almost any school in any town in Finland and get a great education. They say that this is why we need to invest so much more in anti-poverty and welfare programs before we can make any real progress. But, to me, that just shows how much they misunderstand how equality works. The Finns didn't attempt to squeeze everyone to the middle—they set a high bar and expected everyone to rise to get over it. That is the opposite of how we seem to view "equality."

There is also a great analogy in Finland to our controllists' current Common Core push. In the early 1970s, Finland first attempted reform by developing a national curriculum. It was seven hundred pages long. According to the NEA, these changes were "intended to equalize educational outcomes and provide more open access to higher education." It didn't work.

By the mid-'90s, when Finland's real reforms began, they had thrown out the prescribed curriculum and had replaced it with a ten-page document offering guidance to teachers to help them with "collectively developing local curriculum and assessments."

Pasi Sahlberg, a Finnish policy analyst, recently summarized the popular worldwide education reforms that Finland has avoided. See if any of this sounds familiar:

- Standardization of curriculum enforced by frequent external tests;
- Narrowing of the curriculum to basic skills in reading and mathematics;
- Reduced use of innovative teaching strategies;
- Adoption of high-stakes accountability policies, featuring rewards and sanctions for students, teachers, and schools.

When you boil it down, what Finland has basically done is pretty simple. They take extremely smart people, train them well, and then put them in an environment where they can excel.

We are never going to all agree on every detail of what a good education system should look like—and that's okay. There is no perfect formula or recipe. But I think that almost everyone can agree that what we have now is not working.

So, what will work? I believe the answer lies in taking the best practices from countries like Finland and then applying American ideals to them. Americans are not, for example, going to be willing to go from the glut of standardizing testing that we have now to nothing—but maybe there is some middle ground. Likewise, teachers' unions aren't about to go from forcing districts to spend years and hundreds of thousands of dollars to fire a bad teacher to allowing principals total hiring and firing freedom—but, again, maybe there is some middle ground.

This is going to drive progressives absolutely crazy, but the way forward for American education can actually be found in our past.

Before the federal government got so heavily involved in education, things weren't going so poorly. Individual communities hired teachers, chose the curriculum, and managed their own schools. Decisions about education were made as close to the students themselves as possible. Washington bureaucrats didn't dictate test questions or decide which textbooks were best for kids in small-town Idaho; the leadership of individual schools made those decisions. If parents didn't like what their kids were learning, they knew exactly whom they could talk to.

None of that sat well with the "experts" in Washington who didn't like the fact that education—something so vitally important to the country's future—could exist completely outside their control. They did not like the decentralization inherent in federalism. "Why should some towns and cities and states have no standards or low standards and others have extremely high standards when the children belong to all of us[?]" asked Paul Reville, the former secretary of education for Massachusetts, echoing the sentiment of many controllists.

The ironic thing about the government's meddling with states and communities is that the very thing they say they hope to achieve (a "race to the top") is actually causing a race to the bottom. States, now forced to compete for federal dollars by hitting certain national benchmarks, are incentivized to lie, cheat, and steal to get the results they need.

Education Secretary Arne Duncan agrees that this has been a problem. "[A]lmost twenty states dummied down standards on No Child Left Behind to make politicians look good," he told *TheBlaze*. "It's one of the most silly things to happen to education."

Florida is a good example of just how silly it can get. After they raised the minimum proficiency level on the writing portion of their Florida Comprehensive Assessment Test, the percentage of fourth-, eighth-, and tenth-graders who passed fell dramatically. Horrified administrators called an emergency board meeting, where they decided to lower the minimum standard. This ensured that a far greater number of students would be deemed proficient and fewer schools and teachers would see their performance ratings take a hit.

When you tell a state that they'll qualify for all kinds of federal aid if their students achieve a certain score on a certain test, then you'd better believe those students will learn that specific test material inside and out. That may make all of their students test-smart, but does it make them *actually* smart? Data from the last few decades makes it pretty clear that the answer is no—especially when compared with other countries.

Here's an analogy to help explain this phenomenon in another way. Imagine that two ten-year-old kids are put into separate rooms, each with a box full of Legos. Child #1 is given an exact set of instructions for building a spaceship and is told to follow them precisely. Child #2 is instead told to play around with the Legos, learn how they work, and then build something incredible.

At the end of the exercise it's very likely that Child #1 will have built the spaceship. It's also very likely that Child #2 will have built something far better. The difference, of course, is that Child #2 will also have a far better understanding of *how* the Legos work. That child won't have simply assembled pieces together according to a set of instructions, but will instead have discovered how the Legos all fit together; how many of each sized piece are offered, the color patterns that can be created, and many other important details.

In education, we're creating a lot of Child #1 kids—kids who know the *what* but not the *why* or the *how*. Kids who go through life singing "Everything Is Awesome" but who have no idea how to really do anything other than follow instructions given by others.

But it hasn't always been that way.

Prior to the federal government's getting involved with Race to the Top, No Child Left Behind, Common Core, and all the other programs that have come and gone over the years, the states were still forced to compete with each other over dollars—but they weren't *federal* dollars, they were taxpayer dollars. As shocking as this may sound, parents actually wanted to put their kids into great schools, and they actively shopped for them when buying a home. If one state or town or district had a great record of achievement, then parents moved there in droves. The town and state benefited from an ever-increasing tax base.

But now? With some exceptions, most schools are being forced to the middle by these standards that squeeze out the top and bottom. It's almost like what we're doing to the economic classes—we try to move the poor up to the middle class by penalizing the wealthy and moving them down to the middle. In both cases it's a recipe for disaster. With education, families no longer have to vote with their wallets, so states and towns no longer worry much about competing for them. Schools have taken their eyes off those they should be serving—students and families—and are instead focused on serving their masters in Washington.

Fortunately, all of this leads to a pretty simple answer in terms of what it's going to take to reverse the awful trends in education results that we've been seeing.

Competition.

It really is that easy. Let the states compete against each other without a bunch of Thou Shalt and Shalt Nots from the federal government. If states want residents and businesses to move inside their borders, they'll have to create better schools to lure them. If they succeed they'll create more jobs, a better workforce, and a much higher and more sustainable tax base.

This isn't just some libertarian fantasy; it has clear historical precedence. Jay Greene, head of the Department of Education Reform at the University of Arkansas, has studied this history extensively. "The history of U.S. education is filled with evidence of how this competition for residents and tax base has spurred improvements in quality and increases in rigor," Greene wrote. "The economic historian William Fischel carefully documents how the development and spread of high school education in the United States was driven by localities seeking to compete for residents demanding a more rigorous education."

Did you catch the end of that quote? *Rigorous education*. A top-down approach like Common Core that purports to offer a "rigorous" curriculum isn't necessary when you have proper competition among towns and districts for tax dollars instead of federal dollars. Greene points out that states—acting on their own free will—have increased and strengthened high school graduation requirements over time:

In almost half of the states students now have to pass a state test to receive a standard diploma. And 37 states instituted their own testing and accountability systems before [No Child Left Behind] was adopted. The result of these state and local efforts was not always a rigorous education, but they clearly show a trend toward higher standards and quality in response to consumer demand. Competition produces a race to the top as long as it is competition for individual taxpayers and business instead of competition for federal government handouts.

Still not convinced? Consider how competition from charter schools has forced traditional government schools to adapt in order to attract and retain students—along with the state aid that's attached to each one. Researchers have found evidence that the introduction of charter schools into a district leads to "significant changes" in that district's policies and practice, including efforts to "replicate" what the charter schools are doing and to seek out their own innovations.

If competition among schools leads to a better overall educational experience for students within those districts, certainly competition among individual states will do the same.

Local control worked well enough to make America's education system the envy of the world at one time. We started losing that advantage when local school districts started losing their autonomy. As Greene puts it, "The policies, practices, and funding of schools has increasingly shifted to the state and national governments and greater uniformity has been imposed by unionization. The enemy of high standards and improving outcomes is centralization."

With that in mind, there are a few areas where I think we have a real opportunity to change things for the better. Some of them are small and can be done right away, while others are more radical, but I think all of these will help move us back toward a system where parents and communities are empowered to do what's best for their own situation.

Keep in mind that entire books can—and in some cases already have—been written about these ideas. This section is not meant to be comprehensive; it's just meant to show that the kind of thinking that's happening in Washington is not nearly creative enough. As always, I encourage you to do your own research on anything you find interesting, then help spread the word by becoming active in your community and online. Please share what works (and what doesn't) and the lessons you're learning with us so that we can support you and help spread the word to others who are on the front lines. (If you're on Twitter, use #conform with your posts so my staff can be sure to find them.)

Education Savings Accounts

"This is a very large improvement over a 'take it or take it' public school system consigning children to particular schools based on their zip codes. An ESA program represents an important refinement of the voucher concept. . . . The ESA model creates education choice rather than school choice."

—MATT LADNER, FOUNDATION FOR
EXCELLENCE IN EDUCATION

Despite the efforts of government school apologists to fight school reform, the fact is that some of these folks have understood for years that our current education model has devolved into a stagnant, monopolistic system designed to serve union members over students.

The late American Federation of Teachers president Albert Shanker once described the system perfectly:

It is time to admit that public education operates like a planned economy. It's a bureaucratic system where everyone's role is spelled out in advance, and there are few incentives for innovation or productivity. It's not a surprise when a school system doesn't improve. It more resembles a communist economy than our own market economy.

Shanker wrote those words in 1989, which shows you just how long we've been dealing with this issue. *Nineteen eighty-nine!* Twenty-five years and we're just now starting to make serious progress in terms of implementing school choice, bringing accountability to the classroom, and reshaping schools to focus on students.

A few visionaries recognized the need for reform even earlier than Shanker. Chief among them was the late economist, free-market advocate, and father of school choice Milton Friedman. By the middle of the last century he clearly understood that our dynamic free enterprise system, driven by rapid technological advancement, would never be served by an education system devoid of all incentive to innovate and improve. He also understood that working people would never benefit from schools that failed to prepare them for the challenging jobs and financial opportunities created by the new economy.

Friedman first called for publicly funded, private school vouchers in the 1950s, when such a concept seemed foreign and radical to most people. He summed up his views in an editorial published in the *Washington Post* in 1995:

Our elementary and secondary education system needs to be radically reconstructed. That need arises in the first instance from the defects of our current system. . . .

A radical reconstruction of the educational system has the potential of staving off social conflict while at the same time strengthening the growth in living standards made possible by the new technology and the increasingly global market. In my view, such a radical reconstruction can be achieved only by privatizing a major segment of the educational system—i.e., by enabling a private, for-profit industry to develop that will provide a wide variety of learning opportunities and offer effective competition to public schools. Such a reconstruction cannot come about overnight. It inevitably must be gradual.

The most feasible way to bring about such a gradual yet substantial transfer from government to private enterprise is the enactment in each state of a voucher system that enables parents to choose freely the schools their children attend. I first proposed such a voucher system forty years ago.

Many attempts have been made in the years since to adopt educational vouchers. With minor exceptions, no one has succeeded in getting a voucher system adopted, thanks primarily to the political power of the school establishment, more recently reinforced by the National Education Association and the American Federation of Teachers, together the strongest political lobbying body in the U.S.

Friedman would probably be very happy to see that his voucher concept is finally coming to fruition. A total of twenty-one states, along with Douglas County, Colorado, and Washington, D.C., have now adopted some form of school voucher program, either through direct government vouchers given to parents (usually in low-income or poor-performing school districts) or through the more indirect route of tax credits awarded to those who contribute to private school scholarship funds.

Of course the controllists have not surrendered on this issue. Unions continue to legally challenge voucher programs wherever they're proposed or implemented, most recently in Louisiana and Alabama. But serious reformers know that school choice options must continue to increase for American students if they hope to receive the type of education necessary to thrive in an increasingly competitive and interconnected world.

Government school advocates like to argue that only kids in inner-city areas are trapped in less-than-desirable schools. But, according to an article published by Heritage Foundation researcher Lindsey Burke, that's just not true:

> Even in what are traditionally thought of as the higher-performing urban school districts, academic achievement is tragically low. Researcher[s] . . . found "out of the nearly 14,000 public school districts in the U.S., only 6 percent have average student math achievement that would place them in the upper third of global performance." [The researchers] go on to note "People generally think they have escaped the ills of urban public education by moving to the suburbs, they don't usually think that only one or two suburbs actually produce excellent results."

But even as voucher programs continue to expand, a new and more advanced form of educational choice—Education Savings Accounts (ESAs)—has taken root in Arizona, and should be the next wave of reform spreading across the nation.

The accounts, known in Arizona as Empowerment Scholarship Accounts, first became available in 2011. The program initially targeted students with disabilities who attended public schools, but has since been expanded to include students attending low-performing individual public schools or districts, the children of military families, and children in the state's foster care program.

Here's how it works: Instead of receiving a voucher for tuition to a single private school, parents in the program are given

90 percent of their child's share of state education funds, which they can then use in any number of ways. These funds can, for example, be used to pay for tuition and fees for private schools, online learning programs, educational therapy services, textbooks, home-schooling curriculum, or contributions to a qualified college tuition savings account.

Parents receive restricted-use debit cards that can be used to purchase anything on the approved list. They can also "roll over" unused funds from year to year, giving them incentive to shop carefully for the best educational values, and encouraging schools and vendors to make services available at competitive prices. If you're familiar with Health Savings Accounts then you likely see the parallels.

The basic idea is to give parents ultimate flexibility in designing the most effective education program for their kids. For instance, they might like an outstanding math teacher at one school, a great science teacher at another, and a terrific English teacher online. Friedman would've undoubtedly loved it.

Burke explained how these ESAs further the idea of total education choice:

> Arizona has created a model that should be every state policy-maker's goal when considering how to improve education: funding students instead of physical school buildings and allowing that funding to follow children to any education provider of choice. Such control over education funding ensures parents have access to options that meet their children's unique learning needs and ultimately can move beyond the worthwhile goal of school choice to choice among education service providers, courses, teachers and methods.

This is not a "Wild West" model of education; there is still plenty of government oversight involved. To participate, parents or guardians must sign an agreement to provide an educational experience that includes the basics like reading, grammar, math, social studies, and science. The law also allows for random audits of accounts and families can be removed from the program for misuse of funds.

The program, now in its third year, has yet to attract large numbers of participants. (Only 716 children were enrolled in the 2013–2014 academic year.) There are probably several reasons for the lukewarm response, including the fact that the unions continue to challenge the program in court, and that the state has yet to aggressively publicize it.

About 66 percent of those who've taken advantage of the accounts have used the funds to attend a single school, as they would with a regular voucher. But 34 percent have used the money for multiple educational options, including private tutoring, education therapy, and online learning services. Popularity aside, participating parents have reported extremely high levels of satisfaction with the program so far. Ninety-four percent report being "very satisfied," while the other 6 percent said they were "somewhat satisfied."

Given the high marks from parents, it's no surprise that other states are beginning to take notice. In Oklahoma, where a majority of residents say they support ESAs, a bill was recently introduced that would provide families with up to 90 percent of the state funds dedicated to their public education. "Children should go wherever they need to go. Public schools don't work for every child," said one of the bill's sponsors, Rep. Jason Nelson.

While this program is still in its infancy, it has major potential to reshape how people view education in this country—and the government's role in it. If you think ESAs have potential in your state—get active and vocal and make sure your lawmakers study them.

Power Shift

"Every child, regardless of their zip code,
deserves access to a great education. While it
is our goal to help struggling schools succeed,
we need to make sure students and parents can
choose the best option and make sure each child receives
a truly great education."

—WISCONSIN GOVERNOR SCOTT WALKER

School reform activists can complain all they want about the obvious shortcomings of government schools, but as we've seen over and over again, being right often makes no difference. Real change only happens when the people who make the rules are willing to rock the boat. That often means angering wealthy and influential special interests and imposing the changes necessary to make the education process more consumer driven, student based, and transparent.

Unfortunately, most state lawmakers and local school board members seem to lack the courage to challenge these interests, like the teachers' unions, which have demonstrated they are willing and able to make life miserable for public officials.

Sometimes it's not courage that's in short supply but independence. The sad fact is that many school board members and state lawmakers are in the pockets of the unions, which have literally purchased their loyalty through endorsements, financial contributions, and a steady supply of eager campaign volunteers.

But the situation is far from hopeless. Critical change can occur when real leaders stand their ground, impose reform, and ignore the protests of the unions and others in the education establishment. And voters will stand by those leaders when they see the positive change that occurs in their schools.

This cycle has been proven time and again—most recently in Douglas County, Colorado, and in Wisconsin.

The Douglas County school board has become one of the most famous school boards in the nation. It's loved and respected by those who believe that education should meet the needs of children and their families, and despised by controllists who want the unions in charge of everything. The board has evoked these strong emotions through a series of courageous and unprecedented acts over the past few years.

The school district's teachers' union—and many others who make their living through the school—were stunned and angered when the board voted in 2011 to create its own private school voucher program for students. That's right, the school board invited any student in their district to leave and instead enroll in private schools if they preferred. They *voluntarily* surrendered a big chunk of state aid to pay the tuition of anyone who made that decision.

The most interesting thing about this is that Douglas County schools were already academically excellent. This wasn't a decision made in deference to quality; it was a decision about the principle of choice. "[The choice of schools] should be up to the parents of Douglas County, not the school district," said school board president John Carson. "We have very good schools, so there's never been a concern about losing a lot of students. But we set up the voucher program because all students learn differently and their parents should have the freedom to determine the best fit."

The program was challenged in court by the teachers' union and the American Civil Liberties Union, and remains tied up in litigation. But the school board stands ready to implement its plan as soon as it becomes legally possible. "It's not the school district funding the private schools, it's the parents taking their share of state money and funding the schools.

"The school board members have 19 children between us that are, or were recently, in school, and just about all of our kids attend traditional neighborhood schools in the district," Carson said. "But we push school choice because we think it's good for families. It's wonderful to have those choices available in our district. If 10 percent want another choice, I think the school district should make that choice available. The more options students have, the more all the schools improve. They're challenged. It leads to a more dynamic system."

It's refreshing to hear honesty like that, but the voucher program was just the tip of the iceberg in Douglas County. Board members there also:

- Adopted a market-based compensation scale for teachers so they could offer more money to quality educators in hard-to-fill subjects.
- Implemented a pay-for-performance plan to reward teachers who get the best results.
- Encouraged the expansion of charter schools within the district.
- Pushed through a decentralization plan that cut the administrative budget and diverted about $1 million to neighborhood schools.
- Took a public stand against Common Core.
- Publicly opposed a state ballot proposal that would have increased the state income tax to provide more revenue for government schools.
- Ended its recognition of the local teachers' union as the bargaining agent for teachers after months of fruitless labor negotiations.

Many of these reforms were possible only because Colorado law doesn't require school boards to collectively bargain with unions. While that had been common practice for years in Douglas County, the board decided enough was enough once they realized that the unions were a deterrent to free-market reforms. "The board's laser focus was to keep as much money in the classroom as possible and cut fat that doesn't help kids learn," said Carrie Mendoza, who served on the Douglas County board.

Board members wanted union leaders to respect their right to govern the district and establish policies, and to stop trying to interfere with the superintendent. "We would have done a contract with the union if they would have respected proper roles and recognized that policy decisions are made by the elected school board and superintendent, and their role was to represent teachers," Carson, the board president, said. "Their problem is they wanted to run the school district and decide all of those policy issues, and not focus on the interests of teachers."

Board members were also angry about other union-related issues. "We did not want to continue to pay the salaries of union officers who didn't teach," Carson said. "We were paying out $300,000 per year to union officers who were on full-time leave and didn't teach a minute."

Union leaders responded to the school board's rejection by predicting a mass exodus of teachers from the district. It never happened. Meanwhile, the union, assisted by its allies from around the nation, made a major effort to oust three reform-minded school board members who were up for reelection in November 2013.

As radio host Mike Rosen argued in the *Denver Post*, "This is a pivotal election with national ramifications. Teachers' unions are the greatest obstacle to substantive public school reform and want desperately to strangle the Dougco non-union baby in its crib."

Fortunately, the union's efforts failed and all three board members were retained by voters, making a pre-election prediction made by Carson look pretty prescient: "There's a certain group of people who attack the district because they don't like school choice or pay-for-performance," he'd said. "But I'm comfortable we will win because it's pretty clear the community supports parental choice, trimming the bureaucracy, and empowering principals."

The Douglas County school board governs just one district. It would be impossible to force every school board across the nation to take similarly bold steps. State governments, on the other hand, yield a great deal of power over public education, and they have the ability to empower many local school boards to reform their districts with broad legislative action. That's exactly what happened in Wisconsin.

Wisconsin schools were in a huge financial mess in 2010, largely due to the cost of union-negotiated health insurance and pension programs for retirees combined with the unwillingness of a Democratic governor to rein in spending. The recession had caused tax revenue to drop dramatically, which forced the state to reduce its aid to public schools. Many school boards approached their teachers' unions, asking for various concessions to help balance the books and preserve jobs and student programs, but most were met with a definitive "no."

Then Scott Walker was elected governor—and everything changed.

Walker and Republicans in the state legislature quickly pushed through a controversial bill, later known as Act 10, that severely curtailed the power of government employee unions, including teachers' unions. Under the new law, unions were limited to only negotiating salary, and raises were limited to the rate of inflation. All other issues were off the table.

As a result of Act 10, school boards suddenly had new freedom to reshape budgets and reestablish rules to benefit students instead of union employees. They no longer had to operate under cumbersome union contracts as thick as a phone book, or beg the unions for financial concessions to maintain enough money to serve students.

The results have been dramatic.

Prior to Act 10, teachers in the Milwaukee school district who retired at the age of fifty-five with at least fifteen years of experience could maintain their full health coverage until they reached sixty-five and qualified for Medicare. The benefits were very generous, with premiums completely paid for by the district.

The cost of the program had increased sharply between 2004 and 2011, and the future looked bleak for the cash-strapped district. Retiree insurance costs were expected to rise from about $65 million per year in 2011 to about $135 million per year in 2020. It was, in a word, unsustainable.

After Act 10 was signed into law, the board of school directors unilaterally voted to increase the minimum retirement age and years of service needed to qualify for retiree health insurance, and to increase the deductibles, co-insurance, and co-pays. As a result, costs are now expected to rise only from $65 million per year in 2011 to $68 million in 2020.

Retiree pensions were another huge problem. Under the union contract, the district was obligated to pay each employee's share of premiums for pension programs operated by the state and city. Pension costs for the district were expected to rise from about $80 million per year in 2011 to about $87 million per year in 2020.

Act 10 forced all school employees to pay their own share of state and city pension programs, and gave the school board the power to cancel its supplemental pension program. As a result, pension costs are now expected to drop to about $53 million.

According to a report from the Fordham Institute, none of these critical cost-saving changes would have been likely if the union had retained its full collective bargaining powers. "Some relatively minor accommodations were negotiated before Act 10 became effective, as the crisis faced by [the school district] became impossible to ignore," the institute reported. "But the major changes were implemented under Act 10 once [the district] was freed from collective bargaining over benefits. It seems clear that most of the changes would have been more difficult—and probably impossible—without Act 10."

Act 10 helped out financially, but it also improved the quality of education as school districts across Wisconsin were finally free to make practical changes without union approval. Most school districts took advantage of this by dumping the old "last in, first out" union rules about layoffs. Many districts also adopted, or are currently adopting, pay scales based on merit rather than seniority.

Act 10 also did away with "just cause" protections for teachers, meaning that most educators now work under one-year contacts. This allows school administrators to do something their peers in many other states would love the chance to do: fire incompetent or ineffective teachers without having to battle the union for years and spend hundreds of thousands of dollars in legal fees in the process.

"We are seeing some teachers being counseled out of the profession and we're seeing principals move staff around more than they might have in the past," said Barry Forbes of the Wisconsin Association of School Boards.

Deb Kerr, superintendent of the Brown Deer school district, agreed. "Now we can have those heart-to-heart conversations with some staff members and tell them they may need to be in different school districts," she said.

Act 10 clearly works for school boards and administrators, but it also works for teachers—or at least the good ones. With districts now free to start offering big raises—sometimes as large as $10,000 to $15,000 per year—quality teachers are being lured away from other districts where they are paid strictly according to union seniority scales.

It goes without saying that Act 10 was universally despised by unions and their supporters throughout the state. They immediately started collecting tens of thousands of signatures to remove Governor Walker from office, and a recall election was scheduled for June 2012. The unions poured millions of dollars and countless man hours into the recall campaign, and early polls suggested that Walker might be doomed.

In the end, however, voters sided with commonsense reform, even in a traditionally pro-labor state like Wisconsin—the birthplace of progressivism. Walker faced Milwaukee mayor Tom Barrett in his original election in 2010 and won 52.2 percent to 46.8 percent. He faced Barrett again in the recall election and, despite the massive union protests and get-out-the-vote campaigns organized by the left, he won by an even larger margin: 53.1 percent to 46.3 percent.

Like the Douglas County school board, Walker demonstrated that people will support courageous leaders who stand up for children against the special interests. That message cannot be repeated often enough and more states must follow Wisconsin's lead in freeing up their school boards to make the right reform decisions for their communities.

Technology

"We have the technology, the people and the institutions (foundations and think-tanks) we need. Of course in-person will always be better than online teaching—if the teacher is any good. . . . But each newly minted ignoramus is a child we have failed, who will likely lug around the burden of a third-rate education his whole life; who deserved better of this nation."
—DAVID GELERNTER, YALE UNIVERSITY
COMPUTER SCIENCE PROFESSOR

Ever since the mid to late 1800s, the overarching trend in education has been for the state to assume a greater and greater role in training the next generation of students. Education was once the responsibility of each family, but it's been recast as the domain of state government, and slowly but surely, the federal government.

The controllists justified their original takeover of education by arguing that the large number of immigrant children coming into a young and growing America needed to be assimilated into the culture and given a common language and a common set of values.

It wasn't about control back then; it was about giving kids the common tools they'd need to be able to succeed in a new environment. Perhaps that was the original "Common Core."

As a result of their efforts, the "classroom" was moved from the family kitchen table to a community school (which our great-grandparents had to walk eight miles—uphill, both ways—to get to and from). American education has followed that same pattern now for more than a hundred years. In the process, it's become more regimented, more bureaucratic, and more institutionalized.

But that might be about to change.

We're living in the early stages of a technological revolution that could reestablish parents—and the students themselves—as key decision makers in the education process. In fact, it's already beginning to happen. But before I get into specifics, let's all remember that, as scholars Allan Collins and Richard Halverson have noted, there is a big difference between "education" and "schooling": Schooling eventually ends; education goes on forever.

In their 2009 book about education's unfolding technological revolution, Collins and Halverson argued that there are "deep incompatibilities" between schooling and the rapidly evolving technologies:

Deeply ingrained in the structure of schooling is a mass-production notion of uniform learning. This belief stipulates that everyone should learn the same things at the same time. But one of the great advantages of technology is customization.

Virtual charter schools are popping up in numerous states, allowing students to learn at home at a pace and in a style that works for them. With the help of technology, a student in rural Idaho could, for example, take an engineering course from a professor delivering a lecture at the Massachusetts Institute of Technology. Hundreds, if not thousands, of students across the country could learn from the best educators, in real time or by archived presentations. Advances in software mean that knowledge and skills can be tested and improved through adaptive education applications that are based on each individual's learning pattern and capability.

That's a pretty exciting possibility—especially when you compare it to the current system, in which many students are constrained by their zip code or the teachers who happen to be assigned to their school.

Technology can increase access to our most talented educators while helping to eventually displace our most ineffective ones. The only thing keeping this from becoming reality are the teachers' unions and other controllists who want to block this technology and maintain the status quo.

A few school districts, like California's Riverside Unified, have voluntarily embraced digital learning. After that district became one of the first to use digital textbooks, EdSource.org reported that "3 to 4 percent more students tested proficient or advanced in math" compared to students who used traditional paper textbooks. The district also began providing online instruction and online charter schools began to operate there.

But the California Federation of Teachers and their allies in the legislature and bureaucracy weren't impressed. When they saw the online learning threat coming down the track, they responded by fighting fire with fire. First, the state implemented a regulation mandating that students could only enroll in online schools that were chartered in a county that was contiguous to the one of their residence. Second, through collective bargaining agreements, the union capped how many students could learn from a "virtual" lecturer, thereby ensuring a minimum number of jobs and dues-paying members. Writing in *National Review,* Pacific Research Institute scholar Lance Izumi noted that the California Federation of Teachers' model contract (that is, the one every local union should seek to implement) stated no union member "shall be displaced because of distance learning or other education technology."

Stanford professor Terry Moe noted that such rules "go a long way toward eliminating the very features that are distinctive and advantageous about cyberschools, and force them to operate under geographic and staffing constraints that make them more like traditional schools." In other words, these policies completely undermine the core advantages of a digital education. That is not a coincidence.

Meanwhile, some charter school operators, most notably Rocketship Education, blend the traditional classroom with varying hours of student-driven learning in front of computers. Rocketship schools serve low-income communities, and their blended approach to learning is getting results. Two of their three California schools rank among the fifteen top-performing high-poverty schools in the state.

Rocketship schools are succeeding, in large part, because they're customizing education to fit individual students' needs. The downside to this virtual school option—whether it's exclusively at home or as part of a blended classroom—is that many of these schools are supported with tax dollars. As a result, virtual schools will likely be required to educate students according to the same Common Core standards as traditional schools. Until that is changed, many virtual charter schools won't be the answer for families that are looking to escape the failed, top-down mandates of the controllists.

Which bring us to David Gelernter, one of the few visionaries who foresaw the creation of the Internet and all of its potential.

These days, Gelernter, who is a professor of computer science at Yale University, is looking ahead to how technology can be used to restore true parental control over the education process. To do that, he's proposing that Americans redefine the very idea of what constitutes a "public school." His concept is something he refers to as "local internet schools," and he recently explained how they might work:

> The idea is simple: a one-classroom school, with twenty-odd children of all ages between 6th and 12th grade, each sitting at a computer and wearing mike-and-earphones. They all come from nearby. A one-room internet school might serve a few blocks in a suburb, or a single urban apartment house.
>
> In front sits any reliable adult whom the neighbors vouch for—often, no doubt, some student's father (or mother), taking his turn. He leads the Pledge, announces regular short recesses to clear everyone's head, proclaims lunch-time. He hands out batteries and Band-Aids and sends sick children home or to a doctor. He reloads the printers and futzes with malfunctioning scanners, no doubt making any problem worse. But these machines are cheap, and each classroom can deploy several.
>
> Each child does a whole curriculum's-worth of learning online, at the computer. Most of the time he follows canned courses

onscreen. But for an hour every day, he deals directly one-to-one over phone or videophone with a tutor. Ideally there's a teaching assistant on an open phone line throughout the day, each assistant dealing with a few dozen students.

In early years, parents will need to help here, too. And each child needs a "mentor" who advises parents on courses and keeps track of the student's progress. The wealthy conservative foundation, think tank, or consortium that spends liberally to get this idea off the ground will probably provide mentors, in early years, from its own staff.

The online courses (some exist already, but not enough) are produced by teaching maestros. As these new schools gather momentum, they will make use, as tutors or assistants, of the huge number of people who are willing and able to help children in some topic for a few hours a week, but can't or won't teach full time: college and graduate students, retirees, lawyers, accountants, housewives, professors.

Gelernter notes that these "local internet schools" will require a serious commitment from parents—whether it's taking their turn as school supervisor or simply monitoring their child's daily progress. This approach to schooling and learning will work for a great many students, though Gelernter acknowledges that it obviously won't be the answer for everyone.

Commonsense Reforms

The problems I've identified in this book have been festering for decades—they aren't going to be fixed overnight. But that doesn't mean we should stop trying to open up the eyes of our neighbors, friends, and representatives to commonsense solutions that could have a real impact.

One of the simplest and most effective things we can do is push for reform of teacher certification. I wrote earlier about the many problems with teachers' colleges—from the low standards for acceptance to the concerns over the quality of graduates. Educators Barbara Nemko and Harold Kwalwasser believe that the solution shouldn't be to reform this process; it should be to throw it away completely.

"Instead of trying to improve undergraduate teacher training—as experts have proposed for decades," they wrote, "we have another idea: Get rid of it. Or at least end teacher education as we know it."

What they propose to replace traditional education with will make a ton of sense to everyone other than the unions. "[R]equire aspiring teachers to major in something other than education," they explained. "Students who want to be math teachers must major in math, for example, and fulfill the same graduation requirements as the school's other math majors. Same for English and science."

Think about how incredibly effective that would be. By forcing prospective teachers to become subject-matter experts we'd be taking the very best and brightest in each field and helping them transfer their in-depth knowledge to our students. Students should be looked at much more like mini-apprentices who spend their time learning from masters. We wouldn't put a prospective blacksmith in a shop with someone who majored in education, so why do we think it's okay to do that with prospective writers, engineers, or historians?

Use *Your Voice*

"Look, I am being manhandled and shut down because I
asked inconvenient questions. Why won't they allow an open
forum where there can be a debate? We are told to sit there
and be lectured to about how great Common Core is."
—ROBERT SMALL, BALTIMORE COUNTY PARENT

It is easy to complain about how things are; it's another thing
entirely to take action in pursuit of the way you think things
should be.

The fight that's being waged against the Common Core initiative is an unfortunate distraction from advancing choice and freedom in education, but it's a fight that must be waged. The ragtag
army of average parents and students is making a real difference
and showing the controllists that all of Bill Gates's money, Jeb
Bush's connections, and Barack Obama's power still may not be
enough to save Common Core.

Arkansas mother Karen Lamoreaux recently appeared before her state's board of education and asked a simple question:
"If there are 18 students in a class, and the class counts itself by a
number and ends with 90, what number did they count by?"

One member of the board—after dividing 90 by 18—rightfully
answered "five."

Lamoreaux responded that the board member's answer
would be wrong, because it wasn't done the Common Core way.
Lamoreaux then showed the board "notes and drawings totaling
a staggering 108 steps to solve the problem," *TheBlaze* reported.

"This is not rigorous," she told them. "This is not college-
ready. This is not preparing our children to compete in a global
economy."

Lamoreaux later appeared on my television program and explained that "parents have no voice" when it comes to state school boards. She said she's learned that these people are virtually immune from criticism and accountability because they don't answer to the people directly. The good news, according to Lamoreaux, is that she found a group of people who aren't immune: state legislators.

> . . . I think that when our legislators [were] handed the power and the authority to take on these standards back in 2009, they believed what they were told. They believed that it was merely a set of standards and this was all sunshine and applesauce and this was going to be such a great program. I don't believe that they have malignant intentions.
>
> But now, it's starting to roll out and it's been a year or so and we're seeing Common Core for what it is, they're listening. There are 38 bills pushing back against Common Core in the United States of America. Twenty-two states are fighting back, they started with 46, they're down to 41 . . . that have adopted. The legislature is listening, they are just as frustrated by this.
>
> And I think they are putting the big picture together. I think our state House members and Senate members, they see what's going on with healthcare and with all this NSA garbage and they see it in the school system and they have had enough and they are fighting back.

Lamoreaux was wrong about one thing, though: parents do have a voice. Millions heard her and others like her, and she is making a real difference.

We heard Ethan Young's voice, too. According to *TheBlaze,*

the Knox County, Tennessee, high school student appeared before his local school board to "make his case as to why he believes the school district should drop the new national education standards."

> The president essentially bribed states into implementation via "Race to the Top," offering $4.35 billion taxpayer dollars to participating states, $500 million of which went to Tennessee. And much like No Child Left Behind, the program promises national testing and a one-size-fits-all education, because hey, it worked so well the first time.

> If nothing else, these standards are a glowing conflict of interest and they lack the research they allegedly received.

Young also argued that Common Core standards display a "mistrust of teachers," a line that prompted applause from the audience.

His withering attack didn't end there.

"Somewhere our Founding Fathers are turning in their graves—pleading, screaming, and trying to say to us that we teach to free minds. We teach to inspire. We teach to equip, the careers will come naturally," Young concluded.

Millions heard Young's voice.

Maryland dad Robert Small showed up to a Baltimore County School District public forum seeking answers about Common Core. The meeting was billed as a question-and-answer session for parents to obtain information about the new standards that have caused so much upheaval in that district and many others around the country. It was an opportunity for the bureaucratic "experts" to quell the unwashed masses.

But the Q&A involved attendees submitting questions on cards in advance, thereby allowing Baltimore County superintendent Dallas Dance and members of the state board of education to pick and choose which ones they wanted to answer.

This was unsatisfactory to Small. As *TheBlaze* reported in September 2013:

> Small began speaking out against the district's use of Common Core, prompting a security guard, who was also a police officer, to approach him and order him to leave. "Let's go!" he said sternly.

> When Small didn't immediately comply, the officer began pulling his arm and pushing him towards the exit. Some audience members gasped at the cop's use of force.

> "Don't stand for this," Small yelled as he was manhandled for using the most dangerous weapon in the room that night—his voice. "You are sitting here like cattle! Is this America?"

The *Baltimore Sun* reported the officer "pushed Small and then escorted him into the hall, handcuffed him, and had him sit on the curb in front of the school."

Because a parent decided to break the bureaucrats' "rules" of the meeting, he was treated like a criminal. Illegal immigrants aren't even treated that harshly.

Small was charged with second-degree assault of a police officer and faced a fine of up to $2,500 and ten years in prison. All for taking a courageous stand and being unwilling to comply with the orders of a bureaucracy's attack dog.

Charges were dropped after the incident later received national attention. State's attorney Scott Shellenberger told WBAL radio that it was "clear that Mr. Small violated the rules of the meeting and disrupted the meeting."

"It was also clear that the Officer acted appropriately and did have probable cause to make an arrest on both charges," Shellenberger added. "The Baltimore County State's Attorney's Office has just received and reviewed the facts of this case. In the interest of justice, further prosecution will not accomplish anything more. Therefore, the charges have been dismissed."

The controllists wanted to send a clear message: don't cross us or you will pay. As implementation continues, we'll likely see more of this.

We're also starting to see Common Core supporters resorting to old strategies like "change the language, change the debate." They've done this successfully with many different issues over the years (i.e., global warming is now "climate change" and illegal aliens are now "undocumented workers") and now, realizing just how toxic the term "Common Core" is becoming, they're trying it again.

In Iowa, Common Core is now called "Iowa Core." (My guess is that some pollster found that parents objected less when the state name was included, because it implied some sort of local control.) According to *TheBlaze*, Arizona governor Jan Brewer recently signed an executive order to scrub the Common Core name from their math and reading standards. Louisiana is also reportedly considering a name change, and Florida has switched to the "Next Generation Sunshine State Standards."

This is all great strategy, according to the progressives—many of them Republican—who champion the program. "Rebrand it, refocus it, but don't retreat," former Arkansas governor Mike Huckabee told a recent meeting of the Council of Chief State School Officers.

This is yet another reason why it's so imperative that you use your voice to speak out and educate your friends and neighbors about what's really going on here. Others have already scored major victories in this fight—but there are plenty more battles ahead.

Education reformers are even beginning to take aim at the

archaic union contract rules, claiming these policies are violating children's right to a quality education and effective educators. In California, a recent high-profile court case against teacher tenure may have national implications. The *New York Times* describes this case as "the most sweeping legal challenge claiming that students are hurt by employment laws for teachers. The case also relies on a civil rights argument that so far is untested: that poor and minority students are denied equal access to education because they are more likely to have 'grossly ineffective' teachers."

Michelle Rhee, who runs Students First, which pushes for educational reforms, underscored how regular people can force a state into change, even in the face of a compliant and complacent legislature. "In an ideal world you would want policies to be passed in the legislature," she told the *Times*, "but in California there was no movement on that. I think in this case they were tired of waiting."

The importance of this case cannot be understated. Even Randi Weingarten, head of the AFT, is concerned, calling the lawsuit "worse than troubling" and complaining that families are just looking for a scapegoat instead of "rolling up your sleeves and dealing with [the] problem."

As of press time the trial was still under way, but no matter who prevails, the case (known as *Vergara v. California*) will likely end up at the California Supreme Court. This one is worth watching closely and, depending on the final outcome, may have significant consequences for education reform activists all over the country.

Meanwhile, some concerned citizens are already getting involved on the political side of the debate by running for governor or for state superintendent or state legislature or for their local school board with the intention of taking power back from the moneyed interests and federal government. Find out who they are and support them or—better yet—join their campaign.

9/12 Project members and others in the ragtag army have started blogs and Facebook groups, like California school board member Angela Weinzinger's "Parents and Educators Against Common Core Standards." Join them, learn, and inform your friends and family. Not just about Common Core, but about all the important issues surrounding education.

We need more voices in the education debate. You may be a parent. You're definitely a taxpayer. You have every right to have your voice heard. Don't let the "experts"—the very people who produced and profited from this broken, dysfunctional government-run system—tell you to mind your own business.

Between information outlets like *TheBlaze,* Fox News, and EAGnews.org, as well as social media sites like Facebook, we are using our singular and collective voices to defeat the entrenched money and power.

We have the facts on our side and facts help to win minds, but it's the personal stories of those like Lamoreaux, Young, and Small that help win the hearts. Contact the media and share your story with them. Share your child's textbooks and worksheets. Explain to them how you see Common Core changing the teaching and learning process.

Our schools—whether you have children in them or not—*are* your business. Run for the school board yourself or support a candidate who is running and who understands the threat posed by Common Core. 9/12 and Tea Party groups have enormous influence in school board elections. Use that power wisely.

If being a candidate is not your thing, attend your local school board meetings and blog or tweet about them. Address the board like Lamoreaux and Young did. Keep the bureaucrats on their toes like Small did.

You can also play private investigator and follow the money trail. Submit Freedom of Information Act requests for spending documents like the district's check register, employee credit cards, and cell phone bills. Post them online for everyone in your community to see. Ask for no-bid contracts and find out who owns the company that was awarded the project. Are they connected to the administration or board members? The local media is not doing this work so we taxpayers must. Contact Education Action Group (EAGnews.org) and they will help you navigate the bureaucratic school waters.

We all have an obligation to expose what is happening with privacy concerns as well. Find out where your child's sensitive personal information is being shared and who has access to it. The federal government? Private companies? Find out, and then, if you don't like what you found, share it with the community—chances are that they'll be just as outraged as you are.

You can also volunteer for your school district's curriculum committee. Get involved. Ask to review textbooks, worksheets, and other components of the curriculum. It's the best way to root out propaganda and information that are just plain wrong.

Know your rights as a parent and be a responsible one. Get to know your child's teacher, principal, superintendent, and school board. Be engaged in the educational process, reviewing homework, assignments, and what your child is learning each day. Don't take anything for granted. If you don't like what you are seeing—tell someone. If the school tries to marginalize you or cut you out of the process, they're very likely hiding something. Find out what it is.

We have the right solutions. And we have the will to implement them. Now we just need to wrestle control away from the unions, bureaucrats, and politicians who think they know how to run our lives better than we do.

We're ready.

Are you?

NOTES

AUTHOR'S NOTE

PAGE XI: " 'is allowable in each classroom' " Indiana Department of Education (Internal Document), March 21, 2011, http://www.in.gov/legislative/house_repub licans/publications/doecb/doecb.pdf. • " 'Work site' " Yirmeyah Beckles, "Labor Council Decides Not to Sanction Picket Line at Lakeview Elementary," *Oakland North,* July 21, 2012, http://oaklandnorth.net/2012/07/21/labor-council-decides-not -to-sanction-picket-line-at-lakeview-elementary/.

PAGE XII: "it was actually against the law to teach a slave" Kimberly Sambo-Tosco, "The Slave Experience: Education, Arts, & Culture," *Education Broadcasting Corporation,* 2004, http://www.pbs.org/wnet/slavery/experience/education/history2.html.

PART ONE: THE TRUTH ABOUT EDUCATION

CHAPTER 1: YOU CAN'T CRITICIZE PUBLIC EDUCATION IF YOU HAVEN'T BEEN IN THE CLASSROOM

PAGE 3: " 'the experience and knowledge needed to run a school?' " Diane Ravitch, "Why Celebrities Should Not Tell Teachers How to Fix Schools," *dianeravitch.net,* September 23, 2013, http://dianeravitch.net/2013/09/23/why-celebrities-should-not -tell-teachers-how-to-fix-schools/. • " 'you have no business in the [school] board room' " Patricia Fox, "Patricia Fox's Facebook Page," *facebook.com,* August 1, 2012, accessed January 28, 2014, https://www.facebook.com/electpatriciafox. • " 'three thousand local affiliate unions across the nation' " American Federation of Teachers, "About American Federation of Teachers, AFL-CIO," *aft.org,* accessed January 28, 2014, http://www.aft.org/about/. • "no right to criticize U.S. military action in Iraq" American Federation of Teachers, "AFT Resolutions: Iraq," *aft.org,* 2004, http://www.aft.org/about/resolution_detail.cfm?articleid=1314.

PAGE 4: "no business supporting Obamacare" American Federation of Teachers, "AFT Resolutions: In Support of the Affordable Care Act, Medicare and Social Security," *aft .org,* 2012, http://www.aft.org/about/resolution_detail.cfm?articleid=1630. • "union represents many thousands of health-care professionals" American Federation of Teachers, "About AFT Healthcare," *aft.org,* accessed January 28, 2014, http://www.aft .org/yourwork/healthcare/about.cfm.

PAGE 5: "fuzzy names like the 'National Education Association' " National Education Association, *nea.org,* accessed January 28, 2014, http://www.nea.org/.

PAGE 6: "increased nearly 1,500 percent since 1970" "Government Spending Chart," *usgovernmentspending.com,* accessed January 28, 2014, http://www.usgovernment spending.com/spending_chart_1970_2018USb_15s2li111mcn_20t. • "spent by the federal government alone since 1965" Andrew J. Coulson, "The Impact of Federal Involvement in America's Classrooms," *Cato Institute,* February 10, 2011, http://www .cato.org/publications/congressional-testimony/impact-federal-involvement-americas -classrooms. • "now stands at more than $151,000 per student" Andrew J. Coulson, "The Impact of Federal Involvement in America's Classrooms," *Cato Institute,* February 10, 2011, http://www.cato.org/publications/congressional-testimony /impact-federal-involvement-americas-classrooms. • "spent on the graduating class of 1970" Andrew J. Coulson, "The Impact of Federal Involvement in America's Classrooms," *Cato Institute,* February 10, 2011, http://www.cato.org/publications /congressional-testimony/impact-federal-involvement-americas-classrooms.

PAGE 7: " 'the last time that test was administered' " Andrew J. Coulson, "The Impact of Federal Involvement in America's Classrooms," *Cato Institute,* February 10, 2011, http://www.cato.org/publications/congressional-testimony/impact-federal-involvement -americas-classrooms. • "21st in reading globally" The Organization for Economic and Co-operation and Development (OECD), "PISA 2012 Key Findings," *oecd.org,* 2012, http://www.oecd.org/pisa/keyfindings/PISA-2012-results-snapshot-Volume-I -ENG.pdf.

CHAPTER 2: CRITICS OF THE SYSTEM ARE JUST "TEACHER BASHERS"

PAGE 9: " 'When did teacher bashing become the new national pastime?' " Sam Chaltain, "My View: When Did Teacher Bashing Become the New National Pastime," *Schools of Thought* blog at *cnn.com,* March 6, 2012, http://schoolsofthought.blogs .cnn.com/2012/03/06/my-view-when-did-teacher-bashing-become-the-new-national -pastime/. • " 'brought us Fox News and reality television?' " David Siroonian, "Why Mary Thorson's Struggle Is Our Struggle," *theassailedteacher.com,* March 12, 2013, http://theassailedteacher.com/2013/03/12/why-mary-thorsons-struggle-is-our -struggle/. • " 'attacking teachers is the same as attacking children' " Suzanne Perez Tobias, "Teachers Union President: Bills Being Written In Topeka Will Hurt Schools," *The Wichita Eagle,* February 8, 2013, updated October 9, 2013, http:// www.kansas.com/2013/02/08/2667990/teachers-union-president-bills.html. • " 'do a lot of teacher-bashing' " Ashley Killough, "Obama: Romney Is a Teacher-Basher," *Political Ticker* blog at *cnn.com,* September 25, 2012, http://politicalticker.blogs .cnn.com/2012/09/25/obama-romney-is-a-teacher-basher/. • "The NEA" "National Education Assn: Totals," *opensecrets.org,* accessed January 29, 2014, http://www .opensecrets.org/orgs/totals.php?id=D000000064&cycle=2012. • "and AFT" "Ameri- can Federation of Teachers," *opensecrets.org,* accessed January 29, 2014, http://www .opensecrets.org/orgs/totals.php?id=D000000083&cycle=2012.

PAGE 10: " 'want to slash pay and benefits for teachers' " Ashley Lauren Samsa, "Enough With the Teacher Bashing. It's Not Helping Students or Anyone Else," *The Guardian,* July 11, 2013, http://www.theguardian.com/commentisfree/2013/jul/11/ teachers-bashing-does-not-help-students. • "73 percent of people have 'trust and con- fidence' in public school teachers" William J. Bushaw and Shane J. Lopez, "Which Way Do We Go?" *Phi Delta Kappan* 95, no. 1 (September 2013), https://www.au.org /files/pdf_documents/2013_PDKGallup.pdf. • "75 percent of respondents said teach- ers have 'very great' or 'considerable' prestige" Harris Interactive, "The MetLife Sur- vey of The American Teacher, 2006: Expectations and Experience," (report, MetLife, Inc., New York City, September 26, 2006), http://files.eric.ed.gov/fulltext/ED496558 .pdf. • "72 percent of people believe that teachers contribute 'a lot' to society's well-being" Katie Reilly, "Respect for Journalists' Contributions Has Fallen Significantly in Recent Years," *pewresearch.org,* July 25, 2013, http://www.pewresearch.org/fact-tank/.

PAGE 11: "lost about 50 percent of its membership" Daniel Bice, "Membership in Public Worker Union Takes a Hit Under Act 10," *Milwaukee Journal Sentinel,* July 20, 2013, http://www.jsonline.com/watchdog/noquarter/membership-in-public-worker -unions-takes-a-hit-under-act-10-b9957856z1-216309111.html. • **"send volunteers door-to-door to try to collect delinquent dues"** Al Campbell, "Will WEAC Survive?" *Curmudgeon's Corner* blog at *germantownnow.com,* July 25, 2011, http:// www.germantownnow.com/blogs/communityblogs/126112208.html. • " 'thus making school more attractive to students' " Ashley Lauren Samsa, "Enough With the Teacher Bashing. It's Not Helping Students or Anyone Else," *The Guardian,* July 11, 2013, http://www.theguardian.com/commentisfree/2013/jul/11/teachers-bashing-does -not-help-students.

PAGE 12: "took out a full page ad in a local newspaper" Charles Lussier, "Union Claims EBR School System Violated Law with Ad Praising Teachers," The Louisiana *Advocate,* October 6, 2013, http://theadvocate.com/home/7211198-125/union -claims-ebr-school-system. • " 'who may be doing a fantastic job in the classroom' " Diana Samuels, "Baton Rouge School Board Violated Law When It Recognized 'Highly Effective' Teachers, Union Says," *The Times-Picayune,* October 1, 2013, http://www.nola.com/education/baton-rouge/index.ssf/2013/10/baton_rouge _school_board_viola.html.

CHAPTER 3: PUBLIC SCHOOLS ARE UNDERFUNDED

PAGE 14: " 'in order to educate all students to academic proficiency' " Dale Mezzacappa, "Experts: Yes, Philly Are Underfunded . . . by $1 Billion," *The Notebook* 15, no. 2 (Winter 2007), http://thenotebook.org/winter-2007/07369/experts-yes-philly schools-are-underfunded-%E2%80%A6-1-billion. • " 'have served to further undermine their mission' " Diane Ravitch, "Saving Our Public Schools," *The Progressive Magazine* 77, no. 10 (October 2013), http://millermps.wordpress.com/2013/10/05 /diane-ravitch-on-how-to-save-public-education. • " 'other nations are out-investing us in education as well' " "U.S. Education Spending Tops Global List, Study Shows," *cbsnews.com,* June 25, 2013, http://www.cbsnews.com/news/us-education-spending -tops-global-list-study-shows/.

PAGE 15: " 'invest at least $1 billion more each year in K–12 education' " John R. Burbank, "Privileged Should Invest More in Public Schools," *seattlepi.com,* July 28, 2007, http://www.seattlepi.com/local/opinion/article/Privileged-should-invest-more -in-public-schools-1244867.php. • **"named 'funding' as the biggest problem facing public schools"** Dylan Scott, "Biggest Problem for Public Education? Lack of Funding, Poll Says," *governing.com,* August 3, 2012, http://www.governing.com/news /politics/gov-biggest-problem-for-public-education-lack-of-funding-poll-says.html. • **"80 percent of most public school budgets are swallowed up by labor costs"** Arthur Peng and James Guthrie, "The Phony Funding Crisis," *Education Next* 10, no. 1 (Winter 2010), http://educationnext.org/the-phony-funding-crisis/.

PAGE 16: "most recent budget deficit was reportedly $304 million" Hilary Russ, "Fiscal crisis looms for Philadelphia schools as students return," reuters .com, September 7, 2013, http://www.reuters.com/article/2013/09/07/us-usa-phila delphia-schools-idUSBRE9860BQ20130907. • **"1,400 layoff notices to employees"** Kristin A. Graham, "Phila. School District Sends 1,400 layoff notices to blue-collar union," *philly.com,* January 03, 2012, http://articles.philly.com/2012-01-03 /news/30583608_1_layoff-notices-number-of-union-employees-pink-slips. • **"laid**

off another 3,783 employees" Action News, "3,783 being laid off from Philadelphia School District," *abclocal.go.com,* June 7th, 2013, http://abclocal.go.com/wpvi
/story?section=news/local&id=9130566. • "just to open its doors for the start of
the 2013–2014 school year" Vince Lattanzio, "Gov. Corbett to Release $45M in
Funding for Philadelphia Schools," *nbcphiladelphia.com,* October 6th, 2013, http://
www.nbcphiladelphia.com/news/local/Corbett-to-Release-45M-in-Sought-Funding
-for-Philadelphia-Schools-228025001.html. • "district spent $132 million on health
insurance for union members in 2011–2012" Steve Gunn, "For a district on the brink
of collapse, Philly schools still managed to hand out huge salaries and pricey perks,"
eagnews.org, January 31, 2014. http://eagnews.org/for-a-district-on-the-brink-of
-collapse-philly-schools-still-managed-to-hand-out-huge-salaries-and-pricey-perks.
• "$36.2 million paid out in unused sick leave" Steve Gunn, "For a district on the brink
of collapse, Philly schools still managed to hand out huge salaries and pricey perks,"
eagnews.org, January 31, 2014, http://eagnews.org/for-a-district-on-the-brink-of
-collapse-philly-schools-still-managed-to-hand-out-huge-salaries-and-pricey-perks.
• "$5.2 million on the union 'wage continuation plan' " Steve Gunn, "For a district
on the brink of collapse, Philly schools still managed to hand out huge salaries and
pricey perks," eagnews.org, January 31, 2014, http://eagnews.org/for-a-district-on-the
-brink-of-collapse-philly-schools-still-managed-to-hand-out-huge-salaries-and-pricey
-perks.

PAGE 17: "spends right at the OECD average of 2.5 percent" OECD, "Education at a
Glance 2013: OECD Indicators [Table B2.2]," (report, OECD Publishing, Paris, 2013),
http://www.oecd.org/edu/eag2013%20(eng)—FINAL%2020%20June%202013.pdf.
• " 'with better ACT scores or graduation rates' " State Budget Solutions "Study:
States Spending More On Education Doesn't Lead to Better Test Scores," press release, September 12, 2012, http://www.statebudgetsolutions.org/about_us/newsroom
/study-states-spending-more-on-education-doesnt-lead-to-better-test-scores.

PAGE 18: "another $47 million on automatic, annual raises for teachers" Steve Gunn,
"Sucking the Life Out of America's Public Schools: The Expense of Teachers Union
Contracts, Part 5, United Teachers Los Angeles Contract," (report, eagnews.org,
Muskegon, MI, Summer 2012), http://eagnews.org/wp-content/uploads/2012/07
/Los-Angeles-contract-report.pdf. • "was a miserable 61 percent" Barbara Jones,
"LAUSD Sees Fewer Dropouts, But Graduation Rate Dips," *Los Angeles Daily News,*
June 26, 2012, http://www.dailynews.com/social-affairs/20120627/lausd-sees-fewer
-dropouts-but-graduation-rate-dips.

CHAPTER 4: TEACHERS' UNIONS PUT KIDS FIRST

PAGE 19: " 'can't put students first when you put teachers last' " Allison Sampite-
Montecalvo, "Teachers Association, District Head Toward Impasse," *San Diego
Union-Tribune,* November 18, 2013, http://www.utsandiego.com/news/2013/Nov/18
/sweetwater-teacher-association-negotiation/. • " 'our teachers can do what they
do best: teach' " Charles McBarron, "Teachers Support Education Reform Package
That Puts Kids First," *ieanea.org,* April 14, 2011, http://www.ieanea.org/2011/04/14
/teachers-support-education-reform-package-that-puts-kids-first/. • " 'I'll start representing the interests of schoolchildren' " " 'When School Children Start Paying
Union Dues, That's When I'll Start Representing the Interests of School Children,' "
2mm.typepad.com, January 7, 2010, http://2mm.typepad.com/usa/2010/01/when
-school-children-start-paying-union-dues-that-s-when-ill-start-representing-the
-interests-of-sch.html.

PAGE 20: " 'advance their interests as education employees' " Conn Carroll, "NEA
General Counsel: Union Dues, Not Education, Are Our Top Priority," *The Foundry*

blog at *heritage.org,* July 9, 2009, http://blog.heritage.org/2009/07/09/nea-general
-counsel-union-dues-not-education-are-our-top-priority/.

PAGE 22: " 'in the throes of political activism and social justice' " Carolyn Doggett,
"Carolyn Doggett CTA State Council Speech," (speech, Los Angeles, January 27,
2013), California Teachers Association, http://www.cta.org/~/media/Documents
/PDFs/State%20Council/Jan%202013%20Council/Carolyn%20Doggett%20Council%
20Speech2.pdf.

PAGE 23: "70 percent of these districts use seniority as the *sole* factor" Dan Gold-
haber and Roddy Theobald, "Managing the Teacher Workforce," *Education Next* 11,
no. 4 (Fall 2011), http://educationnext.org/managing-the-teacher-workforce/. • "482
younger teachers who faced immediate layoff" Erin Richards and Amy Hetzner,
"Seniority System Cuts Fresh MPS Teachers Amid Budget Crunch," *Milwaukee Journal Sentinel,* June 14, 2010, http://www.jsonline.com/news/education/96349689.html.

PAGE 24: " 'children to keep their teachers' " Pat O'Mahar, "MTEA Interim Executive
Director Makes Statement on MPS Layoffs and Rally," (speech, Milwaukee, June 14,
2010), Milwaukee Teachers' Education Association, http://www.mtea.org/Public/pdf
/statement-on-layoffs.pdf. • " 'or the jobs of 10 other teachers' " Erin Richards and
Amy Hetzner, "Seniority System Cuts Fresh MPS Teachers Amid Budget Crunch,"
Milwaukee Journal Sentinel, June 14, 2010, http://www.jsonline.com/news/education
/96349689.html. • "that successful 'turnaround' elementary" Eleanor Chute, "Pittsburgh Public Schools Board OKs Layoffs," *Pittsburgh Post-Gazette,* July 26, 2012,
http://www.post-gazette.com/news/education/2012/07/26/Pittsburgh-Public-Schools
-board-OKs-280-layoffs/stories/201207260325.

PAGE 25: "teachers walked out for eight weeks in 2013" Donna J. Miller, "Teachers
Return to Strongsville Classrooms After 8-Week Strike," *cleveland.com,* April 30, 2013,
http://www.cleveland.com/metro/index.ssf/2013/04/teachers_return_to_strongsvill.html.
• " 'Rosa Parks would be ashamed!' " Jessica Chasmar, " 'Rosa Parks Would Be
Ashamed!': Ohio Strikers Heckle Substitute Teachers," *Washington Times,* March 6, 2013,
http://www.washingtontimes.com/news/2013/mar/6/rosa-parks-would-be-ashamed
-ohio-strikers-heckle-s/. • "they were living near 'scabs' " Debbie Palmer, " 'Scab'
Posters Turn Up Near Teacher's Home," *strongsville.patch.com,* March 8, 2013, http://
strongsville.patch.com/groups/schools/p/scab-posters-turn-up-near-teacher-s-home.
• "the names and addresses of the fill-in teachers" Cory Shaffer, "Cleveland Teachers Union President Suing Strongsville School Board for Substitute Names, Personal
Info," *cleveland.com,* July 12, 2013, http://www.cleveland.com/strongsville/index
.ssf/2013/07/cleveland_teachers_union_presi.html#incart_river. • " 'erratic and worrisome behavior' " Kim Russell, "A Swartz Creek Teacher Ruled 'Not Mentally Fit'
May Be Put Back in the Classroom," *minbcnews.com,* May 12, 2011 updated May 13,
2011, http://www.minbcnews.com/news/story.aspx?id=616992#.Uuq2jWSwLF9.

PAGE 26: "it ordered her reinstatement" Kayla Habermehl, "Swartz Creek Schools Re-
instates Teacher, Counselor After About Three Year Legal Battle," *mlive.com,* May 19,
2011, http://www.mlive.com/news/flint/index.ssf/2011/05/swartz_creek_schools_re
instate.html. • "a judge ordered her reinstatement" Steve Gunn, "Michigan Union
Fought to Reinstate School Counselor, Despite Mental Health Concerns," *eagnews
.org,* May 27, 2013, http://eagnews.org/michigan-union-fought-to-reinstate-school
-counselor-despite-mental-health-concerns/. • " 'but that is secondary to the other
goals' " Concerned Educators Against Forced Unionism, "Noteworthy Quotes,"
ceafu.org, accessed January 29, 2014, http://ceafu.org/resources/research/688–2/.

CHAPTER 5: TEACHERS NEED UNIONS AND COLLECTIVE BARGAINING

PAGE 27: " 'and to retain those individuals . . .' " The Pennsylvania State Education Association, "The Power of a Great Education: PSEA's 20/20 Vision for the Future," *psea.org*, January 6, 2010, http://www.psea.org/uploadedFiles/LegislationAndPolitics /Vision/Vision_PreserveCollectiveBargaining.pdf. • " 'cannot safely speak out for what is best for students' " Teachers for Social Justice, "PEPP English Booklet," *eagnews.org*, August 15, 2013, http://eagnews.org/wp-content/uploads/2013/09/PEPP -English-Booklet-8.15.20131.pdf. • " 'Teachers Need Strong Unions' " Dick Meister, "Teachers Need Strong Unions," *dickmeister.com*, 2011, http://www.dickmeister.com /id446.html.

PAGE 28: "teachers' union, lost approximately thirty thousand members" Steven Verburg, "Recall Aftermath: Public Unions Face Uncertain Future," *Wisconsin State Journal*, June 10, 2012, http://host.madison.com/news/local/govt-and-politics/recall -aftermath-public-unions-face-uncertain-future/article_82fa0a7e-b25f-11e1-9c50-001 a4bcf887a.html. • "the right to decide if they want to be union members" M. Alex Johnson, "Snyder Signs Michigan Anti-Union 'Right to Work' Measures Over Protests of Thousands," *usnews.nbcnews.com*, December 11, 2012, http://usnews .nbcnews.com/_news/2012/12/11/15842456-snyder-signs-michigan-anti-union-right -to-work-measures-over-protests-of-thousands. • "a 10 percent pay cut for teachers" Derk Wilcox, "Taylor Teachers Fight Union Subversion of Right-to-Work Law," *mackinac.org*, April 8, 2013, http://www.mackinac.org/18500. • "eventually lost in court" "Administrative Law Judge Recommends Dismissal of Taylor Teachers' Challenge to Decade-Long Forced Dues Extension," *mackinac.org*, January 6, 2014, http:// www.mackinac.org/19498.

PAGE 29: " 'continue paying dues or agency fees through 2023' " Gus Burns, "Mackinac Center-Backed Right-to-Work Battle Broils in Taylor," *mlive.com*, March 1, 2013, http://www.mlive.com/news/detroit/index.ssf/2013/03/mackinac_center-backed_right -t.html. • " 'They don't really do anything else' " Steve Gunn, "Dougco School Board President Says Voters Prefer Student-Based Reforms Over Union Greed," *eagnews .org*, October 9, 2013, http://eagnews.org/douglas-county-school-board-president-says -voters-prefer-student-based-reforms-over-union-greed/. • "punished with a forty-five-day unpaid suspension" "Pervy Teachers Must Get the Boot, Even Though Arbitrators Let Them Keep Their Jobs," *New York Daily News*, April 6, 2012, http://www .nydailynews.com/opinion/pervy-teachers-boot-article-1.1057018.

PAGE 30: "in the classroom after paying a $10,000 fine" Rachel Monahan and Ben Chapman, "Sixteen Teachers Singled Out for Pervy Conduct Get to Keep Their Jobs in New York City Schools," *New York Daily News*, April 5, 2012, updated April 6, 2012, http://www.nydailynews.com/new-york/education/dozen-sexually-inappropri ate-teachers-jobs-new-york-city-schools-article-1.1057113. • "they secured $200,000 in back pay for him" La Rae G. Munk, "School Unions Shortchange Students," *mackinac.org*, April 16, 1999, http://www.mackinac.org/1686. • "admitted to molesting a student for three years" Tim Barnum, "Erickson Sentenced to 15–30 Years in Prison," *Ogemaw County Herald*, July 10, 2013, http://www.ogemawherald.com /stories/Erickson%20sentenced%20to%2015%2030%20years%20in%20prison,97478. • "he was due a $10,000 payout when he left the district" Victor Skinner, "Parents Stunned That Union is Seeking a $10K Severance for Teacher Who Molested Their Son," *eagnews.org*, December 11, 2013, http://eagnews.org/parents-are-stunned-that-the -teachers-union-is-seeking-a-10000-severance-for-the-teacher-who-molested-their-son/.

PAGE 31: " 'spending about $4,000 locally for teacher training' " Steve Gunn, "Dougco School Board President Says Voters Prefer Student-Based Reforms Over

Union Greed," *eagnews.org,* October 9, 2013, http://eagnews.org/douglas-county
-school-board-president-says-voters-prefer-student-based-reforms-over-union-greed/.
• "**supporting President Obama's reelection bid in 2011**" "Union Taxes Teachers
$10 for Obama Campaign," *Follow the Money with Eric Bolling,* Fox Business, July 7,
2011, http://video.foxbusiness.com/v/1041566501001/union-taxes-teachers-10-for-obama
-campaign/#sp=show-clips. • " '**not to become a political pawn'** " Association of
American Educators, "Union Member Angered By Obama Endorsement," *AAE*
blog at *aaeteachers.org,* July 8, 2011, http://www.aaeteachers.org/index.php/blog/479
-union-member-angered-by-obama-endorsement. • "**makes $362,644**" Perry Chiar-
amonte, "Average Teacher Makes $44G While Their Top Union Bosses Pull in
Nearly $500G," *foxnews.com,* July 14, 2012, http://www.foxnews.com/us/2012/07
/14/teacher-union-bigs-rake-in-dough-despite-budget-cuts-across-education-sector/.
• "**another $5.9 million on lobbying**" "National Education Assn: Summary," *open
secrets.org,* accessed January 29, 2014, http://www.opensecrets.org/orgs/summary
.php?id=D000000064.

CHAPTER 6: TEACHERS NEED TENURE

PAGE 32: " '**I had reached "tenure" status . . .'** " "Guest Column: Teachers Need Tenure,
and Here's Why: Letters from Readers," *Florida Times-Union,* May 15, 2011, http://
members.jacksonville.com/opinion/letters-readers/2011–05–16/story/guest-column
-teachers-need-tenure-and-heres-why. • " '**that could have a negative impact on
them and the children they serve'** " Randy Turner, "An Argument for Teacher Tenure,"
huffingtonpost.com, December 7, 2012, http://www.huffingtonpost.com/randy-turner
/teacher-tenure-_b_2257120.html. • " '**the larger community that the school
serves'** " Editors of Rethinking Schools, "Editorial: What's Up with All the Teacher
Bashing?" *rethinkingschools.org,* Summer 2010, http://www.rethinkingschools.org//
cmshandler.asp?archive/24_04/edit244.shtml.

PAGE 33: " '**not the only thing that would protect you'** " Alan Greenblatt, "Is Teacher
Tenure Still Necessary?" *npr.org,* April 29, 2010, http://www.npr.org/templates/story
/story.php?storyId=126349435.

PAGE 34: " '**the teacher can be dismissed'** " Ceolaf, "Why K12 Teachers Need
Tenure," *ceolaf.blogspot.com,* April 10, 2008, http://ceolaf.blogspot.com/2008/04
/why-k12-teachers-need-tenure.html. • "**The teacher's pay was suspended for the
first four months**" James Smith, "The Process for Firing a Tenured Teacher in New
Jersey," *eagnews.org,* accessed January 31, 2014, http://eagnews.org/wp-content/up
loads/2012/05/EAGnews-New-Jersey-tenure-process-chart.pdf.

PAGE 35: " '**It takes guts, money and know-how'** " Kyle Olson, "Expensive, Lengthy
NJ Teacher Tenure Process Revealed," *townhall.com,* January 6, 2011, http://townhall
.com/columnists/kyleolson/2011/01/06/expensive,_lengthy_nj_teacher_tenure_pro
cess_revealed/page/full. • " '**do not try to fire bad teachers'** " Scott Reeder, "Cost
to Fire a Tenured Teacher? More Than $219,000," *thehiddencostsoftenure.com,* ac-
cessed January 31, 2014, http://thehiddencostsoftenure.com/stories/?prcss=display
&id=295712. • "**have fired fewer than 1 out of 1,000 tenured teachers**" Alan Greenblatt, "Is Teacher Tenure Still Necessary?" *npr.org,* April 29, 2010, http://www.npr.org
/templates/story/story.php?storyId=126349435.

PAGE 36: "**only two were fired for performance reasons**" Scott Reeder, "Tenure Frus-
trates Drive for Teacher Accountability," *thehiddencostsoftenure.com,* accessed January 31, 2014, http://thehiddencostsoftenure.com/stories/?prcss=display&id=266539.
• " '**risk getting hurt?'** " Fran Tarkenton, "What if the NFL Played by Teachers'
Rules?" *The Wall Street Journal,* October 3, 2011, http://online.wsj.com/news/articles
/SB10001424052970204226204576601232986845102.

PAGE 37: " 'for a variety of untenable reasons' " Matt Coleman, "Matt Coleman: Why Teachers Need Tenure," *gainesville.com*, April 7, 2011, http://www.gainesville.com /article/20110407/NEWS/110409625. • **"about 45 percent of new teachers walk away within their first five years"** Erik Kain, "High Teacher Turnover Rates are a Big Problem for America's Public Schools," *forbes.com*, March 8, 2011, http://www.forbes .com/sites/erikkain/2011/03/08/high-teacher-turnover-rates-are-a-big-problem-for -americas-public-schools/. • " '**mediocrity rather than excellence'** " TNTP, "The Irreplaceables: Understanding the Real Retention Crisis in America's Urban Schools," (report, TNTP, Brooklyn, 2012), http://tntp.org/assets/documents/TNTP_Irreplace ables_2012.pdf.

PAGE 38: "one out of every 57 doctors having their license revoked" "Protecting Bad Teachers," *teachersunionexposed.com*, accessed January 31, 2014, http://teachers unionexposed.com/protecting.php. • " '**shouldn't even be pumping gas'** " George A. Clowes, "Teachers Like Tenure But Admit Its Flaws," *news.heartland.org*, July 1, 2003, http://news.heartland.org/newspaper-article/2003/07/01/teachers-tenure-ad mit-its-flaws. • **"3.25 percent across-the-board pay raise"** Gabrielle Russon, "Sarasota Schools to Hand Out $9 Million in Bonuses," *Sarasota Herald-Tribune*, October 15, 2013, http://www.heraldtribune.com/article/20131015/article/131019774. • **"that practice could save the district $900,000 per year"** Dave Miller, "Phasing Out KISD's Longevity Pay Logical," *Killeen Daily Herald*, April 15, 2012, http://kdhnews .com/opinion/editorials/article_d7b6588a-7252–53f8–8d5f-45ef3f011991.html.

PAGE 39: " 'if that is what I really wanted to do' " Real Life Burned Out Teacher, "What Am I Doing?" *confessionsofaburnedoutteacher.blogspot.com*, April 27, 2010, http://confessionsofaburnedoutteacher.blogspot.com/2010/04/what-am-i-doing.html.

PAGE 40: " '**once the passion has left you, so should tenure'** " Michael Smith, "Teacher Burnout. And Yet, They Still Keep Going to Work." *Principal's Page* blog at *principal spage.com*, September 16, 2010, http://www.principalspage.com/theblog/archives /teacher-burnout-and-yet-they-still-keep-going-to-work. • " '**do that job unless you really love to do it?'** " Ben Flanagan, "Matt Damon Tears into Debt Ceiling, Defends Working Teachers," *Politics* blog at *al.com*, August 3, 2011, http://blog.al.com/tusca loosa/2011/08/matt_damon_tears_into_debt_cei.html.

CHAPTER 7: PAY SHOULD BE BASED ON SENIORITY, NOT PERFORMANCE

PAGE 41: " '**for an extra $5,000 or so'** " Diane Ravitch, "Thoughts on the Failure of Merit Pay," *Bridging Differences* blog at *edweek.org*, March 29, 2011, http://blogs .edweek.org/edweek/Bridging-Differences/2011/03/thoughts_on_the_failure_of.html. • " '**a high quality education that prepares them for their future'** " John Rosales, "Pay Based on Test Scores?" *nea.org*, accessed February 1, 2014, http://www.nea .org/home/36780.htm#. • " '**We're not producing widgets'** " Melissa Jenco, "Merit Pay Opinions Mixed," *Chicago Tribune*, September 13, 2012, http://articles.chicago tribune.com/2012–09–13/news/ct-tl-merit-pay-teachers-20120913_1_pits-teachers -rewarding-teachers-high-school-teachers.

PAGE 42: " '**and all but four passed reading'** " TNTP, "The Irreplaceables: Understanding the Real Retention Crisis in America's Urban Schools," (report, TNTP, Brooklyn, 2012), http://tntp.org/assets/documents/TNTP_Irreplaceables_2012.pdf.

PAGE 43: "if two teachers were hired on the same day" Molly Bloom, "Schools Use Coin Toss to Decide Who Gets Laid Off," *stateimpact.npr.org*, July 17, 2012, http:// stateimpact.npr.org/ohio/2012/07/17/schools-use-coin-toss-to-decide-who-gets-laid -off/. • **"roughly 25,000 teachers in Charbonneau's state make more than he does"** Jami Lund, "25,000 Teachers Paid More Than the National Teacher of the Year,"

Freedom Foundation blog at *myfreedomfoundation.com*, October 9, 2013, http://myfreedomfoundation.com/blog/liberty-live/detail/25000-teachers-paid-more-than-the-national-teacher-of-the-year.

PAGE 44: " 'on fairness and not as much on quality' " Frank Bruni, "Teachers on the Defensive," *New York Times*, August 18, 2012, http://www.nytimes.com/2012/08/19/opinion/sunday/bruni-teachers-on-the-defensive.html?_r=1&pagewanted=all. • "**annual 'step' increases for teachers in 2010–11**" Steve Gunn, "Sucking the Life Out of America's Public Schools: The Expense of Teachers Union Contracts, Part 5, United Teachers Los Angeles Contract," (report, eagnews.org, Muskegon, MI, Summer 2012), http://eagnews.org/wp-content/uploads/2012/07/Los-Angeles-contract-report.pdf. • "**paid out an additional $21.4 million**" Steve Gunn, "Sucking the Life Out of America's Public Schools: The Expense of Teachers Union Contracts, Part 9, Denver Classroom Teachers Association Contract," (report, eagnews.org, Muskegon, MI, Fall 2012), http://eagnews.org/wp-content/uploads/2012/10/Denver-report.pdf. • "**the Detroit district spent $15.6 million**" Steve Gunn, "Sucking the Life Out of America's Public Schools: The Expense of Teachers Union Contracts, Part 3, Detroit Federation of Teachers Contract," (report, eagnews.org, Muskegon, MI, Spring 2012), http://eagnews.org/wp-content/uploads/2012/05/Detroit-contract-report.pdf. • " 'I've been here the longest' " Frank Bruni, "Teachers on the Defensive," *New York Times*, August 18, 2012, http://www.nytimes.com/2012/08/19/opinion/sunday/bruni-teachers-on-the-defensive.html?_r=1&pagewanted=all. • "**teachers' unions**" "AFT: A Union of Professionals," *aft.org*, accessed February 1, 2014, http://www.aft.org/.

PAGE 45: "**teachers being rated 'satisfactory,'** " Jenny Anderson, "Curious Grade for Teachers: Nearly All Pass," *New York Times*, March 30, 2013, http://www.nytimes.com/2013/03/31/education/curious-grade-for-teachers-nearly-all-pass.html?pagewanted=all. • "**motivated by $43 million in federal 'Race to the Top'** " United States Government Accountability Office, "Race to the Top: States Implementing Teacher and Principal Evaluation Systems Despite Challenges," (report, Government Accountability Office no. 13-777, September 2013), http://www.gao.gov/assets/660/657936.pdf. • "**still rated 'effective' or 'highly effective' in 2012–13**" John O'Connor, "2012-2013 Florida Teacher Evaluation Data, By District," *stateimpact.npr.org*, December 3, 2013, https://stateimpact.npr.org/florida/2013/12/03/2012–2013-florida-teacher-evaluation-data-by-district/.

PAGE 46: " 'have been far behind' " Jason Felch, Jason Song, and Doug Smith, "Who's Teaching L.A.'s Kids?" *Los Angeles Times*, August 14, 2010, http://articles.latimes.com/2010/aug/14/local/la-me-teachers-value-20100815.

PAGE 47: " 'approximately 90 percent of the master's degrees' " TNTP, "The Irreplaceables: Understanding the Real Retention Crisis in America's Urban Schools," (report, TNTP, Brooklyn, 2012), http://tntp.org/assets/documents/TNTP_Irreplaceables_2012.pdf. • " 'not solely on seniority and additional degrees' " "Pay Effective Teachers More Money," *studentsfirst.org*, accessed February 1, 2014, http://www.studentsfirst.org/policy-agenda/entry/pay-teachers-substantially-more-for-effectiveness.

PAGE 48: "**develop a 'total merit pay process'** " Tom Gantert, "School District Sees Success Through Merit Pay," *michigancapitolconfidential.com*, August 13, 2013, http://www.michigancapitolconfidential.com/18992.

CHAPTER 8: ONLY PEOPLE WHO GO TO A COLLEGE OF EDUCATION SHOULD BE TEACHERS

PAGE 49: " 'teaching is something anyone can do' " Tim Walker, "Three 'Reforms' That Are Deprofessionalizing Teaching," *neatoday.org*, March 6, 2013, http://neato

day.org/2013/03/06/three-%E2%80%98reforms%E2%80%99-that-are-deprofession
alizing-teaching/.

PAGE 50: " '**requirements for graduation are too low**' " Barbara Nemko and Harold
Kwalwasser, "Why Teacher Colleges Get a Flunking Grade," *The Wall Street Journal,*
October 23, 2013, http://online.wsj.com/news/articles/SB1000142405270230486450
4579143902608329802. • "**Department of Education reports**" U.S. Department of
Education, "The Secretary's Seventh Annual Report On Teacher Quality." *U.S. Department of Education,* September 2010. http://www2.ed.gov/about/reports/annual
/teachprep/t2r7.pdf. • " '**increasing ethnic and socioeconomic student diversity**' "
Associated Press, "Report: U.S. Teacher Training an 'Industry of Mediocrity'," *cbsnews
.com,* June 18, 2013, http://www.cbsnews.com/news/report-us-teacher-training-an
-industry-of-mediocrity/. • "**A recent study by McKinsey reported**" Byron Auguste, Paul Kihn, and Matt Miller, "Education: Closing the Talent Gap: Attracting
and Retaining Top-Third Graduates to Careers in Teaching, An International and
Market Research-Based Perspective," (report, McKinsey & Company, New York,
September 2010), http://mckinseyonsociety.com/downloads/reports/Education/Clos
ing_the_talent_gap.pdf. • " '**we're attracting from the bottom one-third**' " Byron
Auguste, Paul Kihn, and Matt Miller, "Education: Closing the Talent Gap: Attracting and Retaining Top-Third Graduates to Careers in Teaching, An International
and Market Research-Based Perspective," (report, McKinsey & Company, New York,
September 2010), http://mckinseyonsociety.com/downloads/reports/Education/Clos
ing_the_talent_gap.pdf.

PAGE 51: " '**teachers prepared in lower quality programs**' " Arthur Levine, "Educating
School Teachers," (report, Education Schools Project, Washington, D.C., September
18, 2006), http://files.eric.ed.gov/fulltext/ED504135.pdf. • " '**bring in quality that is
also needed**' " Ben DeGrow, "Study: Alternative Teacher Certification Benefits Students," *news.heartland.org,* October 17, 2009, http://news.heartland.org/newspaper
-article/2009/10/17/study-alternative-teacher-certification-benefits-students.

PAGE 52: " '**courses and philosophy do not lead to competent teachers**' " George
Leef, "A Key Reason Why American Students Do Poorly," *Forbes,* October 24,
2013, http://www.forbes.com/sites/georgeleef/2013/10/24/a-key-reason-why-american
-students-do-poorly/. • " '**a downward spiral of falling competence**' " George Leef,
"A Key Reason Why American Students Do Poorly," *Forbes,* October 24, 2013, http://
www.forbes.com/sites/georgeleef/2013/10/24/a-key-reason-why-american-students
-do-poorly/.

PAGE 53: " '**learn how to do the math itself**' " Barbara Nemko and Harold Kwalwasser,
"Why Teacher Colleges Get a Flunking Grade," *The Wall Street Journal,* October 23,
2013, http://online.wsj.com/news/articles/SB10001424052702304864504579143902
608329802.

PAGE 54: " '**heteronormativity, and internalized oppression**' " Carole Grupton, Mary
Beth Kelley, Tim Lensmire, Bic Ngo, and Michael Goh, "Teacher Education Redesign
Initiative," (initiative paper, University of Minnesota, Minneapolis, MN, July 16,
2009, http://thefire.org/public/pdfs/644d7eac9fea37165d1129cb1420163c.pdf?direct.
• " '**based on various theories of social justice**' " K.C. Johnson "Dispositions,
Education Programs, and the Social Justice Requirement: NCATE 2002 Assessment
Guidelines," *cuny.edu,* accessed February 1, 2014, http://academic.brooklyn.cuny.edu
/history/johnson/dispositions.html.

PAGE 55: " '**particularly in an urban environment**' " Sol Stern, "The Ed Schools'
Latest—and Worst—Humbug," *City Journal* 16, no. 3 (Summer 2006), http://www
.city-journal.org/html/16_3_ed_school.html. • " '**direct their lives toward creating**

a just society' " "Teaching Social Justice, Anti-Americanism, & Leftism in the K–12 Classroom," *discoverthenetworks.org,* accessed February 1, 2014, http://www.discover thenetworks.org/viewSubCategory.asp?id=715. • **the 'teaching for social justice' movement"** David Steiner, "Skewed Perspective," *Education Next* 5, no. 1 (Winter 2005), http://educationnext.org/skewedperspective/.

PAGE 56: " '**the creation of classless societies'** " Sol Stern, "Pedagogy of the Oppressor," *City Journal* 19, no. 2 (Spring 2009), http://www.city-journal.org/2009/19_2_freirian -pedagogy.html. • **"the largest group of education school professors and research- ers in the United States"** ed. Omari L. Dyson, Jennifer James, and Teresa Rishel, "American Educational Research Association, Division B: Curriculum Studies," *American Educational Research Association,* Summer 2009, http://legacy.aera.net /uploadedFiles/Divisions/Curriculum_Studies_%28B%29/Newsletters/Summer2009 .pdf. • " '**become agents of social change in K–12 classrooms'** " "Teaching Social Justice, Anti-Americanism, & Leftism in the K–12 Classroom," *discoverthenetworks .org,* accessed February 1, 2014, http://www.discoverthenetworks.org/viewSubCat egory.asp?id=715.

PAGE 57: " '**control of the preparation of public school teachers'** " Eugene W. Hickock, "Higher Standards for Teacher Training," *Policy Review,* no. 91 (September 1, 1998), http://www.hoover.org/publications/policy-review/article/6702. • " '**build- ing a government-enforced monopoly for the purpose of dramatically increasing physician incomes'** " Dale Steinreich, "100 Years of Medical Robbery", mises.org, June 2004. http://mises.org/daily/1547. • " '**significantly restrict entrance to the pro- fession by restricting the number of approved medical schools in operation'** " Dale Steinreich, "100 Years of Medical Robbery," mises.org, June 2004, http://mises.org /daily/1547.

PAGE 58: "**through alternative training programs like TFA"** Associated Press, "Dayton Signs Minnesota Teacher License Bill Into Law," *WCCO Local News,* CBS Minnesota, March 7, 2011, http://minnesota.cbslocal.com/2011/03/07/dayton-to -sign-minn-teacher-license-bill-into-law/. • **"provided TFA with $1.5 million"** Dan Burns, "Dayton Vetoed Teach for America Grant," *tcdailyplanet.net,* May 30, 2013, http://www.tcdailyplanet.net/blog/dan-burns/dayton-vetoed-teach-america-grant. • **"hired TFA teachers with open positions and few other options"** Steve Brandt, "Minnesota Teaching Board Denies Deal for Teach for America," *Star Tribune,* June 14, 2013, http://www.startribune.com/local/minneapolis/211645351.html.

CHAPTER 9: SCHOOL CURRICULUM IS BASED ON A CONSERVATIVE, "WHITES FIRST" WORLD VIEW

PAGE 59: " '**as well as the institutions themselves'** " School Improvement Network, Inc., "The Equity Framework: Schools with No Gaps," (presentation, 2010 CREATE Conference, Green Bay, WI, April 27-28, 2010), http://www.createwisconsin.net /events/2010Conference/1hoursectional/K%20Brown%20Equity%20Framework%20 Intro.pdf.

PAGE 61: " '**I don't think they're aware of the bigger theories behind this'** " Steve Gunn, " 'White Privilege Conference' Reminds Us That Many Teachers Are in the Business of Indoctrination," *eagnews.org,* June 10, 2013, http://eagnews.org /white-privilege-conference-another-reminder-that-many-teachers-work-toward-the -political-indoctrination-of-students/. • **"teacher training offered by companies like Pacific Educational Group (PEG)"** "About Us," *pacificeducationalgroup.com,* accessed February 1, 2014, http://www.pacificeducationalgroup.com/pages/about. • **"learn how to more effectively instruct minority students"** "About," *createwis consin.net,* accessed February 1, 2014, http://www.createwisconsin.net/about/. • **"The**

program costs taxpayers roughly $1 million per year" M.D. Kittle, "Wisconsin Education Program Attacks 'White Privilege' in Classrooms," *watchdog.org*, March 18, 2013, http://watchdog.org/75390/state-education-program-attacks-white-privilege -in-wisconsin-classrooms/. • **"PEG's website listed 185 school districts as clients"** "Clients: School Districts," *pacificeducationalgroup.com*, accessed February 1, 2014, http://www.pacificeducationalgroup.com/pages/clients_districts. • **"state school board associations, and parent-teacher associations"** "Clients: Educational Organizations and Associations," *pacificeducationalgroup.com*, accessed February 1, 2014, http://www.pacificeducationalgroup.com/pages/clients_organizational. • **"taken the theory of 'white privilege' and adapted it to education"** Bill Mullen. *Is there a white skin privilege?* October, 2013. http://socialistworker.org/2013/10/30/is-there-a-white -skin-privilege.

PAGE 62: "There is a huge disparity in overrepresentation, misclassification, and hardship for minority students" "Cultural Considerations in Special Education" (presentation, CREATE Wisconsin, Matt Stewart and Xong Xiong, June 30, 2009), http://www.createwisconsin.net/events/ConferenceHandouts/Tuesday/845am /Matt_and_Xong.pdf. • **"Most American teachers not only do not know how to deal with these students,"** Cultural Considerations in Special Education (presentation, CREATE Wisconsin, Matt Stewart and Xong Xiong, June 30, 2009), http://www .createwisconsin.net/events/ConferenceHandouts/Tuesday/845am/Matt_and_Xong.pdf.

PAGE 63: " 'institutional system supports the dominance of white people' " Karen Ashmore, "Is Your World Too White?" *safehousealliance.org*, http://wp.safehousealliance .org/wp-content/uploads/2012/10/Is-Your-World-Too-White.pdf. • **"More frequently than not"** Karen Ashmore, "Is your World too White?" *safehousealliance.org*, http:// wp.safehousealliance.org/wp-content/uploads/2012/10/Is-Your-World-Too-White.pdf. • **" 'How can you justify it for yourself?' "** Paul Kivel, *Uprooting Racism, How White People Can Work for Racial Justice* (Babriola Island, BC: New Society Publishers, 2002), 46–49, http://www.createwisconsin.net/events/ConferenceHandouts/Tuesday/845am /Costs_of_Racism_to_White_People.pdf. • **" 'making life choices on what will be best for the family' "** Pacific Educational Group, "Courageous Conversation and Courageous Leadership" (presentation, Minneapolis Public Schools, Equity Team Seminar, Minneapolis, MN, February 21, 2008), http://principals.mpls.k12.mn.us/sites /ee869d27–88e5–478a-97e1-b5e41772b8f7/uploads/Feb_21_Powerpoint.pdf.

PAGE 64: " 'shouting out answers or questions' " Cultural Considerations in Special Education (presentation, CREATE Wisconsin, Matt Stewart and Xong Xiong, June 30, 2009), http://www.createwisconsin.net/events/ConferenceHandouts /Tuesday/845am/Matt_and_Xong.pdf. • **" 'children could learn at high levels of expectations' "** School Improvement Network, Inc., "The Equity Framework: Schools with No Gaps" (presentation, 2010 CREATE Conference, Green Bay, WI, April 27–28, 2010), http://www.createwisconsin.net/events/2010Conference/1hoursectional/K%20 Brown%20Equity%20Framework%20Intro.pdf.

PAGE 65: "the University of Northern Iowa and Everett (Wash.) Community College" http://www.whiteprivilegeconference.com/, (archive.org used to find sponsors from previous years). • **" 'maximize the worst part of yourself—greed' "** Steve Gunn, " 'White Privilege Conference' Reminds Us that Many Teachers are in the Business of Indoctrination," *eagnews.org*, June 10, 2013, http://eagnews.org/white -privilege-conference-another-reminder-that-many-teachers-work-toward-the-polit ical-indoctrination-of-students/.

PAGE 66: " 'all other forms of oppression' " "Youth Action Project," *whiteprivilegecon ference.com*, accessed February 1, 2014, http://www.whiteprivilegeconference.com /youth.html.

CHAPTER 10: THE GOVERNMENT EDUCATION SYSTEM CAN'T BE REFORMED UNTIL WE FIRST ERADICATE POVERTY

PAGE 67: " 'toxic combination of poverty and segregation' " Diane Ravitch, "Two Visions for Chicago's Schools," *cityclubvideo.wordpress.com*, video, 49:56, October 15, 2012, http://cityclubvideo.wordpress.com/2012/10/15/diane-ravitch/.

PAGE 69: " 'biggest educational problem of all' " David Sirota, "We Need a War on Poverty, Not Teachers," *Salon,* November 7, 2013, http://www.salon.com/2013/11/07/we _need_a_war_on_poverty_not_teachers/. • " 'math and science within high poverty schools' " Jaela Neal, "Good Teachers Can Make a Big Difference!," *stand.org,* September 12, 2013, http://stand.org/illinois/blog/2013/09/11/good-teachers-can-make-big -difference. • " 'entire math test score distribution' " Dylan Matthews, "Teach for America is a Deeply Divisive Program. It also Works." *Wonk Blog* blog at *washing tonpost.com,* September 10, 2013, http://www.washingtonpost.com/blogs/wonkblog /wp/2013/09/10/teach-for-america-is-a-deeply-divisive-program-it-also-works/.

PAGE 70: " 'inherent condition of the "product" they receive' " Lou Kitchenmaster, "Guest Column: Former Educator Says it's Unfair to Expect High Quality Considering the 'Product' Some Schools Receive," *mlive.com,* April 8, 2013, http://www.mlive.com /opinion/grand-rapids/index.ssf/2013/04/guest_column_former_educator_s.html.

PAGE 71: "American Indian High School ranks *first* among the thirty-three high schools" "Education: Best High Schools: American Indian Public High School," *usnews .com,* accessed February 2, 2014, http://www.usnews.com/education/best-high-schools /california/districts/oakland-unified-school-district/american-indian-public-high-school -2940. • "its college enrollment rate is 77.4 percent, compared to 57 percent for CPS" "Noble Street College Prep," *charterscale.org,* accessed February 2, 2014, http:// charterscale.org/noble-street-college-prep.

PAGE 72: "Lewis, who proudly led twenty-five thousand Chicago teachers on strike in 2012" Noreen S. Ahmed-Ullah, Joel Hood, and Kristen Mack, "Picket Lines Up After CPS, Teachers Fail to Prevent Strike: Walkout is First in 25 Years," *Chicago Tribune,* September 10, 2012, http://articles.chicagotribune.com/2012–09–10/news /chi-chicago-public-schools-chicago-teachers-union-contract-talks-strike_1_picket -lines-teachers-strike-president-david-vitale. • "has blamed everything from poverty" Karen Lewis and Randi Weingarten, "A God Star for the Chicago Teachers Strike," *The Wall Street Journal,* September 23, 2012, http://online.wsj.com/news /articles/SB10000872396390444032404578010731103676940. • "to a lack of funding" William Watkins, "Teachers Continue Fighting for the Children: Interview with Karen Lewis, President, Chicago Teachers' Union," *peoplestribune.org,* January 2013, http://peoplestribune.org/pt-news/2013/01/teachers-continue-fighting-for-the -children-interview-with-karen-lewis-president-chicago-teachers-union/. • "to 'rich white people' " Jessica Chasmar, "Union Boss Karen Lewis Blames 'Rich White People' for Chicago's Education Woes," *Washington Times,* June 19, 2013, http:// www.washingtontimes.com/news/2013/jun/19/union-boss-karen-lewis-blames-rich -white-people-ch/. • " 'They've found ways to work around that' " Rena Havner Phillips, "Calcedeaver Dispels Myth that Poor, Minority Students Can't Learn," *Real-Time News* blog at *al.com,* November 3, 2011, http://blog.al.com/live/2011/11 /calcedeaver_dispels_myth_that.html. • " 'make sure they graduate' " Rena Havner Phillips, "Calcedeaver Dispels Myth that Poor, Minority Students Can't Learn," *Real-Time News* blog at *al.com,* November 3, 2011, http://blog.al.com/live/2011/11 /calcedeaver_dispels_myth_that.html.

PAGE 73: " 'We must do both' " Lynnell Mickelsen, "How I Went from Defending the Teachers Union to Pushing for Reform," *minnpost.com,* October 17, 2013, http://

www.minnpost.com/community-voices/2013/10/how-i-went-defending-teachers-union -pushing-reform.

CHAPTER 11: STATES HAVE FAILED, SO WE NOW NEED NATIONAL STANDARDS; "LOCAL CONTROL" IS JUST A RUSE TO PROTECT MEDIOCRITY

PAGE 74: " 'no longer serving the U.S. well' " Chester E. Finn Jr., "Should All U.S. Students Meet a Single Set of National Proficiency Standards? Yes: It Sets High Expectations," *The Wall Street Journal*, June 22, 2012, http://online.wsj.com/article/SB100014 24052970204603004577269231058863616.html. • "defending mediocrity under the mask of 'local control' " William C. Harrison, "Common Core: 'Local Control' Argument a Guise to Defend Mediocrity," *newsobserver.com*, June 13, 2013, http://www .newsobserver.com/2013/06/13/2961843/common-core-local-control-argument.html.

PAGE 75: "some states have lowered the bar on learning quality and expectations" Paul E. Peterson and Frederick Hess, "Few States Set World-Class Standards," *Education Next* 8, no. 3 (Summer 2008), http://educationnext.org/few-states-set-worldclass -standards/. • "to drive up scores on standardized, fill-in-the-oval state tests" Matthew Ladner, "Anywhere But Here!" *jaypgreene.com*, April 30, 2008, http://jaypgreene .com/2008/04/30/anywhere-but-here/. • "same states had far fewer proficient students" Paul E. Peterson and Frederick Hess, "Few States Set World-Class Standards," *Education Next* 8, no. 3 (Summer 2008), http://educationnext.org/few-states-set-world class-standards/. • "NCLB was the brainchild of George W. Bush and Ted Kennedy" Associated Press, "Promise of No Child Left Behind Falls Short After 10 Years," *USA Today*, January 7, 2012, http://usatoday30.usatoday.com/news/education /story/2012-01-07/no-child-left-behind-anniversary/52430722/1.

PAGE 76: "ensure they win 'bureaucratic approval from the feds' " Jay P. Greene, "Do We Need National Standards to Prevent a Race to the Bottom?" *educationnext .org*, January 17, 2012, http://educationnext.org/do-we-need-national-standards-to -prevent-a-race-to-the-bottom/. • "which concepts to teach kids, grade by grade" "Implementing the Common Core State Standards," *corestandards.org*, accessed February 2, 2014, http://www.corestandards.org/. • " 'be judged by the same mediocre national benchmark' " Michelle Malkin, "Rotten to the Core: Obama's War on Academic Standards (Part 1)," *michellemalkin.com*, January 23, 2013, http://michellemal kin.com/2013/01/23/rotten-to-the-core-obamas-war-on-academic-standards-part-1/.

PAGE 77: " 'achieve the same goals' " J.D. Tuccille, "Common Core Uncommonly Restricts Education Choices," *reason.com*, October 3, 2013, http://reason.com/ar chives/2013/10/03/common-core-uncomonly-restricts-educatio.

PAGE 78: " 'competition for federal government handouts' " Jay P. Greene, "Do We Need National Standards to Prevent a Race to the Bottom?" *educationnext.org*, January 17, 2012, http://educationnext.org/do-we-need-national-standards-to-prevent-a -race-to-the-bottom/.

CHAPTER 12: COMMON CORE IS "STATE LED"

PAGE 79: " 'Council of Chief State School Officers (CCSSO)' " "Common Core State Standards Initiative," *web.archive.org*, accessed February 2, 2014, http://web.archive .org/web/20100305231036/http://www.corestandards.org/. • " 'school boards, school leaders and teachers' " Thomas J. Donohue, "Letter to the Editor: Dispelling Common Core Misconceptions," *Washington Post*, January 17, 2014, http://www.wash ingtonpost.com/opinions/dispelling-common-core-misconceptions/2014/01/17/2b8 ee28a-7ef2-11e3-97d3-b9925ce2c57b_story.html. • " 'That is up to each state' " Jeb

Bush and Joel Klein, "The Case for Common Educational Standards," *The Wall Street Journal,* June 23, 2011, http://online.wsj.com/news/articles/SB1000142405270230407 0104576399532217616502.

PAGE 80: "In 1980, the federal Department of Education opened its doors" "Functions of Department of Education," *education.laws.com,* accessed February 2, 2014, http://education.laws.com/department-of-education.

PAGE 81: " 'either misinformed or willfully misleading' " Press Office, "Duncan Pushes Back on Attacks on Common Core Standards," *ed.gov,* June 25, 2013, http://www.ed.gov/news/speeches/duncan-pushes-back-attacks-common-core-standards.

PAGE 82: " 'a radical proposal into a national agenda' " "About Us," *achieve.org,* accessed February 2, 2014, http://www.achieve.org/about-us. • " 'You never want a serious crisis to go to waste' "** Jim Swift, "Rahm Emanuel: You Never Want a Serious Crisis to Go to Waste," *youtube.com,* February 9, 2009, https://www.youtube.com watch?v=1yeA_kHHLow.

PAGE 83: "state superintendent of public instruction, to adopt the standards" "Evers Unilaterally Approved Common Core Standards," *Wisconsin Daily Independent,* December 12, 2013, http://wisconsindailyindependent.com/evers-unilaterally-approved -common-core-standards/. • **"states to compete for seven-figure education grants"** Adrienne Lu, "Q&A: Common Questions About the Common Core," *huffingtonpost .com,* December 3, 2013, http://www.huffingtonpost.com/2013/12/03/common-core -questions_n_4378643.html. • **"awarded points—40 points out of 500—to states"** Press Office, "Duncan Pushes Back on Attacks on Common Core Standards," *ed.gov,* June 25, 2013, http://www.ed.gov/news/speeches/duncan-pushes-back-attacks-com mon-core-standards. • **"States received 10 points for"** Race to the Top: Technical Review Form, Tier 1, *U.S. Department of Education,* http://www2.ed.gov/programs /racetothetop/technical-review-form.pdf.

PAGE 84: "or other standards that are virtually identical" Press Office, "States Granted Waivers from No Child Left Behind Allowed to Reapply for Renewal for 2014 and 2015 School years," *ed.gov,* August 29, 2013, http://www.ed.gov/news /press-releases/states-granted-waivers-no-child-left-behind-allowed-reapply-renewal -2014-and-201. • " **'tests are aligned to these standards' "** Bill Gates, "Bill Gates— National Conference of State Legislatures," *gatesfoundation.org,* July 21, 2009, http:// www.gatesfoundation.org/media-center/speeches/2009/07/bill-gates-national-conference -of-state-legislatures-ncsl.

PAGE 85: "Kentucky was the first state to adopt Common Core" Scott Wartman, "Ky. Republicans Want to Repeal Common Core," *news.cincinnati.com,* January 17, 2014, http://news.cincinnati.com/article/20140117/NEWS010802/301170078/Ky-Republicans -want-repeal-Common-Core.

PAGE 86: " 'We didn't know who the writers were until the project was complete' " Valerie Strauss, "Former Education Commissioner Blasts Common Core Process— Update," *Answer Sheet* blog at *washingtonpost.com,* February 13, 2013, http://www .washingtonpost.com/blogs/answer-sheet/wp/2013/02/13/former-education-commis sioner-blasts-common-core-process/. • " **'nine unelected individuals' on the Mississippi Board of Education"** Common Core, "Shocking Confession Mississippi Scandal Exposed!" *youtube.com,* November 9, 2013, https://www.youtube.com /watch?v=-xXpmBXkF4o#t=80. • **"the public had no say in the matter"** Jim Stergios, "Common Core is Neither Internationally Benchmarked nor State-Led," *pioneerinsti tute.org,* August 7, 2013, http://pioneerinstitute.org/blog/blog-education/blog-com moncore/common-core-was-neither-internationally-benchmarked-nor-state-led/. • " **'The districts weren't involved' "** Adam O'Neal, "Weingarten: Common Core

Rollout 'Toxic,' " *realclearpolitics.com,* December 4, 2013, http://www.realclearpolitics
.com/articles/2013/12/04/weingarten_common_core_rollout_toxic_120852.html.

PAGE 87: "Common Core–aligned tests administered on computers" The New American Video, "Joy Pullmann on Common Core," *youtube.com,* September 25, 2013, https://www.youtube.com/watch?v=m7WfxJS6iJQ. • **"and funded—by the federal government"** http://www.ed.gov/news/press-releases/us-secretary-education -duncan-announces-winners-competition-improve-student-asse. • **"called this 'de facto federal curricula' "** Trevor Tenbrink, "Resistance to Common Core Grows as Taxpayers Learn How National Standards Could Erode Local Control," *eagnews .org,* May 6, 2013, http://eagnews.org/resistance-to-common-core-grows-as-taxpayers -learn-how-national-standards-could-erode-local-control-of-education/.

PAGE 88: " 'general progressive agenda of centralization and uniformity' " George F. Will, "Doubts over Common Core," *Washington Post,* January 15, 2014, http://www .washingtonpost.com/opinions/george-will-doubts-over-common-core-wont-be-easily -dismissed/2014/01/15/68cecb88–7df3–11e3–93c1–0e888170b723_story.html.

CHAPTER 13: COMMON CORE IS "RIGOROUS"

PAGE 89: " 'set an ambitious and voluntary goal line' " Jeb Bush, "Toward a Better Education System," *nationalreview.com,* August 19, 2013, http://www.nationalreview .com/article/356038/toward-better-education-system-jeb-bush. • **" 'a more rigorous approach' "** "Our View: Common Core is Right Approach," *goerie.com,* August 22, 2013, http://www.goerie.com/article/20130822/OPINION01/308229945/Our -View3A-Common-Core-is-right-approach. • **" 'clear standards as critical to better student results' "** Bill and Melinda Gates Foundation, "Fewer, Clearer, Higher: Moving Forward with Consistent Rigorous Standards for All Students," *gatesfoundation .org,* 2010, accessed February 1, 2014, https://docs.gatesfoundation.org/Documents /fewer-clearer-higher-standards.pdf. • **"these standards are 'rigorous' "** "About the Standards," *corestandards.org,* accessed February 1, 2014, http://www.corestandards .org/about-the-standards. • **"and 'world class' "** "Shaping Rigorous, World-Class Education Standards," *hunt-institute.org,* accessed February 1, 2014, http://www.hunt -institute.org/education-initiatives/shaping-rigorous-world-class-education-standards/.

PAGE 90: "kids will go 'deeper' " "Common Core in Practice: Great Teachers Demonstrate Moving to Deeper Learning," *americaachieves.org,* accessed February 1, 2014, http://www.americaachieves.org/issues/common-core-in-practice-great-teachers-dem onstrate-moving-to-deeper-learning. • **"develop 'critical thinking skills' "** Associated Press, "Common Core Academic Standards Force Teachers to Work on Critical Thinking Over Memorization," *foxnews.com,* December 2, 2013, http://www.foxnews .com/us/2013/12/02/common-core-academic-standards-force-teachers-to-work-on -critical-thinking-over/. • **" 'rapidly changing world of work' "** Oregon Department of Education, "Common Core State Standards: Oregon," *ode.state.org.us,* accessed February 1, 2014, http://www.ode.state.or.us/search/page/?id=3380.

PAGE 91: "create 'college and career ready' students" "Common Core State Standards Initiative Validation Committee Announced," *nga.org,* September 24, 2009, http://www .nga.org/cms/home/news-room/news-releases/page_2009/col2-content/main-content -list/title_common-core-state-standards-initiative-validation-committee-announced .html. • **" 'high-achieving countries give dramatically better results' "** Maggie Gallagher, "Two Moms vs. Common Core," *nationalreview.com,* May 12, 2013, http:// www.nationalreview.com/article/347973/two-moms-vs-common-core. • **"Core is 'not aligned with the expectations at the collegiate level' "** Sarah Carr, "Teachers Feel Urgency of Common Core Standards," *theadvocate.com,* September 4, 2013, http:// theadvocate.com/home/6914390–125/common-core. • **"engineering, or mathematics**

(STEM)" James Milgram and Sandra Stotsky, "Lowering the Bar: How Common Core Math Fails to Prepare Students for STEM," *pioneerinstitute.org,* October 1, 2013, http://pioneerinstitute.org/news/lowering-the-bar-how-common-core-math-fails-to-prepare-students-for-stem/.

PAGE 92: " 'where math education excels' " James Milgram and Sandra Stotsky, "Lowering the Bar: How Common Core Math Fails to Prepare Students for STEM," *pioneerinstitute.org,* October 1, 2013, http://pioneerinstitute.org/news/lowering-the-bar-how-common-core-math-fails-to-prepare-students-for-stem/. • " 'without any mastery of the fundamentals of math' " Michelle Malkin, "Rotten to the Core: Obama's War on Academic Standards (Part 1)," *michellemalkin.com,* January 23, 2013, http://michellemalkin.com/2013/01/23/rotten-to-the-core-obamas-war-on-academic-standards-part-1/.

PAGE 93: " 'How do you know?' " Maggie Gallagher, "Two Moms vs. Common Core," *nationalreview.com,* May 12, 2013, http://www.nationalreview.com/article/347973/two-moms-vs-common-core. • " 'that older people don't know' " "Al Gore: Don't Listen to Your Parents," *wnd.com,* February 5, 2009, http://www.wnd.com/2009/02/88112/. • " 'Common Core standards are not on par' " Ze'ev Wurman and W. Stephen Wilson, "The Common Core Math Standards: Are They a Step Forward or Backward?" *Education News* 12, no. 3 (Summer 2012), http://educationnext.org/the-common-core-math-standards/.

PAGE 94: "best in the nation" "Sandra Stotsky on the Mediocrity of the Common Core ELA Standards," *parentsacrossamerica.org,* April 17, 2011, http://parentsacrossamerica.org/sandra-stotsky-on-the-mediocrity-of-the-common-core-ela-standards/. • "Common Core's focus on 'informational' texts instead of literature" Sandra Stotsky, "Common Core Standards' Devastating Impact on Literary Study and Analytical Thinking," *heritage.org,* December 11, 2012, http://www.heritage.org/research/reports/2012/12/questionable-quality-of-the-common-core-english-language-arts-standards. • "excerpts from a Federal Reserve newsletter" Valerie Strauss, "List: What Common Core Authors Suggest High Schoolers Should Read," *Answer Sheet* blog at *washingtonpost.com,* December 5, 2012, http://www.washingtonpost.com/blogs/answer-sheet/wp/2012/12/05/list-what-common-core-authors-suggest-high-schoolers-should-read/. • "more '*Time* magazine for kids' " Maggie Gallagher, "Two Moms vs. Common Core," *nationalreview.com,* May 12, 2013, http://www.nationalreview.com/article/347973/two-moms-vs-common-core.

PAGE 95: "They're deliberately killing the greatest stories of the greatest nation in history" Terrence O. Moore, "Story-Killers: How the Common Core Destroys Minds and Souls" youtube.com, January 24, 2014, https://www.youtube.com/watch?v=xCoOv_DwaAk. • "present 'informational texts' " Valerie Strauss, "Common Core's Odd Approach to Teaching Gettysburg Address," *Answer Sheet* blog at *washingtonpost.com,* November 19, 2013, http://www.washingtonpost.com/blogs/answer-sheet/wp/2013/11/19/common-cores-odd-approach-to-teaching-gettysburg-address/. • "the only 'experts' who claim that the Common Core standards are of high quality" Jay P. Greene, "My Testimony on National Standards Before U.S. House," *jaypgreene.com,* September 21, 2011, http://jaypgreene.com/2011/09/21/my-testimony-on-national-standards-before-us-house/.

CHAPTER 14: TEACHERS LOVE COMMON CORE

PAGE 97: " 'it'll be the best year I ever taught' " Tim Walker, "10 Things You Should Know About the Common Core," *neatoday.org,* October 16, 2013, http://neatoday.org/2013/10/16/10-things-you-should-know-about-the-common-core/. • " 'support them with "some reservations" (50 percent).' " Tim Walker, "NEA Poll: Majority of

Educators Support the Common Core State Standards," *neatoday.org,* September 12, 2013, http://neatoday.org/2013/09/12/nea-poll-majority-of-educators-support-the -common-core-state-standards/. • " '**right thing to do for our children**' " Allie Bidwell, "Poll: Majority of Teachers Support Common Core," *U.S. News,* September 12, 2013, http://www.usnews.com/news/articles/2013/09/12/poll-majority-of -teachers-support-common-core.

PAGE 98: " '**teach "the standard" or teach the kids**' " Mark Bertin, "When Will We Ever Learn: Dissecting the Common Core State Standards with Dr. Louisa Moats," *huffingtonpost.com,* January 22, 2014, http://www.huffingtonpost.com/mark-bertin -md/when-will-we-ever-learn_b_4588033.html. • " '**new teacher evaluation program will become extinct**' " Elizabeth A. Natale, "Why I Want to Give Up Teaching," *Hartford Courant,* January 17, 2014, http://www.courant.com/news/opinion/hc-op -natale-teacher-ready-to-quit-over-common-cor-20140117,0,6264603.story.

PAGE 99: " '**roughly two-thirds' of teachers**" Tim Walker, "NEA Poll: Majority of Educators Support the Common Core State Standards," *neatoday.org,* September 12, 2013, http://neatoday.org/2013/09/12/nea-poll-majority-of-educators-support-the -common-core-state-standards/.

CHAPTER 15: ALL THIS ANTI–COMMON CORE TALK IS JUST ANOTHER CONSPIRACY THEORY FROM PEOPLE WHO OBVIOUSLY HATE THE PRESIDENT

PAGE 100: " '**Solutions are hard work**' " Ron Matus, "Jeb Bush to Common Core Critics: Drop the Conspiracy Theories," *redefinedonline.org,* October 17, 2013, http:// www.redefinedonline.org/2013/10/jeb-bush-common-core-critics-drop-conspiracy -theories/. • " '**No wonder they don't like it**' " Ron Matus, "Jeb Bush to Common Core Critics: Drop the Conspiracy Theories," *redefinedonline.org,* October 17, 2013, http://www.redefinedonline.org/2013/10/jeb-bush-common-core-criticsdrop -conspiracytheories/. • " '**they have widespread bipartisan support**' " Press Office, "Statement by U.S. Secretary of Education Arne Duncan," *ed.gov,* February 23, 2012, http://www.ed.gov/news/press-releases/statement-us-secretary-education-arne-duncan-1.

PAGE 101: " '**Common Core would not lead to a surrender of local control**' " Maggie Gallagher, "Two Moms vs. Common Core," *nationalreview.com,* May 12, 2013, http:// www.nationalreview.com/article/347973/two-moms-vs-common-core/page/0/1.

PAGE 102: " '**new state assessment tests are going to use these standards**' " Maggie Gallagher, "Two Moms vs. Common Core," *nationalreview.com,* May 12, 2013, http:// www.nationalreview.com/article/347973/two-moms-vs-common-core. • **the highly acclaimed 'Indiana Statewide Testing for Educational Progress**' " Maggie Gallagher, "Two Moms vs. Common Core," *nationalreview.com,* May 12, 2013, http:// www.nationalreview.com/article/347973/two-moms-vs-common-core. • " '**need to worry about** *Ulysses*' " Gerard V. Bradley, "Gerard V. Bradley Letter to Each Catholic Bishop in the United States," files.meetup.com, October 16, 2013, http://files.meetup .com/1387375/Letter%20to%20Catholic%20Bishops%20on%20the%20Common%20 Core%20F.pdf.

PAGE 103: " '**teach the same basic curriculum the same basic way?**' " Maggie Gallagher, "Two Moms vs. Common Core," *nationalreview.com,* May 12, 2013, http:// www.nationalreview.com/article/347973/two-moms-vs-common-core. • " '**The commands of government officials must be obeyed by all**" Perry Chiaramonte, "Common Core lessons blasted for sneaking politics into elementary classrooms," *foxnews .com,* November 10, 2014, http://www.foxnews.com/us/2013/11/10/common-core -lessons-blasted-for-sneaking-politics-into-elementary-classrooms/.

CHAPTER 16: WE NEED BETTER DATA COLLECTION TO HELP US BETTER
EDUCATE OUR KIDS

PAGE 104: " 'great teachers to their schools of education' " Arne Duncan, "Robust
Data Gives Us the Roadmap to Reform," ed.gov, June 8, 2009, http://www.ed.gov
/news/speeches/robust-data-gives-us-roadmap-reform.

PAGE 105: " 'even hundreds, of discrete skills' " Stephanie Simon, "K-12 Student Da-
tabase Jazzes Tech Startups, Spooks Parents," *reuters.com,* March 3, 2013, http://www
.reuters.com/article/2013/03/03/us-education-database-idUSBRE92204W20130303
?irpc=932.

PAGE 106: " 'treating teachers as less than professionals' " Elizabeth A. Natale,
"Why I Want to Give Up Teaching," *Hartford Courant,* January 17, 2014, http://
www.courant.com/news/opinion/hc-op-natale-teacher-ready-to-quit-over-common
-cor-20140117,0,6264603.story.

PAGE 107: "obsessed with using data to make decisions" Tim Murphy, "Inside the
Obama Campaign's Hard Drive," *Mother Jones,* September/October 2012, http://
www.motherjones.com/politics/2012/10/harper-reed-obama-campaign-microtarget-
ing. • " 'deep believer' in data-driven policies" Arne Duncan, *"Robust Data Gives
Us the Roadmap to Reform,"* ed.gov, June 8, 2009, http://www.ed.gov/news/speeches
/robust-data-gives-us-roadmap-reform. • "creation of longitudinal data systems"
Jennifer Cohen, "State Education Data Systems and the Stimulus," *The Ed Money
Watch Blog* at *New America Foundation,* March 26, 2009, http://nces.ed.gov/pro
grams/slds/grant_information.asp.

PAGE 108: "following the 2008 economic crash" U.S. Department of Education, *Race
to the Top Program: Executive Summary,* 111th Cong., 1st sess., http://www2.ed.gov
/programs/racetothetop/executive-summary.pdf. • " 'continue building such systems independently' " U.S. Department of Education, *Race to the Top Program: Executive Summary,* 111th Cong., 1st sess., http://www2.ed.gov/programs/racetothetop
/executive-summary.pdf. • "family's income and voting status" "National Education
Data Model: Student Elementary Secondary," *nces.ed.gov,* accessed February 4, 2014,
http://nces.ed.gov/forum/datamodel/eiebrowser/techview.aspx?instance=studentEle
mentarySecondary. • "track how much students work on the weekends" "National
Education Data Model: Students—Postsecondary," *nces.ed.gov,* accessed February 4,
2014, http://nces.ed.gov/forum/datamodel/eiebrowser/techview.aspx?instance=stud
entPostsecondary.

PAGE 109: "individual states to decide which data points to track" Ben Velderman,
"Medical Laboratory Procedure Results and Religion: Invasive Common Core Data
Mining Worries Parents," *eagnews.org,* May 13, 2014, http://eagnews.org/medical-lab
oratory-procedure-results-and-religion-invasive-common-core-data-mining-worries
-parents/. • "release student records to third-party organizations *without parental
consent*" "December 2011-Revised FERPA Regulations: An Overview for Parents
and Students," *www2.ed.gov,* December 2011, http://www2.ed.gov/policy/gen/guid
fpco/pdf/parentoverview.pdf. • " 'information on free lunch plans' " "Matthew
Calicchio, of Holbrook, Accused of Hacking Sachem S.D. Records and Posting Info
Online," *News 12 Long Island,* News 12 Interactive LLC, November 23, 2013, http://long
island.news12.com/news/matthew-calicchio-of-holbrook-accused-of-hacking-sachem
-s-d-records-and-posting-info-online-1.6485044.

PAGE 110: " 'internal controls needed to secure it' " Jim Ragsdale, "Audit Questions Minnesota Education Department Computer Security," *Star Tribune,* August 30, 2013, http://www.startribune.com/politics/statelocal/221881331.html. • " 'Or
bored?' " Randy Rieland, "Can Facial Recognition Really Tell if a Kid Is Learning in

Class?" *Smithsonian Magazine,* November 1, 2013, http://www.smithsonianmag.com
/innovation/can-facial-recognition-really-tell-if-a-kid-is-learning-in-class-8163550/.

PAGE 111: " 'which kids are tuned in and which are zoned out' " Stephanie
Simon, "Biosensors to Monitor U.S. Students' Attentiveness," *reuters.com,* June 13,
2012, http://www.reuters.com/article/2012/06/13/us-usa-education-gates-idUS
BRE85C17Z20120613. • " 'we were trying to be innovative' " "Polk County School
District Delays Eye Scanning of Bus Riding Students After parent Notification Error,"
10 News, CBS, May 31, 2013, http://www.wtsp.com/news/local/article/319369/8/Polk
-School-District-delays-eye-scanning-of-bus-riding-students.

PAGE 112: "the university sold its program, Degree Compass, to Desire2Learn" Jake
New, "Desire2Learn Acquires Course—Suggestion Software Inspired by Netflix and
Amazon," *Wired Campus* blog at *chronicle.com,* January 24, 2013, http://chronicle
.com/blogs/wiredcampus/desire2learn-acquires-course-suggestion-software-inspired-by
-netflix-and-amazon/41831. • " '**Tough Choices or Tough Times**' " "Tough Choices
or Tough Times State Consortium Publications," *ncee.org,* accessed February 1, 2014,
http://www.ncee.org/publications/archived-publications/tough-choices-or-tough-times
-state-consortium-publications/.

PAGE 113: "standards and the technology are all in place" Alan Singer, "Protest Builds
Against Pearson, Testing, and Common Core," *huffingtonpost.com,* June 13, 2012,
http://www.huffingtonpost.com/alan-singer/protest-builds-against-pe_b_1586573
.html. • " '**career projection' and 'college projection**' " Pearson North America, "A
Vision for Personalized and Connected Learning," *youtube.com,* January 28, 2013,
http://www.youtube.com/watch?v=ZpQCEgEfRyc#t=331. • " '**national system of academic achievement standards for students**' " "History of NCEE," *ncee.org,* accessed
February 1, 2014, http://www.ncee.org/about-ncee/history-of-ncee/.

PAGE 114: " 'try again at the end of their 11th and 12th grades' " Sam Dillon, "High
Schools to Offer Plan to Graduate 2 Years Early," *New York Times,* February 17,
2010, http://www.nytimes.com/2010/02/18/education/18educ.html?_r=1&. • " '**high
school graduates who need remedial courses when they enroll in college**' " Sam
Dillon, "High Schools to Offer Plan to Graduate 2 Years Early," *New York Times,*
February 17, 2010, http://www.nytimes.com/2010/02/18/education/18educ.html.
• "**estimated that K-12 education is a $500 billion industry in the U.S. alone**"
Anna Phillips, "Murdoch Buys Education Tech Company Wireless Generation,"
ny.chalkbeat.org, November 22, 2010, http://ny.chalkbeat.org/2010/11/22/murdoch
-buys-education-tech-company-wireless-generation/. • "**Common Core isn't actually 'state led,' it's 'Gates led**' " Mercedes Schneider, "A Brief Audit of Bill Gates'
Common Core Spending," *huffingtonpost.com,* August 29, 2013, http://www.huffing
tonpost.com/mercedes-schneider/a-brief-audit-of-bill-gat_b_3837421.html.

PAGE 115: " 'galvanic skin response measurements' " Stephanie Simon, "Biosensors
to Monitor U.S. Students' Attentiveness," *reuters.com,* June 13, 2012, http://www.reuters
.com/article/2012/06/13/us-usa-education-gates-idUSBRE85C17Z20120613. • " '**need
universal, valid, reliable and practical instruments**' " Stephanie Simon, "Biosensors to Monitor U.S. Students' Attentiveness," *reuters.com,* June 13, 2012, http://www
.reuters.com/article/2012/06/13/us-usa-education-gates-idUSBRE85C17Z20120613.
• " '**Measures of Effective Teaching**' " Stephanie Simon, "Biosensors to Monitor
U.S. Students' Attentiveness," *reuters.com,* June 13, 2012, http://www.reuters.com
/article/2012/06/13/us-usa-education-gates-idUSBRE85C17Z20120613.

PAGE 116: " 'the type of change that many believe cannot be accomplished' "
Cathlyn Dossetti, "Real Success with the Common Core Will Require Some Fail-

ure," *impatientoptimists.org,* February 18, 2013, http://www.impatientoptimists.org
/Posts/2013/02/Real-Success-With-The-Common-Core-Will-Require-Some-Failure.

**CHAPTER 17: GIVEN THE RISING OBESITY EPIDEMIC, THE FEDERAL
GOVERNMENT MUST SET STRICT STANDARDS FOR IN-SCHOOL MEALS
AND PROVIDE FREE BREAKFAST AND LUNCH DAILY**

PAGE 117: " 'government gets to decide what's for lunch' " Ayala Laufer-Cahana,
"School Lunch: Should the Government Be Feeding Schoolchildren Lunch? (Debate),"
huffingtonpost.com, December 20, 2012, http://www.huffingtonpost.com/2012/12/20
/school-lunch-project_n_2340259.html. • " 'It is possible to create this world!' " Ta-
batha James, "First Lady Gives Tough Love to Parents," *examiner.com,* March 11, 2013,
http://www.examiner.com/article/first-lady-gives-tough-love-to-parents. • " 'we're
going to have to move into a different place as a nation' " BarackObamadotcom,
"Michelle Obama in Puerto Rico," *youtube.com,* May 28, 2008, http://www.youtube.com
/watch?v=afGz0dzVSIU.

PAGE 118: "Citing an obesity 'epidemic' " Daniel J. DeNoon, "Michelle Obama's Plan
to End Childhood Obesity Epidemic," *webmd.com,* May 11, 2010, http://www.webmd
.com/children/news/20100511/michelle-obama-plan-to-end-child-obesity-epidemic.
• " 'Healthy Hunger-Free Kids Act of 2010' " United States Department of Agriculture, Food and Nutrition Service, "Healthy Hunger-Free Kids Act of 2010," *fns.usda
.gov,* accessed February 5, 2014, http://www.fns.usda.gov/cnd/Governance/Legisla
tion/CNR_2010.htm. • "banning brown bag lunches from home" Monica Eng and
Joel Hood, "Chicago School Bans Some Lunches Brought From Home," *Chicago Tribune,* April 11, 2011, http://articles.chicagotribune.com/2011–04–11/news/ct-met-school
-lunch-restrictions-041120110410_1_lunch-food-provider-public-school. • " 'physician's note to that regard' " Trisha Haas, "What the Wha??" *momdot.com,* accessed
February 5, 2014, http://www.momdot.com/a-doctors-note-for-gmos/. • " 'dramatic
step toward reducing childhood obesity' " White House, Office of the Press Secretary, "President Obama Signs Healthy, Hunger-Free Kids Act of 2010 into Law," press
release, December 13, 2010, http://www.whitehouse.gov/the-press-office/2010/12/13
/president-obama-signs-healthy-hunger-free-kids-act-2010-law.

PAGE 119: " 'make them healthier and more productive' " White House, Office
of the Press Secretary, "President Obama Signs Healthy, Hunger-Free Kids Act of
2010 into Law," press release, December 13, 2010, http://www.whitehouse.gov/the
-press-office/2010/12/13/president-obama-signs-healthy-hunger-free-kids-act-2010-law.
• " 'They say it tastes like vomit' " Cheryl K. Chumley, "Kentucky Kids to First Lady
Michelle Obama: Your Foods 'Tastes Like Vomit,' " *Washington Times,* August 28, 2013,
http://www.washingtontimes.com/news/2013/aug/28/kentucky-kids-first-lady-your-food
-tastes-vomit/.

PAGE 120: " 'they are not getting a proper meal' " Erich Schaffhauser, "Students Trash
Veggies Rather Than Eat Them," *keloland.com,* September 18, 2012, http://www.kelo
land.com/newsdetail.cfm?id=137345. • "increase in the amount of food going into
the garbage" Noelle McGee, "Catlin Leaving Federal School Lunch Program," *East
Central Illinois News-Gazette,* June 19, 2013, http://www.news-gazette.com/news
/local/2013–06–19/catlin-leaving-federal-school-lunch-program.html. • " 'some lack
of attentiveness' " Associated Press, "Some Schools Opt Out of Gov't-Subsidized
Lunch Program with Healthier Menu," *cbsnews.com,* August 27, 2013, http://www
.cbsnews.com/news/some-schools-opt-out-of-govt-subsidized-lunch-program-with
-healthier-menu/. • " 'rejected the menu changes and stopped purchasing school
meals' " Jessica Chasmar, "Indiana School District Loses $300K Because Students Re-
fuse to Buy First Lady's Healthy Meals," *Washington Times,* July 11, 2013, http://www

.washingtontimes.com/news/2013/jul/11/indiana-school-district-loses-300k-because-student/. • " 'losing about $100,000 in food sales in one school year' " "Burnt Hills-Ballston Lake Schools Leave National Lunch Program," *news10.com*, July 10, 2013, http://www.news10.com/story/22804698/burnt-hills-ballston-lake-schools-leave-national-lunch-program. • "scathing report in 2013 about the many problems with the program" United States Government Accountability Office, "School Lunch: Modifications Needed to Some of the New Nutrition Standards" (report, Government Accountability Office no. 13–708T, June 27, 2013), http://www.gao.gov/assets/660/655543.pdf.

PAGE 122: " 'not eating all the food that's being offered' " "Students Choose to Go Hungry Rather Than Eat Healthy School Lunches," *foxnewsinsider.com*, September 26, 2012, http://foxnewsinsider.com/2012/09/26/students-hungry-eat-healthy-school-lunches. • " 'we're capable of making in this country' " Emily Goodin, "Michelle Obama Takes Credit for 'Cultural Shift' in U.S. Eating Habits," *thehill.com*, September 6, 2013, http://thehill.com/capital-living/320775-michelle-obama-takes-credit-for-cultural-shift-in-us-eating-habits. • " 'It is possible to create this world!' " White House, Office of the Press Secretary, "Remarks by the First Lady to the Partnership for a Healthier America Summit," press release, March 8, 2013, http://www.whitehouse.gov/the-press-office/2013/03/08/remarks-first-lady-partnership-healthier-america-summit.

PAGE 123: "11.3 million (47.2 percent) getting fed for free or at a subsidized price" United States Department of Agriculture, Food and Nutrition Service, "National School Lunch Program: Participation and Lunches Served," *fns.usda.gov*, January 10, 2014, http://www.fns.usda.gov/pd/slsummar.htm. • "21.5 million of them (70.5 percent) got them for free or at a reduced price" United States Department of Agriculture, Food and Nutrition Service, "National School Lunch Program: Participation and Lunches Served," *fns.usda.gov*, January 10, 2014, http://www.fns.usda.gov/pd/slsummar.htm.

PAGE 124: " 'limiting their weekday television viewing time' " "Family Meals, Adequate Sleep, and Limited TV May Lower Childhood Obesity," *researchnews.osu.edu*, February 8, 2010, http://researchnews.osu.edu/archive/homeroutines.htm. • "government might finally stop categorizing french fries as 'vegetables' " On Air with Ryan Seacrest, "French Fry, Vegetable? Jamie Oliver's Food Revolution: Promo Clip," *youtube.com*, March 1, 2010, http://www.youtube.com/watch?v=q1BOGmBKeAc.

CHAPTER 18: SCHOOL SHOULD TEACH STUDENTS ABOUT SEXUALITY BECAUSE PARETS DON'T

PAGE 125: " 'delude themselves into believing' " Roland Martin, "Sex Education Should Be Mandatory in All Schools," *cnn.com*, October 29, 2011, http://www.cnn.com/2011/10/29/opinion/martin-sex-education. • " 'engaged in conversations about contraception and sexual education' " "New York City Public Schools Offering 'Morning-After Pill,' " *newyork.cbslocal.com*, September 23, 2012, http://newyork.cbslocal.com/2012/09/23/new-york-city-public-schools-offering-morning-after-pill/. • " 'provide age-appropriate sex education, science-based sex education in schools' " Terence P. Jeffrey, "Obama: Sex Ed for Kindergartners 'Is the Right Thing to Do,' " *cnsnews.com*, August 30, 2013, http://cnsnews.com/news/article/obama-sex-ed-kindergartners-right-thing-do.

PAGE 127: " 'orgasms need to be taught in education' " Lauren Funk, "Schools Need to Teach Orgasms Say U.S. Teachers to U.N.," *c-fam.org*, July 7, 2011, http://c-fam.org/en/2011/6853-schools-need-to-teach-orgasms-say-us-teachers-to-un. • " 'STD testing and abortion' " Paul Rondeau, "Obamacare Funnels $75 Million to Planned Parenthood to Push Sex on Kids," *lifenews.com*, March 27, 2013, http://www.lifenews

.com/2013/03/27/obamacare-funnels-75-million-to-planned-parenthood-to-push-sex-on-kids/. • " 'put their mouths down on the vaginas' " Billy Hallowell, " 'Raping Their Innocence': Parents Outraged After School Principal Allegedly Teaches 5th Graders About Oral and Anal Sex," *theblaze.com*, June 14, 2012, http://www.theblaze.com/stories/2012/06/14/raping-their-innocence-parents-outraged-after-school-principal-allegedly-teaches5th-graders-about-oral-anal-sex/. • "was distributing free condoms to students" Carol Kuruvilla, "22 Philadelphia High Schools to Distribute Free Condoms," *New York Daily News*, December 26, 2012 updated December 27, 2012, http://www.nydailynews.com/life-style/health/22-philly-schools-offer-free-condoms-article-1.1227641.

PAGE 128: "three-tenths of one percent of Americans self-identifying as 'transgendered' " Gary J. Gates, "How Many People are Lesbian, Gay, Bisexual, and Transgender?" (report, Williams Institute, University of California, Los Angeles, School of Law, April 2011), http://williamsinstitute.law.ucla.edu/wp-content/uploads/Gates-How-Many-People-LGBT-Apr-2011.pdf. • "provides *all* students with tips on how to 'come out' as transgendered to their parents" "Answer: Sex Ed, Honestly," *answer.rutgers.edu*, accessed February 5, 2014, https://answer.rutgers.edu/product/16. • " 'strategic plan for sexuality education policy and implementation' " "National Sexuality Education Standards: Core Content and Skills, K–12" (report, Future of Sex Education, 2011), http://www.futureofsexeducation.org/documents/josh-fose-standards-web.pdf.

PAGE 130: "In the fall of 2010, McDowell took part in a school observance of 'anti-bullying day' " Associated Press, "Michigan Teacher Suspended Over Anti-Gay Punishment," *USA Today*, November 16, 2010, http://usatoday30.usatoday.com/news/nation/2010-11-16-michigan-teacher-suspended-gay_N.htm. • "violated the student's First Amendment right" "Student Booted from Class for Saying 'I Don't Accept Gays' Wins Federal Lawsuit," *news.yahoo.com*, June 24, 2013, http://news.yahoo.com/student-booted-class-saying-don-t-accept-gays-123034366.html.

PAGE 131: " 'learn how to live' " meaonline, "Jay McDowell—Michigan Education Association's Herman W. Coleman Award Recipient," *youtube.com*, May2, 2012, https://www.youtube.com/watch?v=etuo3HNwadY.

PAGE 132: " 'if we simply punish it severely enough is delusional' " Betsy Karasik, "The Unintended Consequences of Laws Addressing Sex Between Teachers and Students," *Washington Post*, August 30, 2013, http://www.washingtonpost.com/opinions/sex-between-students-and-teachers-should-not-be-a-crime/2013/08/30/dbf7dcca-1107-11e3-b4cb-fd7ce041d814_story.html. • "1962 Supreme Court decision that ended teacher-led prayer in public schools" "What Happened When the Praying Stopped," *forerunner.com*, April 6, 2008, http://www.forerunner.com/forerunner/X0124_When_America_stopped.html.

CHAPTER 19: SCHOOLS SHOULD BE THE CENTER OF THE COMMUNITY, OPEN TWELVE HOURS A DAY, SEVEN DAYS A WEEK

PAGE 133: " 'most successful schools of the future will be integrated learning communities' " Richard W. Riley. "Schools as Centers of Community." *Ed.gov*, April 2000. http://www2.ed.gov/offices/OESE/archives/inits/construction/commguide.pdf. • " 'serve children from age three months old to age 18' " TheBloomergal, "1989 Governors Conference—Lamar Alexander," *youtube.com*, May 3, 2011, https://www.youtube.com/watch?v=SVWDNvJ03FY.

PAGE 134: "The American divorce rate is at a record high" Rick Montgomery, "Baby Boomer Couples are Divorcing at Record Rate," *mcclatchydc.com*, April 2, 2012, http://www.mcclatchydc.com/2012/04/02/143841/baby-boomer-couples-are-divorcing.html.

PAGE 135: " 'twice as likely to repeat a grade in school' " "Statistics on Father Absence," *Father Factor* blog at *fatherhood.org,* accessed February 6, 2014, http://blog .fatherhood.org/statistics-on-father-absence-download/. • " 'and the answer to that is in schools' " "De Blasio: Keeping New York City schools open was right decision," *WABC,* February 14, 2014, http://abclocal.go.com/wabc/story?id=9429997.

PAGE 136: "free 'after school dinner' for kids in six Camden schools" Phil Davis, "Gov. Christie, Camden Superintendent Tout New After-School Dinner Program," *nj.com,* January 23, 2014, http://www.nj.com/camden/index.ssf/2014/01/gov_christie _camden_superintendent_tout_new_after_school_dinner_program.html.

PAGE 137: " 'included child care and dental, medical and counseling clinics' " Sam Dillon, "New Vision for Schools Proposes Broad Role," *New York Times,* July 14, 2008, http://www.nytimes.com/2008/07/14/education/14teachers.html. • " 'particularly in disadvantaged communities' " "Secretary Duncan: Schools Must Become Centers of Communities," *PBS NewsHour,* PBS, December 7, 2010, http://www.pbs.org/news hour/bb/education-july-dec10-duncan_12–07/.

PAGE 138: "soared from 35,451 to 44,672 between 2011–12 and 2012–13" "Secretary Duncan: Schools Must Become Centers of Communities," *PBS NewsHour,* PBS, December 7, 2010, http://www.pbs.org/newshour/bb/education-july-dec10 -duncan_12–07/. • "Texas now spends about $227 million annually" "Texas Public School Districts Spent $227 Million on Disciplinary Problems, School Security: Study," *huffingtonpost.com,* October 30, 2012, http://www.huffingtonpost.com/2012/10/30 /texas-public-school-distr_n_2043787.html.

PAGE 139: " 'Great Society relic has failed to improve academic outcomes' " Lindsey Burke and David B. Muhlhausen, "Head Start Impact Evaluation Report Finally Released," *heritage.org,* January 10, 2013, http://www.heritage.org /research/reports/2013/01/head-start-impact-evaluation-report-finally-released. • " 'federal government funds preschool for all' " Grover J. Whitehurst, "New Evidence Raises Doubts on Obama's Preschool for All," *Brown Center Chalkboard* blog at *brookings.edu,* November 20, 2013, http://www.brookings.edu/blogs/brown-center -chalkboard/posts/2013/11/20-evidence-raises-doubts-about-obamas-preschool-for -all-whitehurst.

CHAPTER 20: HOME-SCHOOLING IS HURTING OUR PUBLIC SCHOOLS AND IS BAD FOR THE COLLECTIVE

PAGE 140: " 'make it harder for less-advantaged children to thrive' " Dana Goldstein, "Liberals, Don't Homeschool Your Kids," *slate.com,* February 16, 2012, http:// www.slate.com/articles/double_x/doublex/2012/02/homeschooling_and_unschool ing_among_liberals_and_progressives_.html. • " 'as a collective and as individuals' " Don McFadden, "Abolishing Home and Private Schools: An Elitist's Dream for the Proletariat," *forcedschool.com,* accessed February 6, 2014, http://www.forced school.com/post/20301664064/abolishing-home-and-private-schools-an-elitists -dream.

PAGE 141: " 'chosen education as their life's work' " OEA, "Homeschooling Parents in Monroe," *Voice* forum at *mainstreetmonroe.com,* May 2, 2011, http://www.main streetmonroe.com/voice/topic.asp?TOPIC_ID=22899. • " 'curriculum approved by the state department of education' " Anne Hendershott, "Homeschooling: Under Fire at Home and Abroad," *catholicworldreport.com,* September 18, 2013, http://www .catholicworldreport.com/Item/2579/homeschooling_under_fire_at_home_and_abroad .aspx#.UvVWHmSwLF-. • " 'Most disturbing is the virulent strain of religious fundamentalism' " Steve Shives, "Homeschoolers Who Don't Learn Science Shouldn't

Receive a Diploma," *voices.yahoo.com,* April 8, 2008, http://voices.yahoo.com/home schoolers-dont-learn-science-shouldnt-receive-1362743.html?cat=9.

PAGE 142: **"number of home-schooled students jumped 70 percent between 1999 and 2007"** National Center for Education Statistics, "Fast Facts," *nces.ed.gov,* accessed February 6, 2014, https://nces.ed.gov/fastfacts/display.asp?id=91. • **" 'You didn't build that' "** White House, Office of the Press Secretary, "Remarks by the President at a Campaign Event in Roanoke, Virginia," press release, July 13, 2012, http://www.whitehouse.gov/the-press-office/2012/07/13/remarks-president-campaign-event-roa noke-virginia.

PAGE 143: **" 'then we start making better investments' "** Michael James, "MSNBC: We Have to Break Through This Idea 'That Kids Belong to Their Parents,'" *cnsnews .com,* April 8, 2013, http://cnsnews.com/news/article/msnbc-we-have-break-through -idea-kids-belong-their-parents. • **" 'the eventual common good' "** Allison Benedikt, "If You Send Your Kid to Private School, You Are a Bad Person," *slate.com,* August 29, 2013, http://www.slate.com/articles/double_x/doublex/2013/08/private_school _vs_public_school_only_bad_people_send_their_kids_to_private.html. • **" 'serve the common good in a vibrant democracy' "** Chris Lubienski, "Whither the Common Good? A Critique of Home Schooling," *Peabody Journal of Education* 75, no. 1 and 2 (April 2000), 207-232, http://www.tandfonline.com/doi/abs/10.1080/0161956X.2000 .9681942#preview.

CHAPTER 21: HOME-SCHOOLERS ARE ACADEMICALLY INFERIOR TO PUBLIC SCHOOL STUDENTS

PAGE 145: **" 'biased and unrepresentative sample of home schoolers' "** Rob Reich, "More Oversight Is Needed," *New York Times,* January 5, 2011, http://www .nytimes.com/roomfordebate/2011/01/04/do-home-schoolers-deserve-a-tax-break /more-oversight-is-needed. • **" 'There is no credible evidence of accomplishment here at all' "** Robin L. West, "The Harms of Homeschooling," *Philosophy and Public Policy Quarterly* 29, no. 3 and 4 (Summer and Fall 2009), http://ippp.gmu.edu/QQ /Vol29_3-4.pdf.

PAGE 146: **" 'scored at the 50th percentile in each subject area' "** "Home-Schooling: Outstanding Results on National Tests," *Washington Times,* August 30, 2009, http:// www.washingtontimes.com/news/2009/aug/30/home-schooling-outstanding-results -national-tests/#ixzz2r9naVr4g. • **" '66.7 percent compared to 57.5 percent' "** Kelsey Sheehy, "Homeschooled Students Well-Prepared For College, Study Finds," *huffingtonpost.com,* June 1, 2012, http://www.huffingtonpost.com/2012/06/01/home schooled-students-wel_n_1562425.html?page=1.

PAGE 147: **"almost half a year ahead in math"** Gwen Dewar, "Homeschooling Outcomes: How do they compare?", *parentingscience.com,* September 2011. http://www .parentingscience.com/homeschooling-outcomes.html.

CHAPTER 22: EVEN IF HOME-SCHOOLED KIDS DO OKAY ACADEMICALLY, THEY SUFFER SOCIALLY BY NOT BEING AT SCHOOL

PAGE 148: **" 'are not well socialized' "** Lana Hope, "It's True: Homeschoolers Are Often Not Socialized," *wideopenground.com,* December 18, 2012, http://www.wideopen ground.com/homeschool-socialization-problem/. • **" 'They learn to be scared of other children' "** sbdivemaster, "Behar on Homeschooling," *youtube.com,* November 20, 2008, http://www.youtube.com/watch?v=8gq9yefHhhI. • **" 'stay home with mom and dad . . .' "** OEA, "Homeschooling Parents in Monroe," *Voice* forum at *mainstreetmonroe.com,* May 2, 2011, http://www.mainstreetmonroe.com/voice/topic .asp?TOPIC_ID=22899.

PAGE 149: " 'homeschool students have as their role models, adults' " Bridget Bentz Sizer, "Socialization: Tackling Homeschooling's 'S' Word," *Parents* at *pbs.org,* accessed February 7, 2014, http://www.pbs.org/parents/education/homeschooling/socializa tion-tackling-homeschoolings-s-word/.

PAGE 150: " 'destructive social skills contribute to negative socialization' " Scott Turnansky, "Social Development and the Homeschooled Child," *homeschool-life .com,* accessed February 7, 2014, https://www.homeschool-life.com/sysfiles/member /custom_public/custom.cfm?memberid=475&customid=4446.

CHAPTER 23: BUT WHAT ARE THESE PARENTS TEACHING THEIR KIDS AT HOME? WE NEED MORE STATE MONITORING TO MAKE SURE IT'S NOT ALL CRAZY CHRISTIAN BIBLE STUFF

PAGE 151: " 'application of any particular educational standards' " "The Third Wave of Homeschool Persecution," *HSLDA: Advocates for Homeschooling Since 1983* XXVI, no. 6 (November/December 2010), http://www.hslda.org/courtreport/V26N6 /V26N601.asp.

PAGE 152: " 'increasing number of educators are motivated to take up the challenge' " Eds. Rob Linné, Leigh Benin, and Adrienne Sosin, "Organinzing the Curriculum: Perspectives on Teaching the US Labor Movement" (report, Sense Publishers, Rotterdam, Netherlands, 2009), https://www.sensepublishers.com/media/733-or ganizing-the-curriculum.pdf. • " 'denigrates poor and working families' " Kyle Olson, *Indoctrination: How 'Useful Idiots' Are Using Our Schools to Subvert American Exceptionalism* (Bloomington, IN: AuthorHouse, 2011), 93, http://books.google.com /books?id=OeHVVebd_c0C&pg=PA93&lpg=PA93. • **leftist American college professor who was born in 1859**" "Robert Rothman Collection of John Dewey, 1935–1959," Southern Illinois University Library Archive, accessed February 8, 2014, http:// archives.lib.siu.edu/index.php?p=collections/findingaid&id=2234&q=. • "**infamous Students for a Democratic Society, the 1960s radical student group**" John Percy, *A History of the Democratic Social Party and Resistance,* vol. 1 (Sydney: Resistance Books, 2005), 201, http://books.google.com/books?id=CEy7xnkwgUgC&pg=PA201& lpg=PA201. • " 'fundamental method of social progress and reform' " John Dewey, "My Pedagogic Creed," *The School Journal* LIV, no. 3 (January 16, 1897), 77–80, http:// infed.org/mobi/john-dewey-my-pedagogical-creed/.

PAGE 153: " 'in every social institution in which we can find a foothold' " Francis X. Gannon, *Biographical Dictionary of the Left, Consolidated,* vol. 1 (Appleton, WI: Western Islands, 1969). • " 'result of John Dewey's teachings' " John Patrick Diggins, *The Promise of Pragmatism: Modernism and the Crisis of Knowledge and Authority* (Chicago: University of Chicago Press, 1995), 305, http://books.google.com/books?id =UJl9EDybv8IC&pg=PA305&lpg=PA305. • "**leftist propaganda disguised as classroom assignments**" Kyle Olson, "Teacher Caught Brainwashing Students with Media Matters Propaganda," *nation.foxnews.com,* accessed February 8, 2014, http://nation .foxnews.com/media-matters/2011/12/05/teacher-caught-brainwashing-students -media-matters-propaganda.

PAGE 154: " 'well-being of these very children and society as a whole' " "The Third Wave of Homeschool Persecution," *HSLDA: Advocates for Homeschooling Since 1983* XXVI, no. 6 (November/December 2010), http://www.hslda.org/courtreport/V26N6 /V26N601.asp.

PAGE 155: "**(mentioned by 17 percent)**" Judy Wheaton, "Homeschoolers: A Snapshot" (report, Austin College, March 2010), http://www.austincollege.edu/wp-content/up loads/2010/03/Homeschooler_A_Snapshot_PPT.pdf. • "**children's standardized test scores, evaluations, and work samples**" Dee Black, "Philadelphia Wants Portfolios

Before Homeschooling Begins," *hslda.org*, July 11, 2013, http://www.hslda.org/hs /state/pa/201307110.asp?utm_source=twitterfeed&utm_medium=facebook.

PAGE 156: **"18 percent are proficient in math"** Kyle Olson, "Philadelphia School District Attempts to Monitor Families Who Homeschool Their Children," *eagnews.org*, July 16, 2013, http://eagnews.org/philadelphia-school-district-attempts-to-monitor -homeschoolers/. • **"only 61 percent of students graduate on schedule"** Paul Socolar, "District On-Time Graduation Rate Surpasses 60 Percent," *The Notebook, Focus on Dropouts and Jobs: A Neighborhood Story* 19, no. 4 (February 2012), http://the notebook.org/february-2012/124482/district-time-graduation-rate-surpasses-60-per cent.

CHAPTER 24: MANY PARENTS AREN'T EQUIPPED TO MAKE THE RIGHT CHOICES FOR THEIR CHILDREN

PAGE 157: **" 'but more autonomy? Really?' "** Julie Mack, "School Choice: Sometimes Less Proves to Be More," *mlive.com*, August 11, 2012, http://www.mlive.com/opinion /kalamazoo/index.ssf/2012/08/school_choice.html. • **" 'abandonment of public schools' "** Jeff Adelson, "Teachers Unions Accuse Gov. Bobby Jindal of Misleading and Inflammatory Rhetoric," *nola.com*, January 23, 2012, http://www.nola.com/edu cation/index.ssf/2012/01/teachers_unions_call_gov_bobby.html.

PAGE 158: **" 'parents are very good in making decisions about their child' "** Brandon Dutcher, "Great Moments In Condescension," *wwwtmrcom.blogspot.com*, May 28, 2010, http://wwwtmrcom.blogspot.com/2010/05/i-n-democracy-in-america-tocque ville.html.

PAGE 159: **" 'best from an education standpoint' "** eagfoundation, "Debbie Squires: Parents Care, They're Just Dumb," *youtube.com*, February 16, 2012, https://www.you tube.com/watch?v=7WpaDkezM7Y.

PAGE 160: **" 'so they don't know how to do that' "** Tom Kertscher, "With school choice funding in play, Racine educator's comments about Milwaukee parents are replayed," *All Politics* blog at *m.jsonline.com*, April 10, 2013, http://m.jsonline.com/more/news /blogs/allpoliticsblog/202352461.htm.

PAGE 161: **"created a tax credit program of $3,500 per year"** Brandon Moseley, "AEA Sues to Block Alabama Accountability Act," *alreporter.com*, September 3, 2013, http://www.alreporter.com/in-case-you-missed-it-2/5071-aea-sues-to-block-alabama -accountability-act.html. • **"filed a lawsuit to end the Louisiana Scholarship Program"** Allie Bidwell, "Louisiana School Voucher Program," *U.S. News*, August 26, 2013, http://www.usnews.com/news/articles/2013/08/26/justice-department-attempts -to-block-louisiana-school-voucher-program. • **"The school board wisely voted to ignore the union and allow the expansion"** Vanessa de la Torre, "Hartford Board OK's 2nd Achievement First Charter School," *Hartford Courant*, August 27, 2013, http://articles.courant.com/2013-08-27/community/hc-hartford-achievement-first -0828-20130827_1_achievement-first-hartford-academy-hartford-democrats-charter -network. • **"forcing public schools to share their half-empty buildings with charter schools"** Bob McManus, "De Blasio's Plan to Kill Charter Schools," *New York Post*, January 14, 2014, http://nypost.com/2014/01/14/de-blasios-plan-to-kill-charter-schools/. • **"threaten the existence of several very successful charter schools"** Joe Tacopino, "Mark-Viverito Leads Charter-Halt Suit," *New York Post*, December 30, 2013, http:// nypost.com/2013/12/30/mark-viverito-leads-charter-halt-suit/.

CHAPTER 25: SCHOOL CHOICE TAKES MONEY AWAY FROM GOVERNMENT SCHOOLS

PAGE 163: " 'give it to private schools' " Lauren Anderson, "Public, Private Schools in Madison Consider the Impact of the Voucher Program," *madisoncommons.org*, May 2, 2013, http://www.madisoncommons.org/?q=content/public-private-schools-in-madison-consider-the-impact-of-voucher-program. • " 'divert essential resources from public schools to private and religious schools' " "Vouchers," *nea.org*, accessed February 8, 2014, http://www.nea.org/home/16378.htm. • " 'poor children suckered into attendance' " Steve Nelson, "School Choice Is a Whale-Sized Red Herring," *huffingtonpost.com*, January 8, 2014, http://www.huffingtonpost.com/steve-nelson/school-vouchers-choice-red-herring_b_4562438.html.

PAGE 166: " 'how to live together, across the board' " Mike Dennison, "Montana 'School Choice' Bill Will Hurt Public School System, Union Chief Says," *missoulian.com*, March 17, 2013, http://missoulian.com/news/state-and-regional/montana-legislature/montana-school-choice-bill-will-hurt-public-school-system-union/article_38ddec18-8f71-11e2-a0fe-001a4bcf887a.html. • " 'taking our children from us' " Patrick Brennan, "La. Teachers' Union President: School Choice 'Taking Our Children From Us,' " *The Corner* at *nationalreview.com*, April 30, 2013, http://www.nationalreview.com/corner/347020/louisiana-teachers%E2%80%99-union-president-education-reform-%E2%80%98taking-our-children-us%E2%80%99.

PAGE 167: " 'expansion of the program is currently being considered' " Susan L. Aud and Leon Michos, "Spreading Freedom and Saving Money: The Fiscal Impact of the D.C. Voucher Program" (report, Cato Institute and the Friedman Foundation, Washington, D.C., 2006), http://hpi.georgetown.edu/scdp/files/Financial.pdf. • " 'This program provides a lifeline to many needy children' " Adeshina Emmanuel, "Much-Debated Scholarship Program for D.C. Students Is Renewed," *The Caucus* blog at *nytimes.com*, June 18, 2012, http://thecaucus.blogs.nytimes.com/2012/06/18/much-debated-scholarship-program-for-d-c-students-is-renewed/?_php=true&_type=blogs&_r=0.

PAGE 168: " 'no conclusive evidence' " "NCEE Study Snapshot, Evaluation of the DC Opportunity Scholarship Program: Final Report," (report, IES National Center for Education Evaluation and Regional Assistance, June 2010), http://ies.ed.gov/ncee/pubs/20104018/pdf/20104032.pdf. • "90 percent of parents were satisfied with the program" "Parental Satisfaction and Program Summary: D.C. Opportunity Scholarship Program 2012–2013" (report, D.C. Children and Youth Investment Trust Corporation, Spring 2013), http://www.dcscholarships.org/elements/file/OSP/2013_11_06%20DC%20OSP%20Parental%20Satisfaction%20and%20Program%20Summary.pdf. • " 'all options should be on the table' " "D.C. Residents Strongly Favor Restoration of Endangered School Voucher Program," *federationforchildren.org*, February 16, 2011, http://www.federationforchildren.org/articles/191. • "funding diverted to the D.C. government school system" "Private School Vouchers for DC," *democraticleader.gov*, March 30, 2011, http://www.democraticleader.gov/floor/private-school-vouchers-dc.

PAGE 169: " '27 percent are enrolled in non-neighborhood public schools' " "Private School Vouchers for DC," *democraticleader.gov*, March 30, 2011, http://www.democraticleader.gov/floor/private-school-vouchers-dc. • "D.C. voucher program was saved" Catalina Carnia, "House Passes Boehner's School Vouchers Bill," *USA Today*, March 30, 2011, http://content.usatoday.com/communities/onpolitics/post/2011/03/john-boehner-school-vouchers-obama-district-of-columbia-/1#.Uvk4tGSwLF9.

PAGE 170: "about 25,000 students this year" "Milwaukee Voucher Program Enrollment Hits New Record," *School Choice Now!* blog at *federationforchildren.blogspot*

.*com*, November 26, 2012, http://federationforchildren.blogspot.com/2012/11/mil waukee-voucher-program-enrollment.html. • **"grown from 3,919 participants to more than 20,000"** Tom Brinkman, "Applications for Indiana Private School Vouchers Double," *indianapublicmedia.org*, September 25, 2013, http://indianapublicmedia.org /news/indianas-private-school-voucher-program-doubles-56215/. • **"Eighty percent of K–12 students in New Orleans attend charter schools"** Charles Chieppo, "How New Orleans is Rebuilding Its Ruined School System from the Ground Up," *governing* .*com*, May 28, 2013, http://www.governing.com/blogs/bfc/col-rebuilding-new-orleans -public-schools.html. • **"In the 2010–11 school year, there were 5,300 charter schools in America"** "Fast Facts: Charter Schools," *nces.ed.gov*, accessed February 8, 2014, http://nces.ed.gov/fastfacts/display.asp?id=30.

CHAPTER 26: EDUCATION SHOULDN'T BE FOR-PROFIT

PAGE 171: " 'not for boosting shareholders' profits' " Mark Schauer, "Mark Schauer: To Improve Education, We Need to Change Way We Handle Charter Schools," *freep.com*, September 5, 2013, http://www.freep.com/article/20130905/OPIN ION05/309050100/mark-schauer-education-charter-schools-reform. • " '**attractive to vulture capitalists like Mitt Romney**' " Ed Schultz, *The Ed Show*, NBC News, September 25, 2012, http://www.nbcnews.com/id/49180945/ns/msnbc-the_ed_show/#. UvlDUGSwLF9. • " '**would somehow solve all our problems . . .**' " Glen Lineberry, "Running Schools Like a Business Is a Crazy Idea," *huffingtonpost.com*, September 14, 2012, http://www.huffingtonpost.com/glen-lineberry/teaching-education-reform -_b_1882808.html.

PAGE 172: " '**out of our public schools would be against our better judgment**' " Milton Gaither, "Home Schooling Goes Mainstream," *Education Next* 9, no. 1, (Winter 2009), http://educationnext.org/home-schooling-goes-mainstream/.

PAGE 173: " '**investing very much in educating children**' " Sarah Carr and Annie Gilbertson, "Schools and For-Profit Managers Don't Mix, Skeptics Say," *usnews.nbcnews* .*com*, February 1, 2013, http://usnews.nbcnews.com/_news/2013/02/01/16797433 -schools-and-for-profit-managers-dont-mix-skeptics-say?lite. • " '**1% Owners to profit from the 99% Serfs**' " War on Error, "Entrepreneurs and Venture Capitalists: Line Up for Your Cash Cow Charter School Profits," *dailykos.com*, August 22, 2013, http://www.dailykos.com/story/2013/08/22/1233120/-Entrepreneurs-Venture-Capita lists-Line-Up-for-Your-Cash-Cow-Charter-School-Profits#. • " '**effort to destroy public education**' " Abby Rapoport, "Diane Ravitch on the 'Effort to Destroy Public Ed,' " *prospect.org*, October 2, 2012, http://prospect.org/article/diane-ravitch-effort -destroy-public-ed.

PAGE 174: " '**meant for public, not-for-profit education**' " "For-Profit Schools," *ms parentscampaign.org*, accessed February 9, 2014, http://www.msparentscampaign.org /mx/hm.asp?id=ForProfit.

PAGE 175: " '**On that point, there can be little dispute**' " "Straight Talk About For-Profit Management Companies," *oapcs.org*, accessed February 9, 2014, http:// www.oapcs.org/files/grassrootsforprofitlongversion.pdf. • "**others suggest they do better**" Ron French, "Study: For-Profit Charter Schools Perform at or Above Non-Profit Peers," *mlive.com*, February 28, 2013, http://www.mlive.com/education/index .ssf/2013/02/for-profit_charter_schools_per.html.

PAGE 176: " '**At least five other charter schools discontinued their management contract**' " Peter Murphy, "Stop Scapegoating 'For-Profit' Charters: Enough Tough Rhetoric—Look at Results," *New York Daily News*, May 20, 2010, http://www.nydaily news.com/opinion/stop-scapegoating-for-profit-charters-tough-rhetoric-results-article -1.448339. • " '**Why would anyone think either of those things a good idea?**' "

Chris Lehmann, "Why I am Against For-Profit Public Schools," *practicaltheory.org*, August 29, 2012, http://practicaltheory.org/blog/2012/08/29/why-i-am-against-for -profit-public-schools/.

PAGE 177: **"only 43 percent of students were graduating"** Steve Gunn, "Rochester District Spent $37 Million on Six-Figure Salaries in 2012–13, while Laying Off Teachers, Cutting Programs," *eagnews.org*, January 22, 2014, http://eagnews.org /rochester-district-spent-37-million-on-six-figure-salaries-in-2012–13-while-laying-off -teachers-and-cutting-programs/. • **"thirty highest-paid administrators made an average of $150,000 in 2012"** Stephen Beale, "Slides: The Top Highest Paid Providence School Employees," *golocalprov.com*, August 31, 2013, http://www.golocalprov.com /news/the-top-30-highest-paid-providence-school-employees/.

PAGE 178: **"math proficiency rates below 5 percent"** Ian Slater and Scott O'Leary, "Chart: RI's High Schools 2012, from #1 to #51," *golocalprov.com*, May 14, 2012, http://www.golocalprov.com/news/chart-ris-high-schools-2012-from-1-to-51/. • **"make more than $200,000 per year"** Jason Hart, "Meet the Bosses: National Education Association," *mediatrackers.org*, January 2, 2013, http://mediatrackers.org /ohio/2013/01/02/meet-the-bosses-nea.

CHAPTER 27: CHARTER SCHOOLS DON'T PERFORM ANY BETTER THAN TRADITIONAL GOVERNMENT SCHOOLS

PAGE 179: **" 'no better than students in traditional public schools' "** Claudio Sanchez, "The Charter School Vs. Public School Debate Continues," *npr.org*, July 16, 2013, http://www.npr.org/2013/07/16/201109021/the-charter-school-vs-public -school-debate-continues. • **"But if you want to fight the union, at least use the facts"** Ben Jovarsky, "Today's lesson: charters do not outperform unionized schools," *Chicago Reader*, October 3, 2012, http://www.chicagoreader.com/chicago/chicagos -unionized-public-schools-outperform-charter-schools/Content?oid=7559748. • " 'we don't want to pay attention to Stanford' " Ed Schultz, *The Ed Show*, NBC News, September 25, 2012, http://www.nbcnews.com/id/49180945/ns/msnbc—the_ed_show /#.UvlDUGSwLF9.

PAGE 180: **".03 standard deviations on math tests"** CREDO, "Multiple Choice: Charter School Performance in 16 States" (report, Center for Research on Education Outcomes, Stanford University, 2009), http://credo.stanford.edu/reports/MULTI PLE_CHOICE_CREDO.pdf. • **".01 standard deviations in reading"** CREDO, "National Charter School Study" (report, Center for Research on Education Outcomes, Stanford University, 2013), http://credo.stanford.edu/documents/NCSS%202013%20 Final%20Draft.pdf. • **"closing dozens of failing government schools"** "UFT Announces Lawsuit Over School Closures," *uft.org*, February 2, 2010, http://www.uft .org/videos/uft-announces-lawsuit-over-school-closures.

PAGE 182: **"85 percent of students now attend charter schools"** Danielle Dreilinger, "New Orleans Charter Enrollment Tops National List for Eighth Year," *nola.com*, December 10, 2013, http://www.nola.com/education/index.ssf/2013/12/new_orleans _charter_enrollment.html. • **"2.5 months of extra learning in math"** Julia Lawrence, "CREDO: Massachusetts Charters Handily Outperform Public Schools," *education news.org*, March 7, 2013, http://www.educationnews.org/education-policy-and-poli tics/credo-massachusetts-charters-handily-outperform-public-schools/.

PAGE 183: **"Charter schools have been graduating students at a rate of about 77 percent"** Mark Lerner, "D.C. Charters High School Graduation Rate at 76.7 Percent, DCPS at 61 Percent," *examiner.com*, November 9, 2012, http://www.examiner.com /article/d-c-charters-high-school-graduation-rate-at-76–7-percent-dcps-at-61-percent. • **"public school graduation rate of approximately 61 percent"** District of Columbia, Executive Office of the Mayor, "OSSE Releases District High School Graduation Rates," press release, November 8, 2012, http://mayor.dc.gov/release/osse-releases -district-high-school-graduation-rates. • " 'one hundred percent of those graduates were accepted into college' " Mark Lerner, "D.C. Charters High School Graduation Rate at 76.7 Percent, DCPS at 61 Percent," *examiner.com*, November 9, 2012, http:// www.examiner.com/article/d-c-charters-high-school-graduation-rate-at-76-7-percent -dcps-at61-percent. • "**100 percent of all graduates of the Thurgood Marshall Academy have been accepted into college**" Thurgood Marshall Academy, Public Charter High School, "Thurgood Marshall Academy One of Five Schools Nationwide to Receive the COSEBOC School Award," press release, April 24, 2013, http://www .thurgoodmarshallacademy.org/newsroom/194/thurgood-marshall-academy-one-of -five-schools-nationwide-to-receive-the-coseboc-school-award. • " ' "two or three grade levels behind their peers" ' " "About: Results and Impact," *kippdc.org*, accessed February 10, 2014, http://www.kippdc.org/about/results-impact/.

PAGE 184: " 'one in five charter schools should be closed because of poor academic performance' " Mary Camille Izlar, "Stanford Study Says Charter School Children Outperform," *Bloomberg Business Week*, June 25, 2013, http://www.businessweek .com/news/2013-06-25/charter-school-children-outperform-peers-in-regular-class rooms. • " 'benefiting lower-income, disadvantaged and special education students' " Carolyn Thompson, "Study: Minority, Poor Students Gain from Charters," *Big Story* at *ap.org*, June 25, 2013, http://bigstory.ap.org/article/study-minority-poor -students-gain-charters.

PAGE 185: "**fighting efforts to lift the cap on the number of charter schools**" James Vaznis, "Bill to Seek End of Mass. Cap on Charter Schools," *Boston Globe*, January 18, 2013, http://www.bostonglobe.com/metro/2013/01/18/groups-urge-bill-aims-lift -cap-charter-schools/zd9HYXmNIKOxKVXZQWwuaM/story.html. • "**mayor wants to stop forcing government schools to share unused classroom space**" "De Blasio Blasts New Bloomberg School Co-Location Plans, Demands Speaker Quinn Support a Moratorium," *billdeblasio.com*, September 3, 2013, http://www.billdeblasio.com/news /in-the-press/de-blasio-blasts-new-bloomberg-school-co-location-plans,-demands -speaker-quinn-support-a-moratorium. • "**ballot referendum was narrowly passed in 2012**" Ann Dornfeld, "WA Charter Schools Initiative Passing Narrowly," *nwpr .org*, November 7, 2012, http://nwpr.org/post/wa-charter-schools-initiative-passing -narrowly. • "**block charter schools on constitutional grounds**" Brian M. Rosenthal, "Coalition's Suit Challenges State's Charter-Schools Law," *Seattle Times*, July 3, 2013, http://seattletimes.com/html/localnews/2021324035_charterlawsuitxml.html. • " 'flimsy reasons on which to base a constitutional challenge' " "Editorial: Teachers Union Should Withdraw Suit to Block Charter Schools," *Seattle Times*, January 8, 2013, http://seattletimes.com/html/editorials/2020087307_editchartersunionxml.html. • " 'disadvantaged children trapped in failing public schools in Washington State' " "Union to File Lawsuit to Overturn Charter School Initiative," *washington policy.org*, January 2, 2013, http://www.washingtonpolicy.org/blog/post/union-file -lawsuit-overturn-charter-school-initiative.

PART TWO: THE WAY FORWARD

PAGE 188: "**Once teachers get placed into a school, they stay for a very long time,**" Justin Snider, "Keys to Finnish Educational Success: Intensive Teacher-Training, Union Collaboration," *huffingtonpost.com*, March 17, 2011, http://www.huffing tonpost.com/justin-snider/keys-to-finnish-education_b_836802.html. • " 'They are very good partners for us' " Justin Snider, "Keys to Finnish Educational Success: Intensive Teacher-Training, Union Collaboration," *huffingtonpost.com*, March 17,

2011, http://www.huffingtonpost.com/justin-snider/keys-to-finnish-education_b_836 802.html.

PAGE 189: "It was seven hundred pages long" Lynell Hancock, "Why Are Finland's Schools Successful?" *Smithsonian Magazine,* September 2011, http://www.smithson ianmag.com/innovation/why-are-finlands-schools-successful-49859555/?all. • " 'provide more open access to higher education' " Linda Darling-Hammond, "What We Can Learn from Finland's Successful School Reform," *nea.org,* accessed February 11, 2014, http://www.nea.org/home/40991.htm. • " 'featuring rewards and sanctions for students, teachers, and schools' " Linda Darling-Hammond, "What We Can Learn from Finland's Successful School Reform," *nea.org,* accessed February 11, 2014, http://www.nea.org/home/40991.htm.

PAGE 190: " 'others have extremely high standards when the children belong to all of us . . .' " Penny Starr, "Panelist at Podesta Think Tank on Common Core: 'The Children Belong to All of Us,' " *cnsnews.com,* February 3, 2014, http://cnsnews .com/news/article/penny-starr/panelist-podesta-think-tank-common-core-children -belong-all-us.

PAGE 191: "would see their performance ratings take a hit" Valerie Strauss, "Test Scores Plummet—so Florida Drops Passing Grade," *Answer Sheet* blog at *washington post.com,* May 21, 2012, http://www.washingtonpost.com/blogs/answer-sheet/post /test-scores-plummet—so-florida-drops-passing-grade/2012/05/21/gIQAzopIeU_blog .html.

PAGE 193: " 'demanding a more rigorous education' " Jay P. Greene, "Do We Need National Standards to Prevent a Race to the Bottom?" *educationnext.org,* July 17, 2012, http://educationnext.org/do-we-need-national-standards-to-prevent-a-race-to -the-bottom/.

PAGE 194: " 'replicate' what the charter schools are doing" Marc J. Holley, Anna J. Egalite, and Martin F. Lueken, "Competition with Charters Motivates Districts," *Education Next* 13, no. 4 (Fall 2013), http://educationnext.org/competition-with -charters-motivates-districts/. • " 'improving outcomes is centralization' " Jay P. Greene, "My Testimony on National Standards Before US House," *jaypgreene .com,* September 21, 2011, http://jaypgreene.com/?s=my+testimony+on+national +standards.

PAGE 195: " 'The ESA model creates education choice rather than school choice' " Matthew Ladner, "Parental Choice 2.0: Elements of Program Administration and Design for an Education Savings Accounts Program," Milton and Rose Friedman Foundation (forthcoming).

PAGE 196: " 'It more resembles a communist economy than our own market economy' " Albert Shanker, "Reding, Wrighting & Erithmatic," *Wall Street Journal,* October 2, 1989.

PAGE 197: " 'the strongest political lobbying body in the U.S.' " Milton Friedman, "Public Schools: Make Them Private," (briefing paper no. 23, Cato Institute, Washington, D.C., 1995), http://www.cato.org/pubs/briefs/bp-023.html.

PAGE 198: " 'one or two suburbs actually produce excellent results' " Lindsey M. Burke, "The Education Debit Card, What Arizona Parents Purchase with Education Savings Accounts" (report, Friedman Foundation for Educational Choice, Indianapolis, August 28, 2013), http://www.edchoice.org/CMSModules/EdChoice /FileLibrary/1015/THE-EDUCATION-DEBIT-CARD-What-Arizona-Parents-Purchase -with-Education-Savings-Accounts.pdf. • **Arizona as Empowerment Scholarship Accounts** "Empowerment Scholarship Accounts," *arizonaschoolchoice.com,* accessed February 11, 2014, http://www.arizonaschoolchoice.com/EDU_ESA.html.

PAGE 199: " 'choice among education service providers, courses, teachers and methods' " Lindsey M. Burke, "The Education Debit Card, What Arizona Parents Purchase with Education Savings Accounts" (report, Friedman Foundation for Educational Choice, Indianapolis, August 28, 2013), http://www.edchoice.org/CMSModules/EdChoice/FileLibrary/1015/THE-EDUCATION-DEBIT-CARD-What-Arizona-Parents-Purchase-with-Education-Savings-Accounts.pdf.

PAGE 200: " 'Public schools don't work for every child' " Heartland Institute, "Oklahoma May Become Second State to Offer Students Education Savings Account," *eagnews.org,* January 30, 2014, http://eagnews.org/oklahoma-may-become-second-state-to-offer-education-savings-accounts/.

PAGE 201: " 'make sure each child receives a truly great education' " Office of the Governor, Scott Walker, "Transforming Education by Expanding School Choice," press release, February 18, 2013, http://www.wisgov.state.wi.us/newsroom/press-release/transforming-education-expanding-school-choice.

PAGE 202: " 'their parents should have the freedom to determine the best fit' " Steve Gunn, "Dougco School Board President Says Voters Prefer Student-Based Reforms Over Union Greed," *eagnews.org,* October 9, 2013, http://eagnews.org/douglas-county-school-board-president-says-voters-prefer-student-based-reforms-over-union-greed/. • **"remains tied up in litigation"** Nancy Mitchell, "Lawsuits Filed Over Dougco Vouchers," *co.chalkbeat.org,* June 21, 2011, http://co.chalkbeat.org/2011/06/21/lawsuit-filed-over-dougco-vouchers/.

PAGE 203: **"more money to quality educators in hard-to-fill subjects"** Sunana Batra, "Douglas County School Board Back Pay-for-Performance Framework," *thecoloradoobserver.com,* May 20, 2013, http://thecoloradoobserver.com/2013/05/douglas-county-school-board-backs-pay-for-performance-framework/. • **"reward teachers who get the best results"** Brittany Corona, "Colorado Teachers Now Paid for Performance, Not Years of Service," *The Foundry* blog at *heritage.org,* June 12, 2013, http://blog.heritage.org/2013/06/12/colorado-teachers-now-paid-for-performance-not-years-of-service/. • **"expansion of charter schools within the district"** "Analysis: Union Criticism of Charter Schools Hits Close to Home in Dougco," *thecoloradoobserver.com,* August 14, 2013, http://thecoloradoobserver.com/2013/08/analysis-national-unions-criticism-of-charter-schools-hits-close-to-home-in-dougco/. • **"diverted about $1 million to neighborhood schools"** Steve Gunn, "Dougco School Board President Says Voters Prefer Student-Based Reforms Over Union Greed," *eagnews.org,* October 9, 2013, http://eagnews.org/douglas-county-school-board-president-says-voters-prefer-student-based-reforms-over-union-greed/. • **"Took a public stand against Common Core"** "Douglas County School Board Resolution Opposes Common Core," *ednewscolorado.tumblr.com,* accessed February 12, 2014, http://ednewscolorado.tumblr.com/post/55703385127/douglas-county-school-board-resolution-opposes-common. • **"increased the state income tax to provide more revenue for government schools"** John K. Carson, "Resolution of the Board of Education of Douglas County School District, RE-1 in Opposition to Amendment 66, Douglas County School District RE-1," accessed February 12, 2014, https://eboardsecure.dcsdk12.org/attachments/a76bc4a2-8873-464b-96df-d1eee3f5ba07.pdf. • **"local teachers' union as the bargaining agent for teachers"** Nelson Garcia, "DougCo School Board Cuts Ties with Union," *9 News,* NBC, September 5, 2012, http://www.9news.com/news/article/287430/339/DougCo-School-Board-cuts-ties-with-union.

PAGE 204: " 'not focus on the interests of teachers' " Steve Gunn, "Dougco School Board President Says Voters Prefer Student-Based Reforms Over Union Greed,"

eagnews.org, October 9, 2013, http://eagnews.org/douglas-county-school-board
-president-says-voters-prefer-student-based-reforms-over-union-greed/. • **"predicting a mass exodus of teachers from the district"** "Analysis: Union Criticism of
Charter Schools Hits Close to Home in Dougco," *thecoloradoobserver.com,* August 14,
2013, http://thecoloradoobserver.com/2013/08/analysis-national-unions-criticism
-of-charter-schools-hits-close-to-home-in-dougco/. • " **'strangle the Dougco non-
union baby in its crib'** " Mike Rosen, "Rosen: Douglas County School Board Leads
the Way," *Denver Post,* September 25, 2013, http://www.denverpost.com/opinion
/ci_24175822/rosen-douglas-county-school-board-leads-way.

PAGE 205: "All other issues were off the table" David Schaper, "Wis. Gov.
Walker Introduces 'Reform Budget,'" *npr.org,* March 2, 2011, http://www.npr
.org/2011/03/02/134187305/wis-gov-walker-introduces-reform-budget.

PAGE 206: "about $135 million per year in 2020" Robert Costrell and Larry Maloney,
"The Big Squeeze: Retirement Costs and School District Budgets, Milwaukee: Save
by Act 10 . . . For Now" (report, Thomas B. Fordham Institute, Washington, D.C.,
July 18, 2013), http://edexcellencemedia.net/publications/2013/20130606-The-Big
-Squeeze-Retirement-Costs-and-School-District-Budgets/Milwauke-Saved-by-Act
-10-for-Now-EMBARGOED.pdf. • **"increase the minimum retirement age"** Office of
the Superintendent, "Meeting the Challenge," press release, December 26, 2012, http://
www5.milwaukee.k12.wi.us/dept/superintendent/2012/12/meeting-the-challenge/.
• **"about $87 million per year in 2020"** Steve Gunn, "Milwaukee School Officials
Won't Give Credit Where It's Due, but the District will Save Millions Through Act 10,"
eagnews.org, August 19, 2013, http://eagnews.org/milwaukee-school-officials-wont
-give-credit-where-credit-is-due-but-the-district-will-save-millions-through-act-10/.

PAGE 207: " **'without Act 10'** " Steve Gunn, "Milwaukee School Officials Won't Give
Credit Where It's Due," *eagnews.org,* August 13, 2013, http://eagnews.org/milwaukee
-school-officials-wont-give-credit-where-credit-is-due-but-the-district-will-save-millions
-through-act-10/. • " **'some teachers being counseled out of the profession'** " Steve
Gunn, "Act 10 Gives Wisconsin Schools More Power to Fire Subpar Teachers," *eagnews
.org,* July 18, 2013, http://eagnews.org/act-10-gives-wisconsin-school-administrators
-more-power-to-remove-subpar-teachers-and-improve-the-quality-of-instruction.
• **"quality teachers are being lured away from other districts"** Steve Gunn, "Act 10
Helping 'Free Agent' Teachers Earn More Money, Attracting Stronger Candidates
to the Profession," *eagnews.org,* July 25, 2013, http://eagnews.org/wisconsin-school
-officials-act-10-helping-free-agent-teachers-earn-more-money-and-attracting-stronger
-candidates-to-the-profession/.

PAGE 208: "recall election was scheduled for June 2012" Lucy Madison, "Scott Walker
Recall Election Set for June 5," *cbsnews.com,* March 30, 2012, http://www.cbsnews
.com/news/scott-walker-recall-election-set-for-june-5/. • **"Walker faced Milwaukee
mayor Tom Barrett in his original election in 2010 and won"** Patrick Marley and
Lee Bergquist, "Walker Wins Governor's Race on Promise of Jobs," *Milwaukee Journal
Sentinel,* November 3, 2010, http://www.jsonline.com/news/statepolitics/106580158
.html. • **"he won by an even larger margin"** "Wisconsin's Walker Survives Recall
by Wide Margin," *foxnews.com,* June 6, 2012, http://www.foxnews.com/politics
/2012/06/05/polls-close-in-wisconsin-voter-turnout-reported-heavy/. • " **'who deserved better of this nation'** " David Gelernter, "The Friendly, Neighborhood Internet School," *The Wall Street Journal,* August 9, 2012, http://online.wsj.com/news
/articles/SB20000872396390443659204577575001746476494.

PAGE 210: "great advantages of technology is customization" Allan Collins and
Richard Halverson, *Rethinking Education in the Age of Technology: The Digital Revo-*

lution and Schooling in America (New York: Teachers College Press, 2009), http://llk media.mit.edu/courses/readings/Collins-Rethinking-Education.pdf. • " '3 to 4 percent more students tested proficient or advanced in math' " Susan Frey, "Riverside Schools Point to Power of Technology in the Classroom," *edsource.org*, December 8, 2011, http://edsource.org/today/2011/riverside-schools-point-to-power-of-technol ogy-in-the-classroom/3915#.Uvpt4WSwLF9.

PAGE 211: " 'shall be displaced because of distance learning or other education technology' " Lance T. Izumi, "States Vs. the Digital-Learning Revolution," *nation alreview.com*, December 9, 2011, http://www.nationalreview.com/articles/285096 /states-vs-digital-learning-revolution-lance-t-izumi/page/0/1.

PAGE 213: "accountants, housewives, professors" David Gelernter, "The Friendly, Neighborhood Internet School," *online.wsj.com*, August 9, 2012, http://online.wsj .com/news/articles/SB20000872396390443659204577575001746476494.

PAGE 214: " 'Or at least end teacher education as we know it' " Barbara Nemko and Harold Kwalwasser, "Why Teacher Colleges Get a Flunking Grade," *The Wall Street Journal*, October 23, 2013, http://online.wsj.com/news/articles/SB100014240527023 04864504579143902608329802.

PAGE 215: " 'lectured to about how great Common Core is' " Jason Howerton, " 'Is This America?': Parent 'Manhandled', Arrested While Speaking Out Against Common Core at Public Forum," *theblaze.com*, September 20, 2013, http://www.theblaze.com /stories/2013/09/20/is-this-america-parent-manhandled-arrested-while-speaking-out -against-common-core-at-public-forum/. • " 'what number did they count by?' " Pat Richardson, "Arkansas Mother Obliterates Common Core in 4 Minutes!" *youtube.com*, December 16, 2013, http://www.youtube.com/watch?v=wZEGijN_8R0. • " '108 steps to solve the problem' " Erica Ritz, "Fed-Up Mother Tackles Common Core in Viral Video: 'Parents Have No Voice,'" *theblaze.com*, January 15, 2014, http://www.theblaze .com/stories/2014/01/15/fed-up-mother-tackles-common-core-in-viral-video-parents -have-no-voice/.

PAGE 217: " 'they lack the research they allegedly received' " Jason Howerton, "This Could Be One of the Best Cases Ever Made Against Common Core—No One Expected It to Come From a High School Student," *theblaze.com*, November 15, 2013, http:// www.theblaze.com/stories/2013/11/15/this-could-be-one-of-the-best-cases-ever-made -against-common-core-no-one-expected-it-to-come-from-a-high-school-student/.

PAGE 218: " 'Is this America?' " Jason Howerton, " 'Is This America?': Parent 'Man-handled', Arrested While Speaking Out Against Common Core at Public Forum," *theblaze.com*, September 20, 2013, http://www.theblaze.com/stories/2013/09/20 /is-this-america-parent-manhandled-arrested-while-speaking-out-against-common -core-at-public-forum/. • " 'sit on the curb in front of the school' " Liz Bowie, "Parent Arrested at Forum After Protesting Use of Common Core," *Baltimore Sun*, September 20, 2013, http://www.baltimoresun.com/news/maryland/education/blog /bs-md-co-common-core-arrest-20130920,0,7127220.story. • " 'violated the rules of the meeting and disrupted the meeting' " Ashley Williams and Robert Lang, "Charges Dropped Against Parent Arrested During Common Core Meeting," *wbal .com*, September 23, 2013, http://www.wbal.com/article/102892/21/template-story /Charges-Dropped-Against-Parent-Arrested-During-Common-Core-Meeting.

PAGE 219: "Common Core is now called 'Iowa Core' " Jason Howerton, "The Sneaky Tactic Some States Are Using Now That Parents Are Standing Up Against Common Core," *TheBlaze*, February 18, 2014, http://www.theblaze.com /stories/2014/02/18/guess-what-sneaky-tactic-some-states-are-using-now-that-parents

-are-standing-up-against-common-core. • **"Jan Brewer recently signed"** Jason How-erton, "The Sneaky Tactic Some States Are Using Now That Parents Are Standing Up Against Common Core," *TheBlaze.com,* February 18, 2014, http://www.theblaze .com/stories/2014/02/18/guess-what-sneaky-tactic-some-states-are-using-now-that -parents-are-standing-up-against-common-core. • **"Florida has switched to the 'Next Generation Sunshine State Standards'"** Perry Chiaramonte "Name game: Amid opposition, states change title of Common Core," *FoxNews.com* February 22, 2014, http://www.foxnews.com/us/2014/02/22/name-game-amid-opposition-states -change-title-common-core.

PAGE 220: " **'grossly ineffective' teachers'** " Jennifer Medina, "Fight Over Effective Teachers Shifts to Courtroom," *New York Times,* January 31, 2014, http://www.ny times.com/2014/02/01/education/fight-over-effective-teachers-shifts-to-courtroom .html?_r=1. • " **'they were tired of waiting'** " Jennifer Medina, "Fight Over Effective Teachers Shifts to Courtroom," *New York Times,* January 31, 2014, http://www.ny times.com/2014/02/01/education/fight-over-effective-teachers-shifts-to-courtroom .html?_r=1. • " **'dealing with [the] problem'** " Jennifer Medina, "Fight Over Effec-tive Teachers Shifts to Courtroom," *New York Times,* January 31, 2014, http://www .nytimes.com/2014/02/01/education/fight-over-effective-teachers-shifts-to-courtroom .html?_r=1.

PAGE 221: " **'Parents and Educators Against Common Core Standards'** " Parents and Educators Against Common Core Standards, "Parents and Educators Against Common Core Standards' Facebook Page," *facebook.com,* accessed February 13, 2014, https://www.facebook.com/ParentsAndEducatorsAgainstCCSS.